WHITE COAL CITY

WHITE COAL CITY

A MEMOIR OF PLACE & FAMILY

ROBERT BOSCHMAN

Printed and bound in Canada at Imprimerie Gauvin. The text of this book is printed on 100% post-consumer recycled paper with earth-friendly vegetable-based inks.

COVER AND TEXT DESIGN: Duncan Noel Campbell
COPY EDITOR: Ryan Perks
PROOFREADER: Rachel Taylor
COVER PHOTO: Marie Funk, courtesy the author

Library and Archives Canada Cataloguing in Publication

TITLE: White coal city : a memoir of place & family / Robert Boschman.

NAMES: Boschman, Robert, 1961- author.

SERIES: Regina collection ; 16.

DESCRIPTION: Series statement: The Regina collection ; 16

IDENTIFIERS: Canadiana (print) 20200360108 | Canadiana (ebook) 20200360116 | ISBN 9780889777965 (softcover) | ISBN 9780889777989 (pdf) | ISBN 9780889778009 (EPUB)

SUBJECTS: LCSH: Boschman, Robert, 1961- | LCSH: Boschman, Robert, 1961-—Childhood and youth. | LCSH: Boschman, Robert, 1961-—Family. | LCSH: Prince Albert (Sask.)—Race relations. | LCSH: Prince Albert (Sask.)—Ethnic relations. | LCSH: Prince Albert (Sask.)—Biography. | LCSH: Prince Albert (Sask.)—Social conditions—20th century. | LCSH: Prince Albert (Sask.)—History—20th century. | LCGFT: Autobiographies.

Classification: LCC FC3549.P75 Z49 2021 | DDC 971.24/2—dc23

University of Regina Press

Saskatchewan, Canada, S4S 0A2
TEL: (306) 585-4758 FAX: (306) 585-4699
WEB: www.uofrpress.ca

10   9   8   7   6   5   4   3   2   1

We acknowledge the support of the Canada Council for the Arts for our publishing program. We acknowledge the financial support of the Government of Canada. / Nous reconnaissons l'appui financier du gouvernement du Canada. This publication was made possible with support from Creative Saskatchewan's Book Publishing Production Grant Program.

For the First Nations Peoples
of Treaties 6, 7, and 10 and
the Métis in Saskatchewan,
who continue to teach me
how to read my own past.

History, like trauma, is never simply one's own . . .
history is precisely the way we are implicated
in each other's traumas.
—CATHY CARUTH, *Unclaimed Experience* (1996)

The organism in its environment
—TIM INGOLD, *The Perception
of the Environment* (2000)

CONTENTS

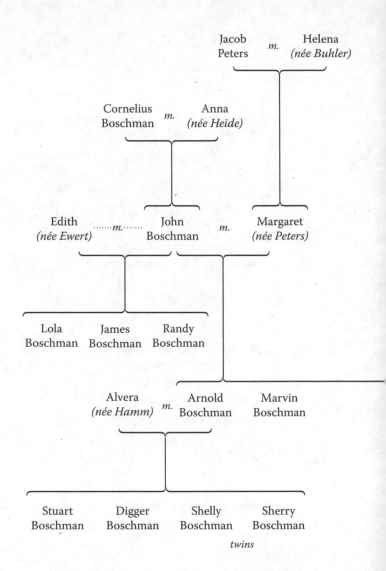

Jacob Peters *m.* Helena *(née Buhler)*

Cornelius Boschman *m.* Anna *(née Heide)*

Edith *(née Ewert)* ·······*m.*······· John Boschman *m.* Margaret *(née Peters)*

Lola Boschman   James Boschman   Randy Boschman

Alvera *(née Hamm)* *m.* Arnold Boschman   Marvin Boschman

Stuart Boschman   Digger Boschman   Shelly Boschman   Sherry Boschman
twins

x

KINSHIP CHART

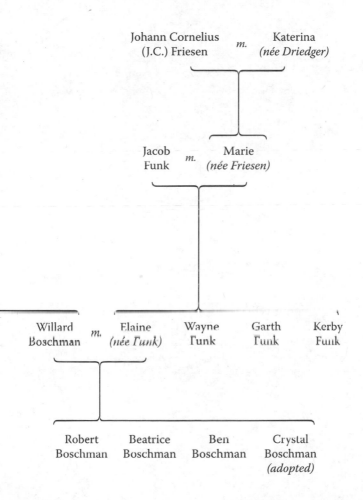

Johann Cornelius (J.C.) Friesen *m.* Katerina *(née Driedger)*

Jacob Funk *m.* Marie *(née Friesen)*

Willard Boschman *m.* Elaine *(née Funk)*   Wayne Funk   Garth Funk   Kerby Funk

Robert Boschman   Beatrice Boschman   Ben Boschman   Crystal Boschman *(adopted)*

SASKATOON CORONER'S INQUEST TRANSCRIPT, JULY 2, 1940

Translated from Pitman shorthand, April 4, 2017

(TRANSLATOR'S NOTE: The following comes from what appears to be a witness statement, which I believe has been taken down by someone as another person conducts the interview. The transcriber is therefore writing at a very fast rate— and in shorthand, no less— and so these outlines appear almost scribbled.)

Just a minute. The car that you saw the deceased woman go round, it was parked?

Yes Sir, it was.

On the south side of Avenue A?

Yes Sir.

That is the hard surface highway?

Yes Sir.

Was it parked on the hard surface or was it partly near on the [gravel shoulder]?

It was parked . . .

Some of it would be on that hard surface?

Yes.

And this northbound car, did you see it move out to pass this parked car?

Yes Sir.

Some distance south of the parked car?

Yes.

And what else if anything did you observe?

I saw that the accident must happen.

PROLOGUE

Over the Dominion Day weekend of 1940—since been renamed Canada Day—eight pedestrians across the country were killed by moving vehicles. Among them, an airman was struck by a hit-and-run driver in Port Stanley, Ontario. At the Belleville train station, a news vendor was run over by an incoming engine, which dragged his body several yards before what was left could work its way loose on the tracks. And in East York, in the same province, a six-year-old boy about to go on summer holiday with his family was crushed by a heavy truck, the driver completely unaware that his wheels had touched anything more than a bump on the road.

Thousands of miles to the west in Saskatchewan, on the Saturday of that weekend, Gilfred Greggain, a constable with the Saskatoon City Police, came on the scene of another of these accidents. It was early evening. What he found was a dark-haired woman in her late twenties lying near the southeast corner of 38th Street and Avenue A (now called Louis Riel Trail), the city's major north–south corridor. In the latter stages of pregnancy, she'd been killed instantly by a car heading north on Avenue A. The woman's name was Margaret and she was my grandmother.

This entire story was born in that instant, when my paternal grandfather John, then thirty-four, looked on in disbelief from across the busy avenue. That moment completely altered the future of my family twenty-one years before I was born. Its effects cross decades and generations and made me what I am as the first-born of Margaret and John's third child. I've seen this ancestral history unfold and reveal itself again and again, enfleshed, without my even knowing a thing about it for the longest time.

BETWEEN TWO RIVERS

A friend from my childhood in Prince Albert got a Prince Albert when his wife left him. He visited a parlour in nearby Saskatoon and said, "Do me—I wanna PA." He showed me what his Prince Albert looked like before (1) I could say anything or close my eyes and (2) the inflammation had subsided. The whole thing looked like a drooping hammerhead shark that had just been finned, or like Boris Karloff's Frankenstein monster hanging upside down. I thought that whoever had named this body modification a Prince Albert could well have known the place and time of my growing up. Or that Karloff himself had once lived in PA before moving to Hollywood. My Prince Albert is a state of mind, a history that marks me, an interior landscape and a town pierced in the most vulnerable places.

My experience growing up in PA during the 1960s and '70s was violent and raw, as though the whole city were growling with the anger of missed chances and dying ends, of things that had shrivelled or would just never be. Geographically, it can still be found within a

circle of pain—ringed and intersected by a federal penitentiary, two provincial corrections units (one for men
and one for women), a former tuberculosis sanitarium,
an old pulp-and-paper mill, and the bankrupt ancient
dam called La Colle Falls.

Walking up my own back alley once I got kicked
so hard in the crotch it rapidly turned red, then blue,
and finally dark purple. I felt I was witnessing my own
murder unfolding in a festoon of colours. I was afraid
to tell my parents because they'd want to look and then
my mom might call Dr. Look and she'd want to look.
The thought of pulling my pants down for a parent or
doctor was more than I could bear. Instead I waited and
watched, checking every twenty minutes, thinking about
the older and much bigger boy, an angry white Jehovah's
Witness who'd caught me alone on a cold day in winter,
me falling down in the snow half a block from home
after he'd kicked me with all his might.

For days I obsessed, afraid my principal and very
private end might die of trauma and fall off and then
I'd regret not showing it to Dr. Look. To show or not
to show caused me almost as much angst as the original trauma. I imagined Dr. Look finally examining the
remains in her office.

"Robbie, you're too late. If you'd come to me right away,
I could have saved your dink. Now you don't have one."

Then she'd look at my stricken parents and add,
"Robbie will have to adjust to this tragic loss and accept
things as they are. I wish you'd called me immediately.
I'm sorry, there's nothing I can do except prescribe
ointment."

The truth in that imagined moment—and in all the
real ones before and after—was that this was my PA and
it needed ointment, a lot of it.

* * *

I didn't go looking for fights. In PA, I knew they were looking for me. It was an awareness that seldom went away, a flow like acid that coursed through my gut, spread to my tubular, pale thighs and knees, eroding my already scant strength and stability. Like many kids before me, I suffered from chronic doubt over my ability to hack what Prince Albert dealt.

PA being what it was back then—a northern Canadian pen-and-pulp town with winters so cold my nostrils froze shut if I didn't breathe through my mouth—hockey dominated life, and violence dominated hockey. Blond Les Jack of the Prince Albert Raiders, our Centennial Cup champions of the Saskatchewan Junior Hockey League, was my hero. In a flurry of green and gold, he was always humiliating some other player from Melville or Kinistino or Moose Jaw.

The PA crowd loved it.

I loved it.

Hockey's fights and its blood were real, unlike Stampede Wrestling, imported live from Calgary once a year. The Stomper, with his cowboy hat and boots and Speedo tights, was unreal and so was his blood. Despite his menacing rhetoric (the colonizer's wet dream)—"I'm gonna teach you sumpin' punk! I'm the boss around here!"—what the Stomper taught me was the difference between an actual blow and a theatrical one. My best friend Barry Henry's grandfather might swear to the hardcore reality of the Stomper's cowboy heel crashing down on Sweet Daddy Siki's skull, but I knew it was an act, beyond what any human could endure.

Hockey and its place in our town were different. The glorified blood and violence shoved its way into everyday life and everyday life shoved right back: it was never clear where one stopped and the other began. Ice hockey, road hockey, hockey on lawns, driveways, and parking lots—it didn't matter. A brawl, with sticks up and fists swinging, was inevitable.

Yet entangled with the game, a fight or some form of altercation could also single me out at any moment or in any place: on streets and playgrounds, in alleys, parks, and school hallways.

I always had to be ready, even though I was never ready.

Aggression was in the PA air like the puke stink of pulp effluent on a forty-below morning in January. Everyone was fascinated by it, laughed at and discussed it, bemoaned its existence, adopted creeds for or against it. But violence was a fact of life, like the penitentiary on the edge of town or the turn-of-the-century jailhouse for men one block from my home. It seemed as basic as the biting insects exploding from the bush after winter finally melted away—torrents of brown runoff sweeping kids' purple- and orange-stained popsicle sticks (the kids themselves running to keep up) all along the roadsides.

2 Saskatchewan is contained by longitudinal lines. These are the second and fourth meridians, which meet each other at the poles. The first meridian runs just west of Winnipeg and was so named because at its inception the spaces beyond were considered wild and empty. Uncontained. Of course, they were none of these things.

Some anthropologists and historians estimate that approximately ninety million human beings lived in the Americas just before 1492. A century later, that rough figure had fallen by 85 percent, the single largest decline in any human population in history. Disease, predation, betrayal, theft. The so-called Columbian Exchange, as though a transaction occurred once and then it was over.

When the Reverend James Nisbet ventured west from Winnipeg in 1866 to establish his mission, perhaps he was unaware that the humans to whom he would deliver his gospel were but a surviving remnant. Debates continue across the years regarding what men like Nisbet really did or didn't know. Some say that men like him are accountable regardless of what they did or didn't know. Some want the names of men like Nisbet removed from important places with long traditions, places like the Nisbet Forest, which stretches between Prince Albert and Duck Lake (and has been subject to logging and garbage dumping). Others oppose changing any names, even though in between these two places there are ancient histories that have nothing to do with James Nisbet. Still, this forested region bears his name and through it runs the third meridian, established by the surveyors who measured and quantified all the geographic space they could find. We live our lives on their terms.

Nisbet crossed the high prairie with the help of Indigenous navigators. He may not have made it otherwise. They crossed the South Saskatchewan north of where Aberdeen would be founded four decades later. They crossed on crude rafts—flotation devices, really—constructed quickly on the riverside. People, animals, equipment, all were carried downstream before the opposite bank could be reached. Then the march northwards till Nisbet saw the place looking out over the North Saskatchewan—the place he gave a name even though it already had one. If he knew it, he ignored it. Naming a place for empire, that was his appointment. He had entered the triangle of land converging on the Forks, where the South meets the North, a point where other humans before him had met at regular intervals for centuries. The water ran clean then—no pipeline ruptures, fertilizers, pulp mill effluents, human sewage, cattle and pig shit—and it teemed with sauger, pickerel, pike, goldeye, and giant ancient sturgeon; it was forded by bear, wolves, and elk; the bison were pretty much gone by then.

So it was named Prince Albert, or simply PA, and soon enough the town fathers laid down roads in all directions, and soon enough those roads were filled with motor cars.

3 Most of the time getting hit by a car occurs along predictable lines. The bumper break comes first. That is, the front bumper of the oncoming machine hits the lower part of the legs and, depending on the speed, may break one or both of them. This is standard stuff in the age of the automobile, documented by police, medics, pathologists, insurers, and safety boards. Besides damage to bone, of course, there is considerable tearing and abrading of skin, flesh, nerves, and muscle. Where precisely this injury occurs depends on the height of the pedestrian. Margaret is about five foot five, and the middle portion of her left leg, ranging from the calf to the mid-thigh, is struck first. She is moving westward, just off the gravelly edge of Avenue A, when Harry Reid hits her.

The bumper break by itself doesn't kill. That occurs in the ensuing stages, when the pedestrian, propelled suddenly upwards and into the oncoming machine, is struck again—and consecutively—by the radiator, grille, headlights, hood, and windshield of the car even as the car continues to move forward, carrying the individual along with it as it travels. Here the lethal damage occurs, first to the torso and then to the neck and head. The radiator sometimes leaves a honeycomb pattern on the clothing and skin (just as bits of clothing and flesh remain on the automobile), and other car parts and fittings, such as hood ornaments and grille, leave their own special signatures. Internal organs in both the lower and upper cavities of the torso may be punctured; certainly they are rapidly compressed and tend to rupture. In an accident of this kind, because of the considerable shearing forces travelling all at once into the legs, the groin is stretched as the body careens upwards over the car. But the deciding damage is done as the head encounters the top portion of the vehicle, the windshield and roof, which now compresses the brain and may snap the neck, after which the body takes to the air. During this time—it happens quickly, in a second or so—various articles of clothing and jewellery fly off, including shoes, taking the same flight path as the body, which is impacted a final time as it hits the ground.

What follows from such a moment has no limits—in time, in the hippocampus where trauma, remembered or not, is stored, in families and among witnesses, or on the ground itself where the event takes place.

It is always there, always taking place.

4 The terrain of Prince Albert was divided into four unequal parts. Viewed on a map or seen from the air, it was a mushroom-shaped grid of streets and avenues. The mushroom's cap faced the powerful North Saskatchewan River flowing east to meet its partner, the South Saskatchewan, at a point called the Forks not far from the city.

In this place named after Queen Victoria's consort, roughly thirty thousand people lived during the 1960s and '70s when I was a child. Most of them made their homes on the south side of the river, a wide flood plain built up over eons stretching half a mile before meeting the river's original worn edge rising into the sky. The primordial riverbank was called the Hill, the flood plain below the Flat. The city's north–south Central Avenue divided these rough halves again: West Flat, East Flat, West Hill, East Hill. Onto the latter neighbourhood, the suburb of Crescent Heights was later added.

In the 1960s and '70s, middle-class people of European descent, for the most part, resided on the Hill, while the Métis, First Nations, and poorer whites mostly lived on the Flat. The broad avenues that took us up and down the West Hill were lined by the city's oldest and grandest homes, where doctors and lawyers and judges, looking out over everything on the Flat, lived important lives I would never touch.

In spring, there were soapbox derbies on one of the wide thoroughfares descending to the Flat. The home-made cars raced through the steep gauntlets of dark and silent early twentieth-century houses.

Farther up the Hill, on the far west side, was All Saints, an Anglican residential school that housed Indigenous children taken from their families and communities in the north for ten months of the year. All Saints seemed to me another world only blocks from my house, though the place where I lived—my family home—couldn't be called a house.

I grew up with my younger siblings in the back of the King Koin Launderette built by my maternal grandfather, Jacob Funk, in the late 1950s. Our family's living quarters were located at the rear of a long, unpainted cement rectangle with a flat gravel roof. There we faced the intersection of two alleys, one running parallel to 2nd Avenue while the other, which met it at a right angle, ran between 27th and 28th Streets West. For over two decades, the King Koin stood its ground on the main corridor through Prince Albert. By a bridge named after its very own prime minister, John Diefenbaker, the avenue connected southern farms and towns to the parklands, lakes, rivers, and shield country north of the North Saskatchewan. The King Koin was a stand-alone grey fortress defending soap and water, a cinder block tabernacle dedicated to clean. Travellers couldn't help but see it.

Our launderette stayed open twenty-four hours a day, seven days a week, and for that reason alone my world stood out on PA's West Hill. Where every other kid had a front yard with a manicured lawn and cement sidewalk and knew what a quiet Sunday afternoon was, I had a gravel parking lot along the avenue. The huge electrified King Koin sign dangled over the vehicles that packed up against our curb, especially on Sunday afternoons, when most folks had time to do their laundry.

Mine was a back-alley world frequented by customers knocking on our heavy wooden door. They were in endless search of quarters and dimes (sometimes in astonishing quantities) to operate the machines that would wash, spin, dry, and dry clean their clothes and bedding. Or else to inform us that a machine didn't work: the dryer blew cold air, the Coke machine was empty, a front-loading washer had stopped in mid-cycle and was now flooding the aisle because an impatient customer had opened the door to transfer their load to another washer.

In summer, this back-facing intersection of alleys lined by old poplars and knotty, angular maples (dusty under a blue sky and a mud hole in rain) was an unvarnished landscape; it was modified partly when my father built an enclosed patio and then a small fenced yard followed by a single-car garage for our white 1970 Ford station wagon.

In winter, the long cement pad my grandfather laid for an outdoor car wash became the theatre for dramatic hockey games that extended into the half-darkness of evenings lit by the floodlights of the King Koin. Many of the boys I knew were regulars outside our living room window, pretending to be Bobby Orr or Bobby Clarke or Dave Schultz, the most violent hockey player we had ever seen.

That living room window, built by Grandpa Funk, created a south-facing picture that was a portal to my outside world. Gazing from it in any season, I read the shifting but fundamental features of my childhood landscape.

In the immediate foreground and descending from right to left was the grey cement stairwell that provided outside access to the basement living quarters. Various members of the extended family lived down there over the years, but eventually, as we entered our tweens and teens, my sister and brother and I took the two bedrooms below.

Just beyond the stairwell was the cement pad sweeping off to the right; and beyond the pad was the back of the Nor-Lite grocery store, which also contained Gil's Barber Shop, all of this fenced with plain sheets of warped and weathered particle board.

A dirt-and-gravel parking lot filled out the upper left-hand quadrant of our picture window. It was lined by a hedge along the alley that intersected with 28th Street. During weekdays, service and supply vehicles visiting the Nor-Lite entered and exited the lot. Large disused cardboard boxes for fresh produce and canned goods piled up against the round cast-iron incinerator, which stood erect like a brown sentinel between Grandpa Funk's car wash pad and the Nor-Lite parking lot.

Fed by the neighbourhood, the incinerator burned all day and into evening, belching smoke from a rusted exhaust stack. Unlatching the blackened door facing our window called for an upward thrust on a heavy bar. The scorching orange semi-circular mouth opened level with a ten-year-old boy's face. It blasted him with heat and fumes but was repaid with a Lysol spray can lobbed in like a grenade, the heavy door slammed shut, explosion forthcoming.

Beneath that maw was a smaller one close to ground level. It, too, opened with a swinging motion, excreting cinders and exploded spray cans.

In winter, fluffy black flakes of ash rode on the wind, fell and stained the snow-covered car wash pad till our boots and beat-up hockey sticks rubbed them out.

5 I wasn't just scrawny; I was cross-eyed too. I wore glasses as soon as I could be trusted to keep them on my face: black horn-rimmed specs, fashionable at the time. Without them, my eyes wandered in different directions, looking for two things at once and causing me no end of trouble. With the glasses, however, my eyes came together and worked nearly in unison, though the doctor said I'd never have proper depth perception, even after two surgeries, one for each eye.

"He'll never fly a plane."

"Nope. And never be a surgeon."

"You said that right. Good thing."

"No guff, eh, bodies everywhere."

People who didn't know me or were being introduced couldn't tell if I was talking to them. They looked at me with puzzlement, hostility even.

"You lookin' at me?" they asked, pointing at themselves. "Fuckin' kid is cross-eyed."

How I'd come to be a cross-eyed kid tortured my parents, who blamed themselves even though my mother's brother suffered from the same thing. In this particular uncle's case, his eyes had supposedly gone crossed after falling down a long set of stairs. So, my parents reasoned, perhaps something similar had happened to me. Once I arched back from my father's arms, diving headfirst onto the floor. This traumatized my parents, who consoled each other by observing that at least the floor wasn't cement. No one in the family seemed open to the possibility that I was born with one eye turned inward.

My crossed eyes, together with my spindly build, anxious temperament, unusual residence, and (soon enough) accelerated education, made me a mediocre hockey player but an excellent target of derision. My sight wasn't true. I couldn't see the puck in space and time and had little sense of anticipation, so crucial to the game. Everyone assumed I was stupid and I agreed, not knowing that I couldn't see what they saw. I could skate but that was it. Like a young sparrow with bad eyes, I was sure to be picked at by the other birds.

Looking out cross-eyed—and in that sense alone, and lonely—from my primary school class photos, I am a child from the large majority of white children of European descent whose grandparents and parents have only recently settled in this place. The only minority in all these photos, taken between the years 1967 and 1974, is Indigenous. These children often come from All Saints, where they've been relocated, forced to live apart from their mothers and fathers, grandparents and great-grandparents, brothers and sisters and cousins, aunts and uncles—and speak a language, English, into which they haven't been born.

I cannot tell their stories or speak for them. I can only say that they were there and tell my own story, giving witness to what I experienced as a white settler child in a town called PA in a place called Canada.

6 One day in June 1997 I took my first-born child, Nina, then three years old, to visit Margaret's grave just outside the town of Aberdeen, not far from Saskatoon. We drove there and parked in the ditch beside the cemetery. It was like a scene from a Canadian version of *Tess of the D'Urbervilles*. In fact, I remembered Thomas Hardy's anger at what he called the "President of the Immortals" as I looked at Margaret's headstone with its sharp edges and dull surface, rough and grey and fierce, like the skin of a shark. I told Nina about her great-grandmother, and as I did she turned away from the stone and buried her face in my neck. Her reaction surprised me. She was too young to read the epitaph, and I didn't tell her what it said—GOD ALONE UNDERSTANDS—or that it was followed by a deeply etched period, as though to indicate John's judgment on the matter. But there it was—and is: an indictment, an accusation, a statement of fact, or faith. Also resignation.

All the above, all the time. John's trinity. His stark period.

GOD ALONE UNDERSTANDS.

I have turned these words over in my mind ever since I first saw them with my own eyes. My kid hugged me while black crickets went chick-chick-chick, grasshoppers hisped and vibrated in the short, crunchy grass, and a robin made a telephone wire song. Sage pervaded the air that day like incense. I looked at the epitaph and considered what it didn't say: "God Understands." That third word, ALONE, carries so much freight through the cycles of the years.

Back home, I transcribed my grandparents' letters on an IBM desktop for my father to review. When Margaret died, he was two—and here I was with Nina, about that same age, and my father now in his late fifties. He'd absorbed the original letters long ago and then dreamed of his mother wrapped in fur and looking at him as she rose from the earth in an urn like an upside-down bell. He later said reading those letters was like knowing his biological mother for the first time.

* * *

The John and Margaret letters were written before the advent of ballpoint, using fountain pens, so called because you have to draw the ink into the pen's reservoir from a well. The ink in these documents is blue.

For John and Margaret, the ink flowed into a nib and onto paper eighty-seven times between 1931 and 1933, pulled along by love and gravity.

This writing technology is undergoing a minor renaissance in the twenty-first century. In specialty shops in North American cities, a fountain pen can cost anywhere from seventy-five to a thousand dollars. Old brand names like Waterman are kept alive by nostalgia, even if the pens themselves are beyond the reach of anyone but the well off.

The red three-cent postage stamp on each envelope in my grandparents' correspondence bears the likeness of George VI, the father of Elizabeth II and patrilineal grandson of Queen Victoria and Prince Albert.

* * *

Sometimes, when I'm rereading an old letter, I find myself in a time slip, like the living past has re-emerged. One such letter for me was written by my Great-Uncle Bill, John's younger brother, who became by sheer happenstance the grandfather I couldn't have in John, because John (1) died prematurely and (2) even had he lived, was just too damaged to give me what I needed. So here I am rereading this letter from the summer of 1938, a time when smoke filled the horizon because of the fires burning in the northern forests around PA, and Bill writes to the older brother he loves two years prior to Margaret's death and John's trauma.

Smoke fills my skies too. The northern forests of Canada are ablaze, and this year everyone knows it. Temperatures are rising. Charred dust gathers on windowsills.

Roland Barthes says that when we see a powerful photograph from long ago, its power comes from time's passage. I look at an image of a child, for instance, who long before I was even born stopped being a child, grew into adulthood, and very likely has died. Perhaps that child's eyes especially speak to me as I view the image. Something happens. Barthes calls this the *punctum*, the element in the image that punctuates emotionally.

Of course, what Barthes is saying here applies to all manner of older things, including letters. They give us pause. The past punctures the present.

In this summer of 1938 John's little brother Bill is a twenty-year-old firefighter. He posts his letter from Connell Creek, Saskatchewan, some miles east of Carrot River, where a tremendous fire is out of control, eating the very land.

> Dear John & Margaret,
>   It is strange what will sometimes cause a person to write a letter. This time it was my collection of souvenirs. I usually give this collection a wide berth as, if I let myself, I can become so absorbed that it takes hours to tear myself away. There are letters galore in this collection, some of them ten years old, snapshots that I keep out of usual sight, newspaper clippings, poems, school records, report cards, Valentines, an old 30-30 shell with bullet, and last but not least, a piece of sweet flag root.

And then Uncle Bill in this letter (itself about objects from the past) quotes John's own words from years before: "Nov. 5/35, 'Margaret wants to come [north] in summer instead of winter. She wants to see the trees in summer garb, holding their arms aloft as if in constant praise for their being.' "

I imagine the following: that Margaret expressed her love of trees to John and then John relayed her words to young Bill, all in a letter Bill found and quoted back to John, who likely gave the letter to Margaret to read and remember. Now my hands hold the letter as fires burn again in the northern forests.

Punctum.

7 Whenever a balloon popped, my father made micro-balloons. He drew a remnant of the shattered balloon into his mouth and twisted it off, thereby producing a tight swelling the size of an adult male's thumbnail. It was perfect for biting. My siblings and I took turns chomping down on the squeaky knobs with our milk teeth until the exploded balloon pieces were riddled with holes. We peeked at each other through the holes too. In time, I mastered the craft of using up a ruined balloon without my dad, enjoying the feel of the hard bubble that formed in my mouth, only to wink out of existence as I bit in, even as my baby teeth fell out and were replaced with adult ones. The miniature explosions concussed the roof of my mouth, and microscopic shards of balloon gave me a taste for bursting perfectly sound balloons just to exercise this talent.

* * *

"Robbie, show me your muscles!"

I was pleased to oblige, a loving repeat sucker for Uncle Kerby from day one.

Good old Uncle Kerby. Kerby Neal Funk, with a nose like Cleopatra's and, eventually growing from beneath that schnozz, a classic moustache over which David Crosby could have wept. KNF. Who for over forty years smoked a pack a day of Du Maurier King Size filter-tipped cigarettes, stopping only once for a few miraculous months while my family held its collective breath, then starting up just as the toxins finally escaped his body. Like a rare but unnerving breakout from the PA Pen, the poisons appeared in his face in a bad case of zits, only to burrow back inside when he lit up again.

Kerby was eight years my senior, my mother's youngest sibling, born to his parents, Jacob and Marie, as a spectacular accidental afterthought, all blue-eyed and sexy.

Kerby and I were in the launderette together selling popcorn out of his newfangled popcorn machine—Kerby's first in a long line of businesses, some great triumphs, others huge busts.

I pumped my bicep as hard as I could.

"Hey, that's chicken muscle," he said, pinching a miniscule fold of skin along my triceps.

He knew I would cry, and I did. Although he cared greatly for me, and would be there in a jam, Kerby loved to taunt. His intense eyes sparkled with promise—the promise of a hidden incendiary device on which I would reliably step.

From the outset of our long relationship, he maintained a certain spin on my birth in Rosthern (a small town south of Prince Albert) in June of 1961, woven from the identity crisis I, the first grandchild to Jacob and Marie Funk, created in him.

Kerby's narrative went like this:

> *Four newborns are presented for viewing on the other side of a pane of glass in the nursery of the hospital. Young Kerby is to choose the*

*one who is his nephew, born to his big sister
Elaine. One of the babies is ugly but the other
three are all quite pleasant looking, so Kerby
chooses the best-looking infant of the three
acceptable ones.*

*His parents, smiling, shake their heads, so
Kerby (disappointed but still hopeful) chooses
the second-best-looking baby.*

"No, Kerby," he is informed. "Try again."

*There are now two babies remaining, one
acceptable and the other a veritable paragon
of ugly: a miniature fat face with puffy eyes
and forehead and little, flattened toad nose.
That one he definitely doesn't choose, hoping
beyond hope that it is not his nephew, the
newly spawned Robert Wayne Boschman. But
it is. I am the toad, and Kerby—with a sly
smile—will announce his chagrin whenever he
and I intersect with an audience of family or
friends in the years to follow.*

Kerby's story scuffled in my mind with another,
that of my great-grandfather, J.C. Friesen, a pillar of
the community in which I was born. Rosthern was a
prairie town fifty miles southwest of Prince Albert, and
the Friesens were its eccentric aristocrats.

As a young man, J.C. had come to Saskatchewan from
southern Manitoba; his father owned and operated a
successful dry goods store in Hague, which J.C. in time
took over. He and his bride raised a family of eight children, of whom Marie, my maternal grandmother, was
the oldest.

Eventually, the Friesens left Hague for the larger,
more active town of Rosthern, eleven miles to the north.

J.C. and his family were stalwarts of the mainstream Mennonite General Conference church. He donated his time and money to Rosthern Junior College, the well-known Mennonite prep school—where Jacob Funk would meet Marie Friesen, my father Willard would meet my mother Elaine, and where my father's father would write letters to the love of his life, Margaret Peters. Everyone in my family, including my siblings, attended this school—everyone but me. I alone refused to go.

On the morning of June 10, 1961, mere hours after my birth, J.C. was seen strolling through town and across the RJC campus, where graduation was taking place, announcing to everyone he met that his first great-grandchild had just been born. Once I was up and running, he told me this story himself, extending a hand to shake mine, repeating my name like I was some kind of miracle. "Robbie Robbie Robbie."

The little finger of the hand I shook was wizened, curled like old gristle. We talk about the finger and its nature, the possible causes of such atrophy, and what might be done about it. I tried with all my might to straighten it for him, but there it was: a dried-out old hook.

Years and years later, when Marie's little finger on the same hand also began to atrophy, she visited her doctor to request its immediate removal. I was startled by her brazen desire to "chop the thing off."

"It gets caught," she complained, "on handles in the kitchen."

Her kitchen was a *sanctum sanctorum* where marvellous creations appeared from unwritten recipes handed down by generations of Mennonites who had come to Canada in the nineteenth century from colonies located north of the Black Sea.

Grandma Funk's fried onions alone smelled like no other fried onions on earth.

Though the doctor complied with her wish to amputate her pinkie, my grandmother complained about its phantom throughout her long life. That smallest of digits never really went away, as though it still might catch on a cupboard door handle.

8 During the early 1960s, my father and his older brother, Arnold, ran their father's dairy and wheat farm a few miles east of Langham, another small town south of Prince Albert, below the confluence of the two rivers, where Grandpa Boschman was still a schoolteacher.

Because my mother was also studying nursing full-time in nearby Saskatoon, I was shuttled back and forth between the farm and the launderette. Here, Grandma Funk cooked while my grandfather fixed an endless series of broken-down washers, dryers, spinners, and dry cleaners. In a falsetto voice, she'd call through the open kitchen window across to the rear entrance of the launderette, "Yoo hoo, Jake, soup's ready! Yoo hoo! SOUP!"

On sweltering days in summer she wore no top, only her large armoured brassiere, and frequently asserted her right to stay cool: "If Jake, Willard, Kerby, and all the other men and boys can go around shirtless on such a hot day like this, why so can I!"

When she wasn't cooking superlative Mennonite meals—borscht, *vareniki* with cream gravy and farmer's sausage—Grandma Funk was writing letters and diary entries. Her letters were legendary, and her daily journal entries span well over half a century.

In the summer of 1963, while my mother was in the hospital in Saskatoon giving birth to my sister, Marie made frequent written reports on my daily activities and general welfare. Kerby and I eventually shared a double bed in the room next to the boiler room. In the thick wall dividing the living quarters from the launderette, with its doors that never locked, Grandpa Funk cut a pair of rough circular holes level with an adult's eye, one in each side of the hollow cement block. Through it, he could scan the boiler room as well as the launderette beyond by way of a screen built into the opposing wall.

Grandma used it too. If she couldn't reach him from the kitchen window, she would *yoo hoo* Grandpa through the hole.

"Yoo hoo, Jake, come for supper! JAKE! SUPPER!"

Its diameter the size of a home telescope, the hole also let in the sounds of the launderette—the chitter, clank, click, and whir of Grandpa's mechanical menagerie mixed with his voice as he made change and managed an insanely complex array of levers and taps. This would continue long after Kerby and I had gone to bed.

Truth be told, Grandpa Funk was already bored with the launderette, turning over new ideas in his big, frustrated brain and wondering even then how he could convince my father, the young farmer, to leave his fields of wheat for long rows of temperamental machines.

As it turned out, this didn't take much enticement at all. The collapse of the farm at Langham made it necessary for my parents and sister to move to Prince Albert and take up residence in the back of the King Koin along with Elaine's folks and younger brothers. My father gave up cows' teats for solenoids and pilot lights, and the barn broom gave way to its launderette equivalent.

9 The Plymouth line of automobiles was announced in July of 1928 by a Chrysler Corporation desperate for sales to match its Detroit rivals, Ford and Chevrolet. By the following year, the low-cost family sedan was a bestseller throughout North America and new models could only be purchased at authorized Plymouth dealerships. It's thanks to this model that Chrysler survived the economic collapse of 1929 and the Great Depression of the following decade. The Plymouth logo showed the *Mayflower* in 1620, loaded with Puritans looking for refuge from religious persecution. Their governor, William Bradford, didn't like what he found on the Eastern Seaboard of the so-called New World; he called it a "hideous wilderness" and the humans there "savages." He named the place Plymouth Rock because the *Mayflower* had departed from Plymouth, England. Apparently, though, the Chrysler Corporation also saw inspiration for the Plymouth automobile in a popular brand of twine made by a cordage manufacturer of the same name.

The 1929 Plymouth sedan that John Boschman purchased used in 1939 was his first vehicle. He needed it badly. He had three young children and a wife and they lived in the country and he was tired of walking, biking, and borrowing his father-in-law's car. The Plymouth cost him eighty dollars. It was dark green. When I think of that car, I imagine it as the minivan of its day. If I bring it into the present, I picture a 1997 Plymouth

Caravan with rust along the rear wheel wells. Production of the Plymouth line ceased in 2001.

10

In my first memory I am shitting my pants. I can feel it still, that unpleasant intrusion, with turmoil to follow. Shit and turmoil, but then honey. A hand like a plate with comb honey held down to me. A voice in a shed. A man's voice. My grandfather, John.

"Try this."

Lying down by the blue salt lick in the corral, cow pie on my brown shoes, in my hair. The smell of purple gas flowing through the black hose into the green tractor. The heavy aromas of cow shit and milk.

Dirt lumps fly across a field. Anger out in that field.

Uncle Arnold.

"Get outahere you god damned sons of bitches!"

In the playhouse with the twins, a sandwich of tomatoes and mayonnaise.

Digger. His dark head hanging upside down from the roof, smoke and fire and voices, and under the turning windmill, water in buckets from the trough.

Waking up next to Aunt Alvera, the late-morning light, the window in the bedroom, I wondered where my mom was. We lived in the small house next to the big house on the farm where the cows were, but I was in the big house with my aunt, her back to me, her crow-black hair spread across the pillow.

My dad milked the cows early in the morning and that's where he was when I woke next to Digger's mother. He would milk them again in the afternoon and I'd watch, sitting on the feedbox attached to the calf's stall.

I ate the feed and watched my father or else played with the kid, but then the kid died. It was tethered in a stall and tried to jump free, only to hang itself.

The farm was a series of small and near disasters before it became one big one and everyone walked away, my parents and Arnold, Digger, Stuart, Alvera, Grandpa Boschman himself. John Boschman was a teacher whose dream it had been to own land and farm it with his sons. In 1956, he purchased a half section with buildings outside Langham, not far from the North Saskatchewan River. He held it for a decade.

Two of his five sons farmed it with him, though it was a rough go during those years, and the provincial government offered no help despite the letters Arnold and Willard wrote requesting assistance. They supported their meager incomes with work found off the farm. For Willard my father, this meant working on the new dam that would create Lake Diefenbaker, on the South Saskatchewan River. Finally, he went to work for his father-in-law, Jacob Funk, at the King Koin Launderette, the wave of the future, in Prince Albert, two hours away by car.

Grandpa Funk asked my father to help him install living quarters in the basement at the rear of the launderette. They panelled the space, otherwise encased in cinder blocks, in dark wood. A small porch with a sliding window enclosed the side entrance so customers looking for change or assistance couldn't just barge in. Beyond the porch, a deep stairwell. Tiger salamanders clung to its dank walls. Small L-shaped windows of sky were trellised in cement at the top of the stairs.

* * *

Though Grandpa Funk was younger than Grandpa Boschman, he knew and respected him. Their years at the Mennonite prep school in Rosthern during the early 1930s had overlapped because John, born in 1905, had returned to school to get his high school diploma in his mid-twenties. They both carved their names in the school's red brick outer walls. Those walls recorded a history of interconnected families, and it was tradition even then for students to etch their names in the brick siding before graduation.

Well before Elaine Funk asked Willard Boschman to marry her, she already knew from her parents the history and identity of the Boschmans. That John Boschman was the teacher at Langham. That Willard had two older siblings, Arnold and Marvin, as well as three younger ones, Lola, James, and Randy. That these six children came from two mothers, Margaret Peters and Edith Ewert—Margaret having been killed in a car accident in Saskatoon in 1940, when my father was two.

Everyone in the Mennonite community of that time knew the genealogy and circumstances of almost everyone else.

By the spring of 1959, when, during a drive to Saskatoon in a car borrowed from John Boschman, my mother surprised my father with the idea of getting married, she no longer really thought of him as the youngest of the trio of Boschman brothers who'd lost their mother in an accident. That bit of news had already been dealt with around the dinner table at home, her father relating the details of the young woman run over by a travelling salesman from Toronto.

Shocking as it first was—the news had spread like an electric current throughout the province in early July 1940—the story had more or less run its course by the time my mother proposed. And yet here was this young man, Margaret's youngest son. My mother was partially through her nursing program at the University of Saskatchewan by this point, while my father was working the farm at Langham with Arnold and John.

When my father requested an audience with Jacob to ask permission to marry Elaine, he was met with a silence lasting an entire day. It wasn't till he and my mother were about to drive away that Jacob finally spoke. He looked at my father through the car window and said, "All right." He liked the John Boschman family, but Grandpa Funk wanted to see his daughter finish her education before plunging into marriage.

John Boschman was another matter. Knowing who Jacob Funk was, and indeed that he was married to the oldest daughter of J.C. Friesen, John cheerfully embraced the idea of marriage between his boy and Elaine Funk. Both the Funks—Americans who had migrated north from Kansas to settle in Drake, Saskatchewan—and the Friesens—renowned in the area for their entrepreneurial spirit—constituted the kind of solid, respectable Mennonite family into which John Boschman wished his sons to marry. And besides, he would intimate with a wink and a nudge, all the boys in Rosthern during his time there were in love with Marie, the rich man's voluptuous and beautiful daughter.

John knew what it was like to wait long years for a home with one's sweetheart, a particular agony he wouldn't wish on anyone. He saw no reason to wait on love unless the wait was clearly necessary, and in this instance he judged that it was not. He set to refurbishing an old, disused portable bunkhouse located on his farmyard. He and second wife Edith cleaned and painted the one-room shanty, furnished it with a bed, table, chairs. Hung curtains. Moved it across the yard and into a grove of mature maples with its backside to the caragana that surrounded the place.

On one side of the love shack where I was conceived was a fabulous vegetable garden with crabapple trees, chokecherry, raspberry, and saskatoon berry bushes, a dense plot of rhubarb with thick red stalks. On the other was the farmhouse proper, where Arnold already lived with his family.

11 By the time a dim self-awareness visited me, Digger had already exploded on to the family scene with the force of a double-barreled 10-gauge shotgun blast. Born two years before me, Digger was my shadow, my me-not-me, my forager and forerunner into the dark.

In an early photo, he mugs behind me in a white T-shirt while my bare belly protrudes like a goiter. His shoulders hover inches above mine, his gaze jetting over my white hair and high forehead as we pose with our backs to the haunchy axle and balding tires of a flatbed truck loaded with two-by-fours and planks.

Digger had thick, ropy muscles and dark hair, skin, and eyes. Early on while running through the peas, he'd tripped on garden string and fallen throat-first onto a stake. The pale scar appeared just below his larynx.

We were solemnly aware of the contrast between us: for Digger a cause for celebration, for me a blend of despair and love.

"Robbie, look," he would say, placing his thick brown forearm alongside my ribbony pale one.

That moment of ritual, repeated on and on into early adulthood, defined us in our knowledge of who we were, together and apart. We'd never fight, and not simply because we both knew the outcome. It wasn't the obvious truth we both knew, but rather what we didn't know, either of us, that drew us into a tight bond. Close enough in age to feel in our bones the power of kinship, we were both also emphatically unaware of the agony and drama into which we'd been born.

No one knew John's tightly guarded secret grief even though it permeated the very Boschman atmosphere.

In the end, only older brother Stuart had the physical and mental strength to stop Digger. Among their earliest battles, Stuart drove a tricycle squarely into and over his brother's body. That incident stood as an emblem of Digger's chronic proximity to calamity, like he didn't know where or what his limits were. Like him, I believed quite simply that he could be driven over. I didn't know the whereabouts of his limits any more than he did, only that being with Digger meant things would happen, but probably not to me. I'd watch.

He was born David Dean, but at some point Stuart called him Digger and the name stuck.

One of his first semi-conscious acts, committed not from fear or bravado but simply because he had to, was to shit in his father's hand. This, for me, was beyond inconceivable, possible only because Digger did it. The sound of Arnold's voice made me panic. The way he laughed, for instance, when I was asked by the adults to sing some old hymn, I was positive he disapproved of my existence.

When I sang "We Three Kings" one Christmas, Arnold laughed and I was humiliated in front of the family.

From far away, I watched my uncle's legs and hips swivel and move. His dusty boots danced in the hooves of cattle or horses, moving with authority, his deep voice rising up amid the jostling animals.

In one memory, I see him with John shooing cows from the barn; John, wearing white coveralls, is impatient. Certainly he was impatient with Arnold, who from a young age insisted on cutting his own swath, eschewing the old Mennonite ways, making fun of them and the singular manner in which Low German made its way into a tripped-up English.

"Throw the cow over the fence some hay."

"Oh that barn is a sore eye."

"Hands off the horn or you'll blow the baby awake."

I was born into a generational guffaw that the five sons of John Boschman shared whenever they came together in any combination. But if Arnold was present, the laughter became more scathing, transcended everything; and Stuart, Digger, and I soaked it up even as we failed to learn the tiniest bit of Low German, the oral tongue all members on every side of our immediate families spoke fluently. Those spoken artifacts were soon to disappear, evidence of a history that had hit the skids. We didn't know why, and though we might have inquired later about why we, too, didn't speak Low German, or even the standard High German, we didn't follow up. We didn't want to speak those languages anyhow. Learning them would involve work, English was easy, and we were lazy.

We watched the brothers laugh, standing in a circle puffing roll-your-own smokes. "It's good to smoke together," Arnold would say, mimicking the heavy accent of an Old World Mennonite.

They called me an *oola näs*, or old nose, and Digger a *vripsbüdel*, a slippery bag, and laughed till tears fell from their eyes. That kind of crying was okay; genuine weeping was of course *verboten.*[1]

"Hey Robbie! Rabbi! Robetai! Robespierre!—you *oola näs*, you!"

My father was especially prone to laughing till he cried, and I'd cry along with him, not knowing for sure why but helpless to do anything else.

My birth had come quickly, early in the morning in June 1961 during the time when lilacs bloom, my mother's water breaking on the front seat of John's new and therefore reliable green Frontenac as my father drove expeditiously to Rosthern, where Dr. Janzen's practice was located.

The birth cost my parents forty dollars and took place without complications, barring the fact that I shat myself as I emerged.

Arnold would learn of this.

"He did, did he! The little bugger."

A few years passed, and I left a gob of excrement on the bathroom floor in the basement of John and Edith's recently constructed bungalow in Langham, a gob that—as luck would have it—Arnold discovered.

"Who in the shitfuckhell left a turd on the floor of that goddamned bathroom down there? Jayzuz Christ!"

By this time, John was dead, out of earshot of all the profanity. The Lord's name was, of course, not to be taken in vain; and "shitfuckhell" originated from the

---

1   Some of these Low German spellings are likely incorrect; at the very least, they're up for some debate (those who speak the language bring a lot of passion to the subject). When, in preparation for this book, I asked my dad and uncles for spellings, they simply laughed. I've opted instead to phoneticize as best I can.

mouth of a renegade Doukhobor who bootlegged on the edge of town. The acronym, SFH, was later employed for use in sensitive company.

And over time, "Let's get the SFH outahere" became simply "SFH."

Time to go. Let's book. We're gone.

Horseshit was one thing, but aloof Half-Horse Arnold, as his father had come to call him in his youth, did not take kindly to having to deal with other people's shit. Digger especially knew this, having gained early notoriety by dumping his load in his sire's hand. Back on the farm, with no indoor toilet, only a two-seater outhouse, he lit on a brilliant scheme to dispose of accidents—pants, briefs, and all—down one of the holes, until Alvera noticed his shrinking wardrobe.

When Digger couldn't be persuaded to mend his shitty ways, Arnold fixed a length of barbed wire across both holes a foot or two down. Anyone using the jacks was responsible for checking those wires before letting their own bombs drop. The pressure was really on to watch one's shit. We all became experts at watching our own and everyone else's.

12 He bursts forth with a roar into a room that has just moments before started teeming with people after I run out into the hall and yell for help.

Before the throng rushes in, during his long last push with his mother, his heart signals disappear and I freak out.

I don't want our first and only son starved of oxygen and possibly damaged, palsied for life, or worse, dead on arrival. The prospect makes me furious.

But the staff in the birth unit respond so swiftly that my anger is swept away and now I have to channel not anger but love, love alone—love so powerful it threatens to undo me in this crowd of strangers—for a son whose name is already Gabriel and whose face is suddenly turned up toward mine as his shoulders are adjusted and his head protrudes, just like that.

The face is the face I have known ever since.

Whenever he howls with fury or is upset, I see his face as I first encountered it, him, Gabriel, on April 1, 2010, at 12:20 p.m. April Fool's had just closed at noon.

On the birth unit, my cell phone has to be turned off in order not to interfere with so many electronic signals, spread out exponentially among room after room of contesting and weighing, birthing and dying.

When I exit the hospital building to turn it on and announce this new life to close family, my first thought is Kerby. When my other two children, daughters, were born, I phoned him.

So now I want to call Kerby, keep our ritual, make it known, but Kerby is dead—died out of the blue three weeks before, just like that, at 4:00 a.m. on a couch in a trailer park in Arizona.

My last exchange with my uncle is an email I wrote just after the second sonogram, when Gabriel's mother, sisters, and I could see the penis.

I still revisit this email: In which I write "Boy" and Kerby writes "You gotta be kidding," like it was the last thing he expects from me.

13

"Hey, Robbie, we don't like you," Digger announced.

"Yeah," Stuart said, "we sure don't like you."

They knew I'd cry, and I did.

"It's okay, Rob, we're just joking. We like you."

The grief subsides.

"No we don't. We lied. We really, really don't like you."

The weeping resumes with a vengeance.

"Just kidding. We like you, we like you, honest, cross my heart hope to die. Stop crying!"

On the farm where these words were said, there were three horses: Patchy Mac, Cisco, and Blondie. Digger led me around on Patchy Mac, not a horse really but a retired pinto who, after a lifetime spent pulling a wagon in a circle, could only turn right. Once Patchy Mac dragged Digger down the road looking for right-hand turns all the way.

Cisco was Arnold's treasured stallion, a Welsh-Standardbred cross. "A mighty little piece of horse," Arnold said. "Cisco—on command!—would jump right into the box of the old International." The truck was a blue 1950 edition, at one point the only vehicle on the yard.

Blondie was my father's horse, a stately palomino. There are black-and-white family photos of my father astride Blondie and holding John's single-shot bolt-action .22. The gun was used to take down coyotes and foxes; the pelts brought in needed extra income. Arnold and Cisco, naturally athletic and curious about everything, would ride ahead as trackers.

Heading north out of the farmyard toward a field—and beyond that the North Saskatchewan—was a lane bordered by poplar and maple. To the east of the lane, Grandpa Boschman kept bees, about six hives, which by August climbed into the sky as he added supers. In a good year, each hive grew tall enough that he needed a stepladder to remove the supers laden with as much as fifty pounds each of honey and wax. It was a wonder these could be handled coming down a ladder, but John had both strength and balance even then—indeed, could walk on his hands, on request.

The bees milled about his head, smoke billowed from his smoker, and everyone stayed away, especially my father, who was allergic to their stings. I saw his face swell after an encounter with a single insect, a reaction to years of indirect contact with John's equipment, bee suits, gloves, and veil.

* * *

Two photos taken the week before the pivotal moment of the twentieth century for our family: to wit, 6:30 p.m., Saturday, June 29, 1940, on an avenue in Saskatoon.

The photos are typical of the era—small black-and-white rectangles with rough white edges.

Margaret and John have taken turns with the camera. In one, he is seated on the running board of the Plymouth, Willard my father on his knee and the two older boys standing on either side, hanging from his shoulders. Wearing a fedora, John smiles brilliantly, the handsome guy nuzzling my father's round, blond head with his chin. The four of them are looking at Margaret behind the camera. They don't take their eyes from her even when she herself poses on the running board of the Plymouth. On his mom's knee, my father turns his face toward her neck, while Marvin looks on with his mouth open, as though exclaiming something to Willard. Arnold, on the other side of his mom, his right arm around the back of her neck, covers his mouth with his left hand as if to stop himself from laughing too hard.

All three boys have blond hair and dark eyes, though not as dark as their mother's. Great with the fourth child, she, too, is smiling.

14 Hockey caught hold of me on the floodlit car wash pad next to the King Koin, and in my first season playing for the Tigers of the East Hill Pre-Squirt League, which scheduled four games and a playoff beginning January 1969. As it had for many before me, it helped to endure seven months of winter, with its mountains of ploughed snow piled in parking lots and ranged along PA's bituminous streets.

In a photo from this time, my sister and I face off, sticks crossed, while our four-year-old brother drops the puck. We are "bundled up": heads covered with toques and hoods, necks wrapped in thick, knotted scarves. The long blue shadows of late afternoon flow out behind us in the snow toward the big white house and the Henry bungalow with its red and white siding. Towering poplars and twisted maples stand bone bare under the sky. I squint into the sun while my sister grins, holding her stick proudly. There were only two sticks to go around, the little brother forced to settle for a long ruler and presiding over the puck drop. There'd been bawling over who held a hockey stick and who a ruler.

On a cold day like that one, tears were to be wiped away fast. The adults frequently warned, "Hey, dry your tears or they'll freeze on your face!" I puzzled over this, especially on a bitter day when the wind made my eyes water. Why my crossed pair didn't freeze when it was forty below was a mystery. If a tear did freeze to my cheek, what would happen really? I was convinced nothing really bad, like dying, could happen to me. If I stepped in front of a car, it'd bounce from my body or I'd fend it off like Underdog. I didn't yet know the truth of my dad's family.

He often took me aside and informed me I had a loud voice. He advised a career in preaching, auctioneering, or arguing before the court. He heard my voice carry from the ruckus of kids on the car wash pad, especially when our big wooden door opened for a customer. Shinny players came from the four-block radius around the King Koin, kids whose dads worked at blue-collar jobs and whose moms stayed at home. The boys with well-to-do professionals and respected business leaders for dads lived farther west on the hill. I knew they played their own game with real nets. Ours were imaginary, burned tin cans and exploded aerosols from the incinerator marking the posts.

A third group of players who lived at nearby All Saints and dispersed throughout the city to various schools during the weekdays played by themselves, using equipment provided by the federal Department of Indian Affairs, which assumed jurisdiction over All Saints in 1968. We never played shinny or organized hockey on the same surface.

Tension had existed in PA right from its start one hundred years before, on the south bank of the North Saskatchewan where River Street now met Central Avenue.

The Reverend James Nisbet, whose original little rectangle of a house I saw at least once a week as I passed through Bryant Park, had named the place Prince Albert after a faraway monarch's dead husband. Standing in

the area that during my childhood would be occupied
by the fire hall, Nisbet told a small group of skeptical
Cree that he was there to help "by teaching them what
will be useful . . . in this life, and what will fit them for a
better life to come."

The Cree, who called the area kistapinânihk (the
"sitting pretty place" or "the great meeting place"), said
Nisbet had come to steal land and buffalo. They told him
so to his face right then and there.

15 When my parents bought their first car (so
they wouldn't have to depend on the International or on John's Frontenac or Jacob's second
car, a 1957 Pontiac station wagon, to travel to Langham,
Saskatoon, and—increasingly—to Prince Albert), I stood
between them on the front seat. It was a sand-coloured
1952 Chev four-door sedan and from where I stood I
could just see my face in the rear-view mirror. We were
driving down the grid between the farm and the little
highway to Langham, along which stood windbreaks
Grandpa Boschman had planted. There was my face
looking back at me. I didn't approve, even when I tried
smiling. That actually made it worse. My lips were too
big, eyes crossed, glasses taped up and crooked. None
of it looked right.

The early 1960s were drought years. The year of my
birth was so dry nothing grew and there was no harvest.
Letters to the provincial government went unanswered;
no farm aid was forthcoming to the Boschman boys
because their land base—a half section—wasn't big
enough. At the 1953 Royal Winter Fair in Toronto, while
my father was still in high school, John's hard red spring

wheat had taken first prize, for which he received a fat ribbon in regal purple. Telegrams and letters of congratulations poured in. The *Saskatoon Star-Phoenix* ran an article, "Wheat Champ Farmer-Tutor, Near Langham— First Entry," describing John's good showing of Thatcher seed with its "rust resistant qualities." But this early promise, captured in the eighteen-pound seed sample sent to Toronto, failed to head out under the arid conditions that arose nearly a decade later.

John was an idealist and a romantic, unlike the hard-headed and practical Jacob Funk, whose mind naturally gravitated toward things that ticked and whirred and produced a constant stream of cash, like the Philco Bendix front-loading washing machines that lined the large rectangular central island of the launderette, bringing in crowds from Prince Albert and beyond, day after day after day and at any hour.

"I need quarters, eh."

"Dimes for the extractor . . . please."

"My dryer is cold."

"One of your poor gimpy washers popped open, water's all over the place."

"Gimme my money back, and no guff."

"Toilet don't flush. Plugged. Better hurry."

Despite boasting that he came from a line of Jacob Funks that could be traced to the eighteenth century, Grandpa Funk was anticipating the future—while Grandpa Boschman, with one major exception (a dark veil pulled taut over the death of Margaret Peters) was mostly looking to the past, dipping his hand into the soil around Langham, saying, "Boys, come and look at this, this is fine soil, the product of eons!" My father, throughout his life, could not see good soil without hearing John's voice.

Often John went on long walkabouts across the land, either alone or with any of his children or grandchildren who cared to come along. He found medicine wheels and arrowheads in the dried-out pastures around Langham. Sage crunched underfoot, releasing its singular scent while John expounded on the Peoples who had lived on the land before Europeans arrived.

"Imagine, boys, the complex culture that existed here for thousands of years." He stood on a pile of lichen-carpeted rocks pushed into place by some recent farmer.

"Imagine! No barbed wire, no surveys, no roads."

Such talk would impact Arnold and Willard for the rest of their lives, pushing them away from their Mennonite roots faster and farther than their father could have wanted.

By 1966, with Willard off to Prince Albert finally and Arnold working odd jobs and passionately pursuing the lore of the Standardbred horse, John dejectedly sold the farm.

Stomach ulcers had plagued him for decades and would kill him in 1968, a year into retirement.

16 After years of searching, I found someone who knew the kind of shorthand employed to record the proceedings of the coroner's inquest on July 2, 1940.

When I wrote to the Saskatoon City Courthouse in the late 1990s, I had hoped beyond expectation to see a copy of the autopsy report and find out if the family rumour of a male fetus was really true. What I received surprised me. Yes, there was a medical report that

confirmed the existence of an unborn male on the verge
of his third trimester—but in addition to this, and quite
unexpected, was a sheaf of over sixty pages of shorthand. And in searching for someone who could translate this document, I came up empty. The sixty pages
of squiggles stayed in their manila envelope for over a
decade; in that whole time all I could discover was that
shorthand, once prominently employed across the legal
systems of the civilized world, came in two forms: Gregg
and Pitman. To my shorthand-illiterate eye—after examining samples of the two—I thought I detected Gregg,
so started looking on the Internet for a capable translator. A woman in California informed me that she knew
Gregg and would charge me approximately two thousand dollars to translate the document, but after sending
her the first page I never heard from her again. Despite
my repeated attempts over several years to contact her,
she went silent; I thought perhaps she had passed away.
No one else, it seemed, knew Gregg.

Finally, I contacted a woman in England whose
website indicated that she knew and could translate Pitman. In desperation, I emailed her to inquire
whether she might know anyone anywhere who could
translate Gregg. Or maybe this was Pitman, I thought,
hoping against hope that something might break my
way. I attached the first page of the text, at the top of
which were the only words that didn't require tran-
scription: "Mrs. Margaret Boschman died." A few
days later, the woman in England responded by saying
that the document was Pitman and for four hundred
pounds she would translate the lot. To demonstrate
her ability, she attached the following translation of
the first page:

Were you in the city on the 29 June?

Yes.

Do you know what day of the week that was?

Saturday.

Did you witness an accident on that day?

Yes Sir.

From memory where did this accident take place?

Between 37 and 38 Street on Avenue A.

Avenue A runs in which direction?

North, this was on Avenue A North.

And Avenue A runs?

North South.

What was your venue at that time?

I came from a party on B and 7 into Avenue A.

You came from Avenue B?

Yes.

Towards what street?

I don't know.

When you arrived on Avenue, did you arrive North or South of the accident?

North.

And on arriving on Avenue A was it your intention to go North or were you going South?

No, I was going South.

And how far on Avenue A did you [travel] South before you witnessed this accident?

Well, 100 [yards]? Or 50? About, about 80.

17 Around the western end of Prince Albert the Nisbet Forest folds, pressing the Saskatchewan Penitentiary into the city's side like a wound that'll never heal. The history of the Sask Pen is also the history of Prince Albert, of things that could've been but aren't. Early on, the city was presented with the opportunity to establish either the central campus for the University of Saskatchewan or the maximum-security holding facility for men convicted of major crimes. By 1910 PA had been awarded the latter. That decision shaped the city's future.

Just as important was the 1909 bid to build La Colle Falls, the failed hydroelectric project on the North Saskatchewan River. Just before the First World War, PA was dubbed White Coal City, as speculators and the city fathers hyped the Falls as the infallible source of future wealth and glory. Convinced that hydroelectricity production would make Prince Albert rich, the city council took a large ownership position; citizens revelled in the rising value of real estate. Clean "white coal" would replace the bitumen mined from the earth in towns like Drumheller and Canmore, in the neighbouring province of Alberta. But the Great War and several fatal financial missteps plunged PA into a monetary crisis that meant oiled rather than paved roads for the rest of the twentieth century. Every spring saw a grid of dusty streets till the rank odour of road tar replaced the dust in our nostrils.

The daunting red brick pen to its west, the crumbling cement edifice of the Falls abandoned halfway across the grand North Saskatchewan off to the east, PA was geographically pincered by its poor decisions and bad luck. It was broke, its population nearly static, roads covered in sticky oil, when my parents finally moved us there for good in 1965 to work and live in the King Koin Launderette.

My father had a diastema, a strong gap between his two front teeth, inherited from the Peters clan on his mother's side. The bottom half of his left front tooth was capped with gold, the legacy of a disastrous teenage attempt to open a bottle of beer with his teeth. The beer part of that incident had to be kept from John, who was told instead that Willard had broken his tooth on a pop bottle, which was bad enough.

The gold cap glinted in the sunshine as I stood beside him, his little ridealong, on the front seat of the car and watched him try to dodge tar-filled potholes. Cursing those cauldrons of black stew, my father delivered parcels for the post office, supplementing his income from the King Koin. He drove a sky-blue 1960 Chevrolet Impala, long and finned out, which he'd reluctantly taken in trade from Jacob for a beautiful maroon Oldsmobile Dynamic 88. My father swapped down to please Grandpa Funk, who coveted that Olds as soon as he laid eyes on it, delighted to give up the blue Chev he'd bought brand new.

I, too, had a thing for cars and car culture. Their grilles were living faces made for counting during parcel delivery trips. Corvairs, Studebakers, Ramblers, Metropolitans—I knew and loved them all, obsessively lining up rows of Dinky Toys on the living room floor or watching customers wash the real thing clean in summer at the outdoor car wash Grandpa had built on the side of the launderette.

The grave-shaped sump under each vehicle stall filled with heavy silt until the silt pressed up on the cast-iron grate. With a long-handled spade or a crowbar, my father would pry the grate up from the sucking muck and tar and begin to shovel the stuff into a wheelbarrow. Soon he'd be down inside the sump, heaving muck like dull clods of evil Jell-O above his shoulders and into the barrow—then roll it away, grunting and sweating and groaning as the soft rubber tire bounced over the potted ground, the result hefted upright in the back alley, muck sliding malodorously into a shivering pile.

His face started to bear the look of chronic pain, a clenched grimace of suffering, as the ulcers that would soon kill John also broke out in a frenzy in my father's gut. He drank so much milk, the only relief available then, that he took his five-foot-ten frame well above 190 pounds, the most he would ever weigh.

Then his appendix became inflamed as well, and threatened to burst. I saw him gagging over the toilet in the bathroom in the basement, a look of abysmal pain and misery on his face.

I asked him what was wrong.

"There's a turd snagged in my appendix and the doctors are going to cut me open and take it out."

"What's an appendix?"

"It's a tiny little finger of intestine down here." He pointed to the affected area just above his right hip, then spat into the toilet.

"It's useless anyway and now it's plugged with that little turd and got all infected."

I felt feverish on his behalf, as though I could throw up too, just like I felt when I saw a silverfish scuttle out of the drain in the tub while I was sitting there naked waiting to take a bath. My mother came to draw the water, and then called my father to remove the silverfish: the tip of its slimy head writhed at the lip of the drain, and neither of us dared to insert the plug.

My father wasn't the only one of us to lie on his back in a surgeon's theatre. Dr. Hussein, an ear, eye, and mouth man, examined my crossed eyes and declared that he could straighten them. At the Holy Family Hospital down on the West Flat, in two successive surgeries set a year apart, he popped out my eyes and adjusted the muscles behind each one. While he was at it, he also removed my tonsils and adenoids.

Twice I was cradled in a nurse's arms while a suffocating black rubber mask covered my nose and mouth and the sour ether swept me away as a voice counted down from a hundred. I lay blindfolded in a hospital crib for a week or so after each operation. Every day during visiting hours my parents would come up to the ward where I lay, homesick, blind, unhappy. I reached out to touch their faces as they stood by my crib. I tried to tell them about the mean nurse who flipped me over in the crib to give me a shot in the ass because I cried too much and wouldn't shut up.

After my surgeries, I no longer had to wear glasses, though Dr. Hussein informed my parents that my eyes weren't fully tethered and never would be. I lacked proper depth perception. I was told, for instance, that I'd never pilot an aircraft because there were things I just couldn't see and I'd never know I couldn't see them. Runways and pucks were high on the list.

18 The outdoor car wash on the side of the King Koin was such a success Grandpa Funk built another, a stand-alone building across the avenue from the launderette. He'd contemplated this for a long time through blue clouds of smoke courtesy of Number 7 cigarettes: how a car wash also called the King Koin would be built containing four bays with cement walls and a pump room in the middle, roofed with sheets of corrugated aluminum. For the grand opening, he'd buy ads in the local newspaper emphasizing the slick new automatic bay lined with giant rollers bristling in red and white. YOUR CAR CLEAN AS A WHISTLE IN JUST TWO MINUTES. A sign outside this bay would state NO TRUCKS, but occasionally trucks would enter anyhow and get tangled in and damaged by the rollers. The customer would complain and Grandpa Funk would point solemnly toward the sign, refusing all requests for a refund. Those trucks, he would say, bugger up my rollers so it takes half a day to get 'em working again.

Now, there was so much muck to shovel my father and grandfather got down in the sumps every day, sweating and groaning as they heaved jiggling masses of sediment into wheelbarrows. I walked beside the barrows and helped to push them upright, engulfed in the harrowing smell. Mounds of drying mud grew on the car wash lot along with quack grass and ancient leftover caragana circling the yard. Kerby made change, mowed grass, and sprayed cement pads, picking up drenched trash and stinking, ruined chamois rags.

Grandpa's favourite thing was to collect coins from his car wash and launderette. He moved from machine to machine, a ring of keys attached to his belt by a retractable chain. The coins fell in a bib around his waist. He rolled them into brown paper and placed them in a dried-up brown leather satchel. Knew from day one that his King Koin launderette and car wash were money-makers. He'd calculated his break-even down to the nickel.

Behind the car wash there was a slough. Four or five worn-out shacks and little houses dotted the landscape on the far side of the water. Frog song drifted across 2nd Avenue to the hot launderette with its cacophony of driers and spinners and washers; stepping out, you could listen instead to the slough going full bore, a parallel universe. Early and late in the day the two cosmoses rubbed up against each other as the amphibious singers vied with the whirring launderette.

I wandered over and stood on a warped old plank and gazed down into the algal, mosquito-breeding murk, mesmerized, waiting for something to move. Tadpoles, leopard frogs, salamanders, toads, and garter snakes crept and slithered and swam in those green waters. Muskrats criss-crossed them and in certain seasons appeared on the road after sunset, hurrying toward some mysterious destination, thick, scaly tails trailing. In late childhood, I rode my bike beside them, talking as they hustled along the darkened streets—primitive and odd under the glow of the occasional street lamp— until they stopped and reared up, pivoting on their tails, baring their long yellow incisors, sick to death of my pestering ways.

19 We often took the two-hour drive south to Langham to see John and Edith, who were building a bungalow around the corner from the old white one where family members still gathered on weekends. To pass the time, we sang songs or counted cars.

> We are going to Langham,
> We shall not be moved,
> We are going to Langham,
> We shall not be moved,
> Just like a tree that's
> Standing by the water,
> We shall not be moved.

Standing on the hump in the back seat, I watched my father's cigarette shrink as it burned and the ash grew correspondingly long and crumbled into the ashtray. I asked him why the cigarette got smaller.

"It's burning away, son."

The smoke curled out of his mouth and disappeared up his nose. The cigarette shrunk, the smoke curled up and in and out again.

"Why? And why doesn't Mommy do that?" Of the Funks, only my mother and Marie didn't smoke.

My father smoked Sweet Caporal King Size and sometimes Rothmans and sometimes a pipe. The rich spicy smoke from the pipe filled the space around him with an aroma of Christmas. He'd tap it on the brass pedestal ashtray till the blackened bowl coughed up its offal in the tray's centre. Grandpa Funk extinguished a pack a day of Number 7s, but my father scheduled his smokes, year in and year out. Grandpa Funk consumed his in a series of quick, fluid motions, sucking hard on the filters so they took on a crushed look, but Willard my father savoured his allotted intake, standing by the mantel or gazing out the window as the blue fumes travelled from mouth to nose and out again: out and in, repeat.

Langham, a town of five hundred, had sidewalks on both sides of each street, all paved. Not like PA, where sidewalks appeared and ended arbitrarily and the streets were midnight blue with sticky gravel gathered on the edges. My sister and I took turns walking between our parents as they each held a hand and swung us back and forth while walking.

Grandpa Boschman's new bungalow had a single-car garage with a baby-blue door attached to one end, making the whole edifice seem the longest house ever.

A golden wood plaque with Gothic lettering hung in the foyer; it was the first thing you noticed.

> The beauty of the house is order;
> The blessing of the house is contentment;
> The glory of the house is hospitality;
> The crown of the house is godliness.

The clock ticked in the new house just as it had in the old one. A silence of some kind held in the air above the din of children's voices and uncles laughing till they cried. Grandma Edith brought out her large wooden platters purchased from the Mennonite Central Committee and the uncles ate her mincemeat tarts while the kids looked for cherry or butter tarts—anything, really, but loathsome mincemeat.

Lola Margaret, the only daughter, silent and stoic and born to Edith, sat at the dining-room table playing Scrabble, and there also was Aunt Ann, the wife of Willard's younger brother James (also born to Edith), her face a lattice of scars, her jaw wired, sucking on soup and talking through her teeth about the wicked car accident she'd survived with James, who'd emerged unscathed. Ann's brother had married Lola, making their combined progeny, my first cousins, double first cousins.

In the backyard, Edith planted a large garden scented in spring by tulips from Holland, not seeming to mind that they were shipped to Canada each year in gratitude for the role Canadian soldiers played in liberating Holland from the Nazis. Every spring in Langham, the Dutch tulips sparked debate and muttering about whether peace-loving Mennonites should accept and grow them. Some were angry and thought it hypocritical.

In the intense heat of summer, cucumbers and dill dominated the air in Grandma Boschman's garden. The yard was never fenced. It faced the gravel parking lot of the Zoar Mennonite Church, and on Sunday mornings we all walked the hundred yards to morning service.

There, under the spinning fans high above our heads, John and Edith celebrated their silver wedding anniversary. Arnold, their oldest, stood at the pulpit, the master of ceremonies. On the wall behind his head, in large Gothic font, were words like hieroglyphs, runes of a stern code into which every one of us had been born: "Selig sind die Gottes Wort hören und bewahren!" (Luke 11:28).

At night as I lay in bed in that long house, waiting to fall asleep, the silence interrupted only by a clock's ticking far off in another room, I repeated a prayer my parents had taught me:

> Now I lay me
> Down to sleep.
> I pray the Lord
> My soul to keep.
> If I should die
> Before I wake
> I pray the Lord
> My soul to take.

As I grew older, I wondered in that dark hum of silence when everyone else was asleep what it would be like if I died then, there in the night after I said that prayer and then finally dropped off into sleep and dreams. Would the Lord, whoever that was, come to take my soul, whatever that was? And if not, what then?

At home in PA, in the basement of the King Koin where the furnace kicked in and out and the boilers and machines never stopped, there was a picture of Jesus on the wall next to my bed. It was brown and plastic, framed by a rustic hem of leather stitching. Jesus's face looked kind and considerate; his brown hair and beard flowed softly down and surrounded his eyes, soft and brown like a white-tailed deer's.

If he was this Lord, I asked myself later, did he really choose some of us and not others?

Next to this plastic image of Jesus was a framed photo of me sitting in a small rocking chair in my pyjamas, my blond hair neatly combed to one side, my eyes still slightly crossed despite the surgeon's best efforts, my cheeks still toad-like and chubby, just as Kerby said. I thought I looked like a little old man rocking in his chair. Could I do something at some point, perhaps much later in my life when I had grown up, that would anger this Lord enough that he would not choose me if I died in my sleep?

It was my distinct understanding from the earliest age that though children were not generally considered sinners, they could be, they could do wrong, and definitely when they reached a certain age they became accountable. But what that age was—ten? eleven? twelve?—wasn't totally clear to me.

I was beset with such questions; they hung around me. Even Grandma Funk—so bird-like and energetic and nothing like the truculent Boschmans, who boldly took off her blouse on a hot summer day and padded around in her brassiere making change for customers— even she had a plaque on one wall behind the King Koin.

> Only one life,
> 'Twill soon be past,

Only what's done
For Christ will last.

"The moments of your life are passing you by, Robbie!"
She would point at their German cuckoo clock or at one of Grandpa Funk's many watches, which fascinated me, their second hands clicking faintly along.

"Every second that ticks by is gone, gone forever! It never comes again! With every second you are closer to the end of your life!"

She'd pick up her diary and describe the weather and what was on for supper that night. Marie's intense concern with time was, however, almost completely secular—she saw only the transient details of daily living, not spiritual torment or eternal punishment or abandonment in the night when the soul might flutter free.

20 When my paternal grandparents' full story first came to my attention, John's words, written in a hand I came to know well, pierced my brain. Bookish kid that I was, living at the back of a launderette sandwiched geographically between All Saints and the jail, I felt my dead grandfather's first words like a nine-inch nail through my identity.

The drama of his life and death, and especially the existence of a grandmother named Margaret, about whom I had heretofore known nothing, changed my life. I was never the same kid after that. I'd carry their story through all my subsequent years, visiting their graves, reading their letters and journals, having dreams about them.

My finding out about Margaret was the result of a question I asked Grandma Edith at Christmas 1970 at her house in Langham, two years after John's death. I was sitting with my cousins and siblings at her dining-room table and I asked Grandma if she believed in ghosts and, if so, whether she had felt or seen Grandpa in that long house with its ticking clock.

I was reluctant to ask such a question for fear of seeming impertinent, but the need to ask overwhelmed me, and so I did.

To my relief, she answered me without hesitation.

"Yes, I often feel Johnny's presence," she said, almost nonchalantly, as though it were an everyday thing.

She disappeared into the basement for a few minutes and returned with a dark-brown wooden box about the size of a small treasure chest. She placed it on the dining-room table, removed the lid, and invited us all to look.

That was when I saw the notebook with the boy on the cover, the bright-yellow box stuffed with letters, the framed photo of John and Margaret on their wedding day, the yellowed and desiccated wedding veil all balled up, the bag of hair, the photograph of Margaret lying in her coffin.

There were many other items in this box, but these were the things that caught my attention the first time the box appeared before our family.

She was a real person, that lady in the coffin. She looked like my dad. There was her actual hair in a small bundle inside a crumpled brown paper bag. I recognized the little brown bag as a grab bag, the kind that was usually filled with assorted candies and cost a nickel. This one contained dark hair from my father's mother, who I had always assumed was Edith—which was not the case, and I'd have to sort it all out, which would take time. For now, I felt this Margaret enter my life as a real person, speaking to me through that swatch of hair and through a photo of her lifeless in her coffin in a parking lot, clothed in a white dress, surrounded by a crowd looking at her.

What a scene.

Margaret, perennially young and my grandmother, twenty-one years before my birth—run over, Edith said, by a travelling salesman from Toronto on his way through Saskatoon.

The date would stick in my heart and mind from then on, as would the name of the driver, Harry D. Reid.

Was it the power of kinship through genetic inheritance that I felt in that moment and that changed me? This was an important question that arose later, to persist in various forms. In this moment of life-altering discovery, I was entranced by the new knowledge of my paternal grandparents and unborn uncle. John, Margaret, Edith, the boy who wouldn't be. I'd never unsee or undo any of this. But I'd carry a torch for them, come to understand my grandfather, and somehow or other find a way to "map" what had happened, that I knew for sure.

Do we have such experiences that shift our being at the cellular level? And, if so, do these occurrences ripple and swell beyond and through us, whether or not they're acknowledged or even known? In an age when terms like post-traumatic stress disorder are regularly invoked, such questions may seem naive, but sometimes the things we assume are self-evident, or have heard and overheard many times, are the things that need recounting.

Then and there, in Edith's dining room, I was a child with a child's instincts. To me, Margaret's hair had agency. I touched it and it touched me; molecules inter-twined; atoms uploaded; I stared at the photo of her standing next to John on their wedding day; I stared at the picture of her lying there dead; I saw Willard my father as I never had before—and I was altered.

* * *

The word *epigenetic* literally means that which is "on top of the genes." I think of it as gene skin. It refers to an idea developed (before the word itself was coined) by a man named Jean-Baptiste Lamarck who, decades before Darwin, surmised that "soft inheritance," or the inheri-tance of acquired traits, plays a role in the relationship between generations.

Two centuries after Lamarck, Susan Merrill Squier describes the "exciting promise" of epigenetic theory by way of questions now opening up about the generations before us. She asks, for instance, "Did our grandmothers face starvation during pregnancy, leaving us a legacy of weight problems or undernourishment?"

For me the question looks like this: Did my paternal grandfather, John, leave a legacy of extreme trauma that was absorbed by his children, including my father, then a toddler, and subsequently passed on? In particular, I've been wondering about the impacts on the men in my father's family: Arnold, the oldest son, and his sons, especially Digger, my me-not-me, as well as Marvin and my father. I've also considered the real possibility that I, too, have been profoundly affected in ways I will never know for sure.

Epigenetic theory opens the door to such questions by relaxing the hold of strict genetic determinism—we are only what our genes dictate—and thereby inviting us into "a new understanding of biological organization that stresses plasticity."

As philosopher Ada Jaarsma puts it, this affects "how we place ourselves in time, especially in relation to ancestral figures."

In addition to culture, environment, and genes, the epigenetic dimension of heritability presents itself as an important factor in each individual's development, but more significant still, it also impacts the formation of whole communities and landscapes, with their histories of power, dispossession, betrayal, and violence in particular places and times.

21 When my mother informed me that the sun was bigger than the moon, I lashed out in frustration. How could this be? Thus far, I'd spent my conscious life looking at the sky and seeing plainly that the gentle moon was obviously larger than that little orb of fire. I tearfully argued with her in the living room of the big white house where she was painting a tree arching diagonally across one entire wall. For a while, I was angry at the moon for deceiving me.

We'd moved from the basement at the King Koin into the white two-storey house across the back alley. Grandpa Funk's eye had long been on the white house, so when the opportunity to purchase appeared, he took it. Often when we looked over at the white house from the King Koin we saw the brown insides of the bluff, then the green sward of the empty lot rising up to the street, and finally the white house with its roof red like arterial blood. Farther on was a little red and white bungalow. No fences, no manicured lawns or paved driveways, no flower beds, no signs of care or class or moneyed ways entered this scene—only two tall, wild poplar trees right at the intersecting alleys plus two maples and a lilac bush with a path through the middle. All had taken seed long ago with or without helping hands.

The big white house smelled of cat piss. At the back door off the L-shaped galley kitchen, the odour attacked and never let up. My father, incensed, investigated the source; he found it down in the claustrophobic cellar, where one wall of red brick gave way at his nose level to an earthen crawl space. He instantly set to hauling out the tainted soil and the odour dissipated, almost but not quite. Always a residue of the original problem haunted our noses and memories.

This fact only fed the Funks' distaste for animal life. Unlike the Boschmans, who were intimately connected to most non-humans, both wild and domesticated, the Funks rejected most anything animal. If the subject came up, they'd snort and regale you with the story of the one pet they'd ever had—a lame greyhound named Legs, a loiterer of the first order. Till Grandpa Funk could take no more and shot him on the back step while the kids looked on and Marie stayed inside with her ears plugged.

Oldest boy Wayne, after whom I took my second name, backed a truck up to the step, loaded Legs, and drove him off to the dump.

* * *

We lived in the big white house for about a year before swapping dwellings with Jake and Marie, who grew tired of the constant interruptions from customers looking for change and assistance. Even after we moved back across the alley in the late summer of 1967 to occupy the main living quarters of the King Koin, though, my territory had forever expanded to include the rough-hewn area around that house, with its sandbox, grass, trees, and empty lot.

The ancient maple between the white house and the bungalow next door leaned out over the bluff facing 27th Street as though some giant hand had pushed the trunk closer to the earth. We kids could easily walk up the knotted trunk and into the upper branches, which draped alongside the bay window of our living room where my mother had painted her tree just like it, leaning down invitingly.

It was on this old living tree, hanging over the hill facing the street, that my siblings and I met the children of our next-door neighbours Louis and Margaret Henry—Linda, Rickie, Barry, and Suzie, plus two First Nations kids from the far north, Cecile and Marlene. I first saw Louis atop a ladder fiddling with something at the edge of his roof, a cigarette dangling from the corner of his wide mouth. I called up to him and then ran off to find my father and brought him over just as Louis climbed down to the ground.

Older than my father, he had black hair and high cheekbones and was always smoking and often smiling. A dark blue and red and green tattoo on one forearm caught my eye, the indelible mark of his stint in Korea, where he was wounded and then sent home with an honourable discharge. Somewhere on his body Louis bore the scar left by a bullet, and I always wanted to see it but was too shy to ask. After his return to civilian life in Saskatchewan, he contracted tuberculosis and wound up in the sanitarium north of Prince Albert where Margaret was a nurse.

Louis and my father were instant friends and our two families merged and melded into one: one household, one lawn, one big barbeque. Louis had grown up at Batoche on a narrow riverfront parcel owned by the Henrys along the South Saskatchewan. His father's name was Napoleon and the Henrys had survived the Riel Resistance of 1869–70, which had taken place right on their doorstep. In his high-pitched singsong voice Louis spoke Michif, the French-Cree hybrid language of the Métis people, and never had a harsh word for anyone.

Laughing and smoking his Export "A" Plain, Louis drew my father into another world and another history, introducing him to his siblings, Roy, Clara, Alfred, Joe, and Johnny, and taking him to a party or two where the men would suddenly and without warning break out in a brawl, only to stop just as quickly and all laugh and start drinking and playing cards again. Watching one of these scraps, my father saw Louis's glasses fly off, landing in the middle of many moving feet—and he intrepidly crawled into the scrum and retrieved them before they were crushed.

All of this came as a longed-for release from the theological and cultural burdens with which my father wrestled and under which he had suffered, in part because of the sudden tragic death of his biological mother. With Louis, he could drink the locally brewed Bohemian lager and say whatever came to mind. Arnold and Marvin, his brothers by Margaret Peters, were the only others with whom my father could be himself completely.

* * *

My family took a summer vacation to British Columbia in our new car, a wine-red 1966 Chev Bel Air with a

427 V8. We stopped to see Arnold and his family at the Brad Gunn Standardbred Horse Farm, where mares were bred to the great stallion Adios Pick, from Adios and Pick Up, and Arnold worked as the farm manager.

Entering the tiny living room where Digger was watching a black-and-white television brought me an electric thrill, the deep satisfaction of reunion with someone I'd come to love profoundly—who was me-not-me, linked by blood and family history but with instincts and a prowess that to me were exotic and sometimes even alien.

Stuart was working alongside Arnold, absorbing his father's equine lore. Hardly older than ten, his thick and crazy brown hair was starting to streak on one side like a patch of cold white ash. He walked like his father, with the same fluid sway of the hips, altogether masculine and powerful yet feminine at the same time. Somewhere deep down, I wanted to walk that way too.

Grandpa Funk and his sons, by contrast, walked in the signature Funk style—a bobbing lope with the head jutting forward like a horse. If indeed there was one animal they could appreciate it was the horse—but only from a distance—and Arnold's and Stuart's keen ways with the musky brown Standardbred earned their arms-length admiration. Besides, there was money to be made buying and selling horses.

I didn't see Grandpa Boschman often, but he loomed over my life in the things my father did. One Christmas morning, I woke to a miniature farmyard with a replica of the barn on the Langham farm. It had a high central gable descending gracefully to a low point on either side. The lower edges of the roof lifted on hinges inserted partway up on both sides. It was grey with red trim and surrounded by the usual tableau, a complete array of tiny vehicles, implements, animals, and supporting structures. I still have this barn.

I didn't know then that I was a settler on this land, a newcomer. I hadn't yet come to realize how entire nations of humans, each with its distinct language and culture, had already been here for millennia and been lied to, betrayed, and injured beyond anything I could imagine. I'd come from four patriarchal Mennonite lines—Boschman, Funk, Friesen, and Peters. These families had fled the Old World in the nineteenth century to join a then three-hundred-year-long diaspora that began just after the Reformation. They had originated in the Netherlands and in Flanders before the fracturing of the Catholic Church and their subsequent immersion in the Anabaptist movement, setting out on a series of flights from religious persecution that would eventually bring them to Canada as refugees hundreds of years later.

22 When it comes to John and Margaret, I'm the well-behaved boy sitting quietly in the back seat of the 1929 Plymouth on June 29, 1940.

Since the day I learned of their existence as a couple, it's seldom been any other way. I keep coming back to it, this day that changes everything, taking it in again and again as though some part of my mind could be likened to a sensor inside a digital camera, the shutter opening and closing faster and faster:

The man from Toronto in the big car.
The policeman, Sergeant Greggain.
The Reverend Henry Rempel and his wife.

Susie Heide screaming her lungs out.
The slab in the morgue.
My grandfather clenching his jaw
   and Arnold receiving the news.
The lilac blossoms lingering still.

Then to high-density video as I watch the scenery pass
while the road angles east and south toward Saskatoon,
just before that moment—because the mind doesn't
follow the conventions of linear narrative. It just doesn't.
Farmland, pasture, barbed-wire fencing. Domesticated
animals. The old Plym (John's term) has a top speed of
forty miles an hour. My grandparents' destination is the
Eaton's store at 21st and 3rd Avenue. Margaret is talking
cheerfully. She has what John calls a "sunny disposition."

John has just been paid. Late as usual. He's been a
rural teacher for six years and in that time he has never
been paid on schedule. The Great Depression and all
that. Their pantry is bare and Arnold (four), Marvin
(three), and Willard my father (two) need clothes for
the summer. The evening before, a kindly neighbour
brought over a pail of milk.

They've left the boys in the care of the local preacher
and have set out on the road later known as Highway
16, the Yellowhead, so named after a blond-haired fur
trader, Pierre Bostonais, nicknamed *Tête Jaune*. Two
years after Margaret's death, crews of Japanese Canadian
men interned by the Canadian government during the
war will complete this national highway route, but the
name *Yellowhead* won't be inaugurated till the seventies.

* * *

In a terrifying dream I had (and have never been able to forget, however much I've wanted to) I'm standing outside a warehouse that looks like a building from the 1930s, like the old buildings still standing here and there in downtown Saskatoon. I see people crawling over the outside of the building, like insects appearing from and disappearing into its many windows.

Then I'm inside the building, in a room with one of those very windows. The room is empty. No furniture. Its ancient walls and floors worn and blackened by feet.

There has been so much traffic here in this empty place that there are clearly demarcated and well-worn paths.

Three or four people clomp up the stairs toward a door that opens into the room where I stand. I hear them before I see them, and when I do see them I don't know them. They are faceless, anonymous. They enter the room carrying a heavy box and, to my astonishment, they flip it over. It lands upside down on the tarry floor at my feet. Then just like that they lift the box with an upward thrust and exit the room, taking the box with them.

There on the floor is a box-shaped clod of earth (blacker than the black floor beneath it), which falls away from a larva-like white body that I realize with horror is Margaret's—a grub buried for so long, muffled in gumbo.

Whatever she is now, I am deeply afraid. The faceless porters, or pallbearers, have left me alone with her, her alabaster skin glistening like the *schönes* land where John (using the German word for *shining*) imagined she had gone in that instant when everything changed.

She lies like a creamy baby bee in her heap of dirt, which, as it falls away, exposes her hands. I can see her perfectly preserved fingers, her manicured nails stained purple as though the last thing she did was eat saska-toon berries.

Here's where I wake up: When Margaret opens her eyes and looks at me.

23 Longhaired, bearded paddlers in freighter canoes appeared from the west on the North Saskatchewan. They camped in Bryant Park, one block east of the King Koin, and spoke to me in frag-mented English with Québécois accents, their water-craft turned over on the grass serving as shelter from the elements. They were retracing the journeys taken by early European explorers by canoeing across Canada to Expo 67 in Montreal.

I wondered why they were camping in Bryant Park, up on the hill and so far from the river—how they'd managed to get their canoes there and how they'd get them back down to the water.

I was riding a bicycle, a red one with a red banana seat. My parents had found it second-hand and surprised me. They taught me to ride in the alley that emptied onto oily 1st Avenue, across which was the south end of Bryant Park, rimmed by a stand of tall spruce three or four rows deep.

As I rode my bike through the trees, the ground dropped to a grassy pitch used for soccer. I was alone, my own pilot. Off to my right was the covered Kinsmen Arena and outdoor public swimming pool. To my left the park stretched north all the way to 22nd Street. There were ball diamonds, paved lanes, a paddling pool; the original house of PA's founding father, the Reverend James Nisbet; tall old ash, maple, and spruce trees; as well as complex growths of caragana and lilac containing warrens that were menacing after dark.

My parents didn't have to tell me not to enter Bryant Park at night, where it was rumoured the unmarked graves of prisoners lay.

Across 28th Street from the rink the old provincial jail, built in 1886 immediately after the Riel Resistance, stood like some medieval fortress grimacing voyeuristically at the passersby on foot and the steady line of family vehicles driving in and out of the parking lot that fed the pool and arena.

My father insisted on using the word *Resistance* rather than the usual *Rebellion* to describe the conflict between Métis and First Nations and the federal government led by John A. MacDonald, Canada's first prime minister, who announced from Parliament that Riel would "hang though every dog in Quebec bark in his favour."

The face of that old jail was bleak and foreboding. I couldn't pass it without feeling myself watched by suffering eyes. I could well believe dead prisoners from its earliest days lay in the park in unmarked plots, and partly for that reason I didn't travel in its unlit depths. The other, more realistic reason for avoiding Bryant Park at night—that I might get mugged—wasn't far from my mind either. A good friend of my dad's, a young Danish landscape painter, had been severely beaten for his case of beer. His jaw broken and wired shut. Soon enough he'd also drive into a moose; the huge animal joined him in the front seat of his car, shredding his face like minced beef.

Our own prime minister, John Diefenbaker, had famously quipped that Prince Albert consisted of "persons of conviction," referring to the unpleasant fact that the city held the penitentiary and provincial jail (he made these remarks before the correctional centre for women came to town).

The mouldering old jail might always be there, I thought, just a block away, the place for men who'd been sentenced to two years less a day, or so said my father when I asked him who was inside its walls and behind its barred windows.

"What's two years less a day?"

"It's the maximum sentence given to men who commit minor crimes."

"What's a minor crime?"

"Stealing smaller things, worth at the very most a few hundred dollars."

"Like my bike?"

"Yes, like your bike."

"What about our car?"

"That would be more serious."

"If someone was caught stealing our car, what would happen?"

"Well, the judge might send him to the pen."

"Isn't that where murderers are?"

"Yes."

During the late summer of 1967, a drifter named Victor Hoffman murdered almost the entire Peterson family at Shell Lake, Saskatchewan, not far from PA. He walked into their house with a .22 rifle and shot nine people, seven of them kids. One girl hid beneath a bed. After he was caught and sent to the asylum at North Battleford, Hoffman explained that he'd let her live because she had "the face of an angel."

I lay awake at night thinking about this man Victor Hoffman—directed, he said, by Satan—and tried to picture how the events of that day transpired. The Sask Pen warden lived right across the street from us. He had his black belt in judo and that gave me some comfort as I tried to sleep, but still my mind returned to the Peterson family. I tossed in bed in my upstairs room listening to the sounds of our old house, wondering what the mom had said and done, what the dad had said and done, what the seven poor kids had said and done, as Victor Hoffman shot them one by one. I knew without a doubt that had I been there that day, playing perhaps with the Peterson kids, I would be dead. Victor Hoffman would have taken one look at me with my slightly crossed eyes and known immediately that I didn't qualify for mercy. I felt immensely sorry for the girl under the bed. During that autumn, as I started grade school, she was never far from my mind.

The following summer on our way to Turtle Lake we drove slowly past the Peterson homestead, forlorn and abandoned and bone white, a husk of a house by the highway. It stood by itself at the end of a long driveway, already becoming derelict. Waves of loneliness, despair, and panic reached out from that scene, pulling at our car as we left it behind us.

I wanted never to see it again.

Not long after I got it, my bike was stolen from our yard and then recovered in Bryant Park, its tires and seat slashed. My mother sat at her sewing machine and made a cover of dark-brown vinyl. She pulled it down like a toque over the banana seat mutilated from front to back. My father replaced the tires and bought me a lock.

Although my bike was never the same, I was able to go out riding again in the sunshine, east toward the park and past the jail.

* * *

Why I was "accelerated" remains a great mystery, but it's interesting how terms connected to speed pervade our culture.

My grade 2 report card gave no indication of a mind at work, only that I was a Squirrel (the name given to my cohort of accelerated students) who'd unwittingly completed the grade by Christmas.

Like a pilot ejected from the cockpit, I was jettisoned from grade 2 across the hall, landing with dramatic precision in Mrs. Lensen's classroom. My parents said little and apparently had no real input in the matter, though my being accelerated immediately altered my stars' alignments. The farther time carried me along from that apparently innocuous event, the more I realized its impact. The line of dominoes that began to shuttle at conception in the love shack on the farm at Langham shifted because someone made a choice. The old line still stands covered in dust in some other cosmos, a life unlived about which I've had nothing to say until now.

Tall, cool, blond Mrs. Lensen wielded a range of teaching methods that literally stuck in one's head. She was silent and swift. I don't remember her voice, only the sight of her pencil planted liked a nail on some kid's skull and the book she employed to hammer it home. Fortunately, I—Robbie Boschman, moved up from grade 2 halfway through the year—didn't merit a shard of lead in my scalp, though I certainly witnessed Mrs. Lensen's modes of persuasion: a knock on the head with a pile of textbooks, a whack with a yardstick, a sharp pinch of the trapezius delivered from behind with precision and force. Star Trek's Mr. Spock could not have done better.

"Onward Christian Soldiers" was a staple of morning exercises, when the school gathered in the gym to kick off the day with prayers, gladness, and rectitude. One year a grade 1 child stood up in the first few rows at the front of the auditorium when we started to sing "Stand Up, Stand Up for Jesus" and the whole school laughed. Even the principal, Mr. Reed, who never, ever laughed, broke out in the smallest smile. The program for morning exercises was reliable: first the singing of "O Canada" and "God Save the Queen," then a resounding hymn ("The Blood of the Lamb" being yet another) followed by remarks and announcements by the vice-principal, Mr. Sopatyk, and the recitation of the Lord's Prayer. Before heading off to class, we asked to be forgiven our trespasses.

That word—*trespass*—was confusing and no one ever explained it. On farm properties outside PA I saw signs saying NO TRESPASSING. What did it mean to ask God the Father to "forgive us our trespasses as we forgive those who trespass against us"? That going on someone's lawn was bad and that if I, say, walked on the nicest lawn on my block, Mr. Mossman's—a man who yelled at us if we even looked at his lawn from across 27th—I was offending the Creator? I had no problem forgiving anyone who walked on my lawn. Unless you counted the green stuff around the big white house (but that was just regular grass), I had no lawn. Certainly not Mr. Mossman's Kentucky blue.

Every day, dozens of people marched up to the heavy wooden door of our living quarters at the rear of the King Koin, asking for this or that. A constant flow of people and vehicles permanently, it seemed, outside our living room window. And over at the white house, too, kids and neighbours came and went, criss-crossing over yards, broken sidewalks, dirt driveways, with no thought of trespassing.

Yet here I was each weekday morning and once on Sundays in church saying this prayer with *trespass* in it. Six days of every week I said that prayer and ratified that contract, asking God to forgive my trespasses and promising to forgive anyone who trespassed against me. I guessed that Victor Hoffman had trespassed on the Peterson family's property, but he'd done far more than that. Would he be forgiven? When that little girl who hid under the bed said the Lord's Prayer, what did it mean to her? I for one didn't want her to forgive Victor Hoffman for coming on to her family's property and taking all their lives away. I didn't want anyone to forgive him, ever.

24 Growing up I guessed that Willard my father was on pretty good terms with the First Nations people who came to the launderette from the reserves surrounding PA—Muskoday, James Smith, and Beardy's and Okemasis to the south, Little Red River, Mistawasis, Sturgeon Lake, and Montreal Lake to the north. Most of these folks were Wood Cree, although the Wahpeton Dakota were present in small numbers as a legacy of the so-called Indian Wars in the United States a century before. Except for those who either lived in PA or resided as students at All Saints, taken from homes in the far north, the First Nations people who visited our launderette lived on land under the terms of Treaty 6, as all Prince Albertans do today.

My father took me to Fort Carlton, to see the place where the treaty was signed in the summer of 1876. All the chiefs of the Cree, Assiniboine, and Dene had gathered there in that year—and those who couldn't make it met days later at Fort Pitt to place their X next to their name. The lands of Treaty 6 are described in detail in the text of the treaty itself, or at least the borders— very important these, to the colonizers—of this territory that stretches across what are now the provinces of Saskatchewan and Alberta, but weren't then during that summer. The land between the rivers (the North and South Saskatchewan meeting at the Forks), where my story takes place, is a small portion of this great territory.

I never heard my father make a racist comment like the kind frequently said on the streets of white PA. My parents knew and taught us that First Nations Peoples had been invaded, had negotiated and signed Treaty 6 in good faith, and were the subjects of an ongoing cultural genocide—though not in those precise words. My parents weren't intellectuals, but their instinctive sense of justice and history was self-evident and they weren't shy about stating plainly what they thought had happened on the very land where we were living. My father read every book on the subject he could find during those years, including Farley Mowat's *People of the Deer*, which he spoke of often at the dinner table. He waded into pitched battles with friends and foes alike regarding the cultures, status, and histories of the various First Nations in Canada, as well as Indigenous Peoples throughout North America.

While the Mowat book influenced his thinking about the relationship between humans and their environment, as well as the destructive impact of European colonialism on the landscape, animals, and Peoples of the Arctic, Maria Campbell's *Halfbreed* made an even bigger impression on my father and thus on our household. These two books so expanded the grievance he carried in his heart that it was impossible not to feel their effects even though I wouldn't read them myself until my later years.

One summer night I lay awake in my bed in the room off the boiler room—the one with the hole in the wall—and listened as my dad, with his typical calm intensity, debated with a close Mennonite friend about the intelligence of Indigenous people. The friend maintained they were stupid because they couldn't apparently assimilate and be like the rest of us. Even then, I'd heard this line of argument before. I lay there a long while, a silent, unseen witness to my father's passion for justice as he took his friend, a prosperous farmer and landowner and someone I liked very much, ruthlessly apart. When it came to that issue, all bets were off for Willard my father.

Every morning as I left the back of the launderette to go to school, I saw kids from All Saints making their way down 28th Street on foot. When the weather was bad and I couldn't ride my bike, we walked together. Maynard Whitehead, Roderick Rat, George Tate were all boys I knew who lived in residence ten months of the year and attended Vincent Massey. I wondered where their homes were but they didn't tell and I didn't ask. We walked mostly in polite silence, only a few words here and there, and at recess played soccer or softball. When the ground wasn't frozen and covered with snow, they ran in black canvas runners with white toes, issued by All Saints. I wouldn't wear their shoes, I thought, and then immediately felt ashamed. I wanted Adidas, white leather ones with blue stripes or blue suede ones with white stripes. I bugged my mom to buy them for me, to take me to the shoe store on Central Avenue, but she never did. I promised her I'd eat fried liver and onions (with ketchup) and not complain. She wouldn't have to tell me about the starving kids in Biafra either.

* * *

Just around the corner from the Co-op along River Street, Carney Nerland, a white supremacist and KKK member, shot and killed Leo LaChance, a fur trapper from the Big River Reserve.

LaChance, forty-three, had hitchhiked south to PA to sell some pelts at the Hudson's Bay Trading Post on January 28, 1991. When he found the store closed, he tried the pawn shop next door, owned and operated by Nerland. Instead of buying the pelts, Nerland shot Leo LaChance, who collapsed on the street and later died in the hospital. Nerland was found guilty of manslaughter and sentenced to four years.

When this happened, I felt my heart break. I was nearly thirty years old and long gone from home. All my father's teachings, his relations with people at the launderette, came back to me in a rush, even as the Kanien'kehà:ka resistance and uprising at Kanehsatà:ke (the Oka crisis) was happening. Nothing had changed. PA had learned nothing from its past.

25 Checking out the King Koin's gutter was my favourite job. My father knew this, so he had me perform other after-school and weekend chores around the launderette first. I swept the floor with our wide-bristle broom, first spreading oily blue sweeping compound to trap the dust. A launderette couldn't be dusty, so this had to be done twice a day. Garbage cans were dumped in the incinerator, the fire lit. The tops and fronts of all twenty-four front-loading washers were wiped down. Neither a dribble of coffee nor a sopping patch of powdered soap could be seen.

Willard my father would slap me on the back and say, "You're a good man."

Then I made my signature move and entered the gutter.

The gutter ran the length of the central island of twenty-four washers, twelve per side with their backs facing one another. These were built into a slightly higher wooden structure covered in white Arborite, the entire structure standing atop a foot-high rectangular base of cement. Beneath the pale shining Arborite shell and running down the middle of the base, the gutter received the complete discharge, including that of a big sink at the head of the island. At the foot was the entrance consisting of a small door, also of wood and Arborite, secured by a clasp and padlock.

Going into the gutter required key, flashlight, rubber boots, and a small plastic pail. Only one person could enter at a time. If, though, a machine broke down and could be repaired without tilting it right off the base, then Grandpa Funk and my father could always remove the roof of the gutter, allowing them to reach their tools on the surrounding washer tops. But I didn't need or actually want the roof removed. I loved stepping into the dank dark, the beam of my light on the backs of the machines and dirty, sudsy water.

I knew that our customers would forget to check their pockets and that whatever was in those pockets would drain with the water at the end of a cycle, flowing at intervals through the rank chutes that stuck out like long greasy tongues behind each machine. From the larger mass of bobby pins, washers, paper clips, slugs, silt, and sludge, I found coins, dollar bills, rings, brooches, jackknives, even watches. The occasional bullet or red shotgun shell appeared in the turbulence.

The whole trove was lifted up and placed in the pail to be scrutinized and sorted in the light of day.

My father, meanwhile, was usually engaged in other tasks around the King Koin. The outsized green dryers forming a bank against one wall held giant traps that lifted up and out to reveal sheets of lint like multicoloured quilts. The gas pilot lights were notorious for winking out if a nor'wester was blowing, in which case customers came to our door on the hour. Each time my father squeezed along the wall behind the bank of dryers to reignite yet another pilot.

In winter, the wall at his back would be caked with frost and he'd be shivering by the time he re-emerged.

On the other side of the launderette, another bank of machines was even more troublesome than the dryers: the tall yellow dry cleaners with their space-age look, as though NASA and not Philco Bendix had manufactured them. Unlike the washing machines, which were fifty cents a load, these needed two dollars in quarters to put through a cycle because they used a modified hydrocarbon, perchloroethylene (or perc), to "dry" clean men's suits and ladies' formal dresses.

My father and grandfather hated perc, invented in the 1940s and not recognized as a carcinogenic until the 1990s. It didn't take rocket science to know this stuff was bad.

"Never touch perc," my father commanded, and I never did, though I liked the smell. It had a mesmerizing odour, like airplane glue or gasoline. It made me dizzy.

My father posted signs on the bank of dry cleaners requiring customers to have their loads inspected first; too often he'd had to deal with a breakdown in mid-cycle because some "pinhead pig farmer" had elected to throw in his barn boots and green sewer parka along with the wife's drapes.

This meant my father had to touch perc.

26 I saw Grandpa Boschman alive for the second-to-last time in February of 1968 when he and Grandma Edith came to Prince Albert to attend the annual winter festival down on the frozen North Saskatchewan. Unlike Grandpa Funk, expansive and outgoing, his nose and hairy nostrils much larger than Kerby's, his legs splayed as he stood in the kitchen of the big white house, arms waving back and forth, a cigarette burning in the ashtray—unlike that, John was grim, contained, and undemonstrative, but determined nonetheless to visit the festival.

In his little green Frontenac, he and I drove in silence down to the river and parked on the dark ice where a large area of snow had been cleared away. I saw other vehicles parked there also, and this gave me comfort as I anxiously considered the thickness of the ice and the weight of so many automobiles and concluded finally that we were safe. Beneath my feet dangerous currents powered eastward and yet here we were, along with many other people and dogs and sleds, held up by a thick slab of ice.

To the east, the river disappeared into a distant wall of coniferous forest partly created by Bateman Island some ways off; to the west, it passed under Diefenbaker Bridge, beyond which the late afternoon sun reflected off the snow in a shimmering plume of light.

The red-brick fire hall stood above us on the south bank of the river. To its left was the long white hall of Lund's Wildlife Exhibit, an extended narrow house stuffed from end to end with a taxidermist's paradise, or someone else's nightmare, of dusty specimens of every mammal, reptile, insect, amphibian, and bird in the region. It was a cabinet of biological curiosities. Once or twice already I had paid a quarter to traverse that silent hall with its cadaverous throng of non-human forms staring through glassy eyes at nothing. Bears and wolves, coyotes and badgers, and my favourite, the wolverine— all the local predators right down to the elegant ermine— bared their lacquered teeth in grimaces of fury. It was a tableau of aggression created for visitors to Prince Albert, billed far and wide as the Gateway to the North and an endless bounty of nature.

Outside on the river, long teams of silver-eyed dogs pulled tough northerners in long-celebrated races whose winners would be announced the next morning in the *Prince Albert Daily Herald* and on Jack Cennon's *Wake Up, Shake Up Show* on CKBI. I'd be getting dressed and hear Jack's voice coming from the kitchen along with the smells of oatmeal, coffee, and toast. Trappers and furriers and hewers of wood talked to Jack throughout the day, informing Prince Albertans and visitors from the surrounding region of the schedule of events.

The festival would close with a huge bonfire of Christmas trees collected and stacked on the ice throughout the week. For part of a day, Grandpa Boschman and I wandered wordlessly around the festival site. We watched the dog pull, the king trapper event, the beard derby; marvelled at the mukluks and moccasins on display, as well as the winning entries in the Winter Festival poster contest. Everyone donned that year's Prince Albert Winter Festival button with its sled dog logo.

As we were leaving, John offered to buy me a candy floss. It was my mistake to accept. How others had made similar mistakes before me was something I thought about only long after I'd left PA, and John's cement headstone had eroded and been replaced by a tougher one made of dark granite. The original bore the epitaph "He Has Kept the Faith" before it was covered over with dusky stone bearing his name, the years of his birth and death (1905–1968), and the small emblem of the honey bee. I was so taken by the pink cotton adhering magically to the paper cone that I couldn't help but nod my head, even though I'd never eaten this kind of sweetness before and didn't know how to put in my mouth. I botched it right away, covering my lower face in a disastrous web of sticky pink sugar. The pressure was too much, as it would be later when I was playing organized hockey and simply collapsed. Where another boy or girl of different disposition might well have shrugged off this early mistake and continued trying this new thing— eating candy floss—I lost control and cried. And my grandfather reacted by walking me back to his car with a stern reprimand, "What's the matter with you?"

And then the words, "I'll give you something to cry about," words I heard again that summer as we crossed pasture near Langham and I got tangled in a barbed-wire fence and, alas, began to cry. We were on a walkabout with John and this was the last time I saw him alive. Our family had driven down to Langham to visit Arnold's family in the house they were renting on the eastern edge of town, backing onto open prairie, a few tufts of stunted poplars here and there. Their German shepherd, Pat, who'd lived with all of us on the dairy farm, waited at the end of the dirt driveway till she could see our Bel Air approach on the little highway from the east, clearly visible from Arnold's green bungalow.

WHITE COAL

27 Don't look back. Forget about it.

In hockey, the past is in the past: another shift, next period, new game tomorrow. Hockey people thrive on this mentality even while they remember *everything* and get all misty-eyed over key events, especially the ones that either elevated or shamed them, their team, neighbourhood, town, city. Canada swallows this whole and documents it. The public record of events that matter. Many things must be remembered, it's true, and some can't be forgotten, while others shouldn't be but are. Or the stricture to forget is made in earnest. Bury it. Entomb it. Nail it shut. Leave it crumbling out on the river east of town, like La Colle Falls, for future generations to think about, if by chance they travel out that way.

Seeing and knowing matter.

Did Grandpa Boschman play hockey? I asked the question many times, knowing the answer already but wanting to hear it anyhow. Like all the men in our family except me, John went to Rosthern Junior College; but unlike most of the young males who spent ten months of the year at RJC, he didn't play the game. In fact, he was a poor skater. Born in 1905, the middle child of fourteen, John was in no position to take up hockey or even skate much, and when the stock market crashed in 1929 he still hadn't attended school beyond grade 8. This wasn't uncommon during that era, but after the sudden economic collapse, John had no prospects other than to finish his schooling. In November 1931, six weeks before his twenty-sixth birthday, he went to RJC to get his diploma. He wasn't happy about this—in fact, he was downright sullen—but he saw nothing better. The plan was to graduate quickly and go to Normal School in Saskatoon for his teacher's certificate.

There are no old photos of John hunched gallantly over a hockey stick, smiling for the little Brownie camera, flashing a grin. But there are photos of my maternal grandfather Jacob Funk and his younger brother Mervin, and a generation later of Wayne Funk and his brother Garth, as well as Willard Boschman and his brother Marvin. All played the game for RJC. Jake Funk happened to be at the college himself when John arrived. He looked up to John as an older man he could admire, even as he, Jacob, fell hard for Marie Friesen, also a student at RJC that year.

I discovered a remarkable tiny photo in one of Marie's voluminous annotated albums that records a scene no one else in our family ever noticed. The picture shows a group of teenaged students sitting on the expansive college lawn. Off in the bottom-left corner, far from the centre, two of them appear, a boy and a man. The man lounges face forward on his stomach, ruminating on the grass before his face. This is Johnny Boschman, his hair combed back and piled up high on his head, his brow slightly furrowed, unsmiling. The teen boy sits beside him, and like John is turned toward the left edge of the photo but looking off, smiling, looking almost deliriously happy. This younger dark-haired student, the driver's cap on his head turned backward, is Jacob Funk, thinking perhaps of the lovely Marie, who also appears in the tableau.

If three of my grandparents appear in an image in the spring of 1932, it's John who's out of joint with time, the older man returning to school, feeling embarrassed. His temper can flash fire. If you tease him about his poor skating, as a cocky male student does one afternoon on the school rink, you run the risk that Johnny Boschman might skate up on those weak ankles and pop you. He can throw junk, swing from barn rafters, and handle a team of draft horses, so he needs to strike only once to knock you out, catching the side of the jaw where a cranial nerve descends. The story of John's fellow student being carried unconscious from the ice lives on in our family. It's been repeated with some irony by his three oldest children, who loved their dad but were beaten black and blue by him. They heard the story from John himself, a steadfast Mennonite dedicated to pacifism. His ambivalence and guilt about committing an act of violence linger in the dark green notebook where he named the individual who'd incited his fury.

My ankles were weak too. My on-ice life began just as John's life ended and the grown-ups noted my flimsy ankles. The first time I laced on skates, I felt shame before I'd even stepped on the ice. My ankles wobbled like two metronomes. Walking barely from the dressing room to the ice was bad enough; the split-second transition to the ice was almost unimaginable that first time. Like being swallowed—like what I thought it'd be to leap from the John Diefenbaker Bridge into the North

Saskatchewan with its mid-current eddies and unfath-
omable murky ways.

Adding to my doubt and fear was the brilliant skating
of a boy my age gliding around the rink, his father
watching with pride. This boy schooled me in how to
skate at the indoor Kinsmen Arena located up the alley
from the King Koin and facing the old jail on 28th. My
father must have noticed those powerful strides and
measured them as I did against my metronomes because
the next time I skated was different. I'll never forget his
easy solution to my unworthy ankles: U-shaped supports
that slid inside each boot and allowed me to get my
stride without worrying about my ankles. They were
cream-coloured and pinched against my ankles when
Willard my father wrapped the thick laces twice around
each brown leather high-top and tongue, cinching hard.
My job was to place a thumb firmly against the first tie at
the summit of the laces as he formed the first loop and
passed the second through it and brought the double
bow into tight formation.

"How does it feel?"

"Okay."

As we repeated and refined the procedure, I learned
to say "Okay" even if my foot hurt a bit. My skate would
relax and feel better, though sometimes one boot would
loosen and I'd have to ask for help again. Then he'd
partially unlace it and we'd repeat the ritual, correcting
the fault.

28

This box John chose is originally and
outwardly a wooden artifact of industry,
from a time before cardboard. Faintly

visible on the exterior flanks are the words *Champion Chemicals*, finely impressed in scarlet.

The box is memory. It is large enough to hold other, smaller boxes made of paper bearing designs and colours used in the 1940s. With its dovetail corners, brown paper lining, and pair of holes—one on either end of the lid—where John placed small nails, it is a private repository, a cache of intimacies.

Also a vault: the hair and the death photo are there, along with two *Saskatoon Star-Phoenix* newspapers, amazingly preserved given the fragility of newsprint, dated July 3 and 6, 1940. Other things are there as well. It takes time to get to know them.

The box also represents family history, not just because it holds records of births and deaths. On the underside of the lid, a child has drawn a map of North America in crayon. The whole underside has been reinforced with plywood, and it's on this plywood, secured with many small golden screws, that PACIFIC and ATLANTIC are inscribed on either side of the continent.

The box is additionally a familiar, a personal relation, something one holds close. It's travelled with me in my own household for many years. It represents and contains the dead. They need a spot that is dry and dark.

Once, from sheer anxiety, I placed the letters in a safe deposit box at my bank. Then I lost the key. Finding it again relieved my panic, and I used that moment to retrieve the letters and put them back in the box.

The box is to me—as a living being is—a unity that can't be replaced. As I get older, I think about its future.

This brings me to a final thought. The box exemplifies a future promise contained within the past. It is not simply the past, important though that is; the box holds a historic future desire recorded in actual events.

A vision and expressed wish (followed by the reality) that is found in the past, my past and my extended relations' past. This has turned out to be—is always becoming—now. It records a litany of future promises, promises that turned into people, of whom I am one.

I will, we shall, let it be so.

Faith in a semi-benevolent and capricious God accompanies these promises, carried out in word and deed by settler actors with their spasms of passion, hope, grief, rejection, violence, and fear.

29 When Narcisse Blood (Tatsikiistamik), a Kainai Elder, visited Calgary's Mount Royal University, where I have taught since 1998, he filled the classroom until there were no seats left and students, faculty, and community members stood at the back and sides of the space. Narcisse showed us a short film of his recent visit to a museum in England, where sacred Blackfoot artifacts have been kept for over a century. He spoke as we watched a group of Blackfoot from both Canada and the United States witness their belongings being brought out of archival storage and presented for them to see and touch during their short visit.

A young Blackfoot warrior holds up a sacred shirt while his Elders encourage him to put it on. He does. The joy and grief are palpable in Narcisse's video; they transmit into the classroom where Indigenous and settler students and faculty sit and stand. We are all profoundly impacted. People are weeping quietly.

Then I hear Narcisse state: "We went to England because we wanted to see our stuff. Now we just want our stuff returned. We want it back. We want to bring it home."

30 John died on December 2, 1968, just short of his sixty-third birthday. His last words were two, "That's enough." He'd spent six weeks in the Swift Current hospital with a perforated stomach that wouldn't heal. It's hard to discern whether he knew he was going to die or decided. When he emerged from surgery to sew up the lining of his stomach and informed Edith he wouldn't leave the hospital alive, she scoffed.

"Oh Johnny, don't be silly, ulcers don't kill people."

"I've seen Jesus. He's waiting."

Swift Current was a long drive south of PA and Langham. John lay on what was indeed his deathbed. In that fall of 1968, he and Edith had made the drive in his little green Frontenac to volunteer at the Swift Current Mennonite Bible College now that John was a retiree. But John's old ulcer broke and started oozing. The surgery revealed extensive scarring. Throughout November, he received transfusions for the constant blood loss, grew thinner and less substantial; the ancient wound this time wasn't going to heal. Peritonitis set in. Edith stayed at his side and the six children visited frequently; finally, he said no more transfusions, he was going home—by then Edith realized this was really it.

We drove south in the red Bel Air to visit John a last time. The young adults and Edith gathered around his bed while my siblings and I waited in the car outside the hospital. I looked up at the hospital window, curious about the drama going on up there but not really understanding what it all meant. It'd be years before I learned about those moments when John addressed his family and said he was going to die and pointed at his youngest son, sixteen-year-old Randy, as his main regret.

"I know he needs me."

Soon after the death of his father, Randy would run away, wild with grief.

My father has a Polaroid from the late spring of that same year showing John fishing in Otter Rapids on the Churchill River in northern Saskatchewan. Named after a seventeenth-century governor of the Hudson's Bay Company, the Churchill is a magnificent river traversing the province from west to east. Its headwaters are found in Churchill Lake, fed in turn by the Beaver River Basin in Alberta: it flows east through countless bodies of water into Cedar Lake in Manitoba, where it empties at last into Lake Winnipeg, which in turn flows into Hudson Bay. The Woodland Cree called the great river *Missinipe*, Big Waters. Longer than either the North or South Saskatchewan, and containing nearly twice the volume of those two rivers after they combine to become the Saskatchewan, the Churchill is the ninth-longest river in Canada, eclipsed in total size only by the Mackenzie, Saint Lawrence, and Columbia.

Six kilometres north of the village of Missinipe, John relaxed for a few days, fishing for walleye, yellow perch, and northern pike in the torrent of rapids where the Churchill's volume squeezes into a narrow channel about a half mile in length. A high cast-iron bridge spans the rapids at the midpoint, providing access as far north as Reindeer Lake. Beyond that huge lake, back in 1968, the grid road known as Highway 102 petered out, and those wanting to travel farther north either flew by bush plane or took a winter road as far as Uranium

City, an Eldorado mining town on the north shore of Lake Athabasca.

Past the roar of Otter Rapids, European voyageurs had portaged their canoes, guided by First Nations men and women who knew the way. John talked about that. He seemed happy. He even drank a few Boh, something he rarely did unless away from Langham, usually on a country road with a Hutterite neighbour and it was a cold beer consumed almost urgently, as though someone might see him. Selecting lures, tying lines, feeling all that river moisture hanging in clouds of fine mist, watching Louis and Willard smoke and catch fish, John let it all go for a few days.

31 For a decade after John's death, Edith lived in the centre of Langham in the house John had built, while Digger and his family held a succession of homes scattered throughout town. There would be four houses in all that would inform my childhood. Two of these, both green, were found on the outskirts, while the other pair stood closer to Edith. Like satellites or small moons, Arnold's houses were held in her orbit. Only her immense gravity kept them from spinning away.

Arnold was nothing if not restless, his one constant the Standardbred horse, especially the trotter who raced unfettered. The pacer was faster but required hobbles to regulate her gait. Stuart, the oldest, his full name actually John Stuart, had now become a teen. His band of white hair, which first appeared in childhood, interrupted an inky hirsute mass like the Milky Way seen against the dark matter of night on the edge of Langham.

In the green houses out on that edge (one to the east, the other to the west), the family also had two dogs in succession, Pat and Angus, one for each house (and in between a stint in PA living with us that was dogless).

I worshipped at the altars of my cousins Digger and Stuart, both of them it seemed to me sleek and brimming with animal grace and menace. I fantasized that one or both intervened on my behalf to prevent some approaching danger or apprehend a villain and beat him senseless. I think my cousins and their dogs represented in my child's mind a hazy drama of justice, retribution, revenge even. There seemed to be a submerged energy working through all of us that was directed at payback.

I was also a part of this—I who was cross-eyed and born with a tremor, as though wired so tightly something might snap at any moment. I was so taut with relentless anxiety my hands had a permanent tremor, as though Parkinson's or some other motor neuron disability had taken over my nervous system, and my father took to calling me Shaky Rob. He must have seen me twitching as I arrived on earth partly out of his own father's drama.

"Hey Rabbi, forget about ever being a surgeon, someone will die." And they all laughed and my dad cried.

"Yeah Robitai. No bein' a mechanic either."

"Yep, someone will for sure die."

Through the dogs Pat and Angus, our family drama appeared in different ways the whole town could see. In fact, it exploded. I can describe the first explosion here.

Pat the German shepherd was a tragic dog, a dog who fell from grace, unlike the second dog, Angus the basenji, who had no vocal cords and was poisoned. Even as Pat performed wonderful and mysterious acts, like waiting for hours out on the driveway, knowing we were coming all the way from PA, she was flawed by an absolute hatred for all non-humans. Another dog or a cat or kittens meant instant death, and not for her. Once, on a visit to the white house in PA, Pat killed a litter of kittens hidden behind a sheet of plywood leaning against the Henry bungalow. There was chaos and much weeping. This was but one of a series of such incidents after all us Boschmans were off the farm and John was dead.

In the unfenced yard of the first green house on Langham's outskirts, Pat finally went too far. She bit a hole in a neighbour girl's dog and the girl, Dagmar was her name, went to her parents and the parents demanded Pat's death. So right then and there Arnold, his name actually John Arnold, took his father's old single-shot bolt-action .22—the one they'd all used for years growing up in the Neuhoffnung School District where John was a teacher south of Langham—and shot Pat. A head shot was best and the old rifle had deadly sight.

This took place—and Digger told me all about it, broken-hearted and hating Dagmar—immediately after our drive down in June 1968 when I walked into the living room and there he was, waiting for me. The T V was on with everyone gathered round, watching the funeral train of Robert F. Kennedy. My parents were upset. Only two months before, Martin Luther King Jr. had been shot in the face while standing on the verandah of a motel in Memphis, Tennessee. Now the younger brother of John F. Kennedy, also assassinated, had been killed by a man with a grudge and a gun.

But we were Canadians and Canadians didn't do stuff like that; we were nice.

Sitting on the floor in front of the television, as we kids all watched black-and-white images of a train crossing the continent and crowds of people standing and waving and weeping all along the tracks, I learned that when I clenched my fists hard enough my knuckles popped, every one of them.

32 We call him Gabe most of the time. Gabriel whenever trouble arises.

He's the only son I have and I cannot imagine having another. His mother calls him "the most alive person I have ever met." We thought about calling him Jude but decided we didn't want the Beatles' "Hey Jude" following him around all his life. These things happen.

I had a dream about my son seven years before his birth. I saw him lying on a bed with his mother. Brown hair, about three years old, fast asleep on my side of the sleeping arrangement, no room for me. I stood by a window and looked out on a medieval city in Flanders, where the Boschmans had once lived before the Reformation. They were Catholics then; they likely spoke both French and Dutch. The name Boschman is an old one and literally signifies *man of the bush*. Somewhere in Flanders there was, I imagine from this distance five centuries later, a stand of timber where a folk lived who became known as *those people who live in the trees: Boschmans.*

On a trip to Bruges in 2013, we wound up staying in an eighteenth-century house. We occupied the low-ceilinged timber-framed rooms at the top: a garret actually.

Bruges is in Flanders and everywhere we went I thought I saw my father or one of his brothers or Uncle Bill or John.

I didn't make the connection to my dream of a decade before until the first evening, when Gabe and Sari fell asleep and I stood by the window and looked out on this ancient place. Dark tower outside the window just the same as in my dream; sleeping and room arrangement within also just the same. It unnerved me. I'd remembered this dream so vividly and spoken of it to my family circle after Gabe's birth in 2010, when that thick shock of dark-brown hair reawakened my memory of a dream in which a brown-haired boy would enter my life.

Earlier that week as we'd visited other parts of Belgium, we'd gone to the permanent Bruegel exhibit in Brussels because I wanted to see *Landscape with the Fall of Icarus*. I stood before it for a long time, thinking about the English poet W.H. Auden. During the 1930s, he'd also visited this masterpiece and responded with his own poetic one, "Musée des Beaux Artes," with its famous first lines: "About suffering they were never wrong, / the old Masters." In the painting's foreground a man ploughs the earth in a long furrow stretching off into the distance. His head of hair dominates—thick and dark brown—as he drives his plough away from the viewer, into the future.

33 The Boschman and Peters families were close neighbours till 1931, when the financial crisis of two years earlier forced the Boschmans off their land and they moved to an old growth forest in the northeast of the province, a forest they would help to cut down. The farms lay between the village of Aberdeen and Clarkboro Ferry, six miles west on washboard road that after the crossing met Highway

11 connecting PA and Saskatoon. The Boschmans numbered sixteen, including the parents, Cornelius and Anna, who had settled in 1903. The younger Peters family consisted of Jacob and Helena and their growing brood, who had moved onto their place in 1924.

Born at the tail end of 1905, John was the seventh child of ten boys and four girls. In the twenty-four years between 1895 and 1919, his mother Anna Heide Boschman gave birth on average every twenty months, many of these taking place in the farmhouse built by Cornelius. By 1931, three children had predeceased John, including the oldest, also named Margaret, who contracted tuberculosis and died a hard death just as the older Boschman boys departed for the bush at Carrot River in a caravan of jalopies, Bennett buggies, wagons, and farm animals.

Although John's family had auctioned off their eight-hundred-acre spread, with its two-storey house, hip-roof barn, orchard, machinery, and assorted smaller dwellings where relatives and friends could stay, seven of them remained behind: John and Anna; her three youngest sons, among them Uncle Bill, and one older boy, Jake, who had just married his sweetheart, Justina Nickel. They were waiting till the new home and outbuildings were built, at which time Cornelius would come and get them—but there was another reason. The oldest Boschman girl, Margaret, was on her deathbed.

During this time, Anna and fourteen-year-old Bill went down to the ferry house almost every day to see thirty-five-year-old Margaret. Anna couldn't leave her to the care of her husband, the ferryman, David Dyck. As Anna was heard to say during her long life, "The old must die; the young may die." She'd brought her daughter into the world; she was determined to see her out of it too. She'd stared down death and grief before; this wouldn't be the last time.

Only after her oldest girl finally passed away on the day before Halloween did Anna make the long trek to join the clan.

John stayed back even longer, working at a nearby dairy operation through the winter of 1930–31. The job extended into the summer and early fall so he was able to remain close to Margaret Peters. He and Margaret had been going together and enjoyed a set of young friends. On Sunday nights throughout that year, the Peters farmhouse was crammed with young people. After the 1931 harvest, John finally had to head north as well, searching out prospects. He couldn't marry on the wages of a lowly hired man with his hands at the teat till his dying day. But when he arrived by train in the muddy town of Carrot River and from there made his way, mostly on foot, some fifteen miles into the bush at Petaigan, where the Boschman crew had built a log house and were preparing for their second winter in close conditions, John discovered that that was a dead end too.

34 In mid-December 1968, I crossed the alley and parking lot from Grandma Edith Boschman's back door to the Zoar Mennonite Church in Langham where John lay in his coffin. I was seven and John was dead and I'd never seen anyone dead before. What would happen when I looked on him, like I knew I would do? I couldn't not look, as some choose to do when the departed are on display.

There he was, wizened, shrunk, still, such a contrast from the man who'd bought me candy floss on the river ice and warned me not to cry.

Edith stood beside him at the front of the church. We looked at him together. I asked her why he still wore glasses: Would he need them?

Edith said no, he wouldn't need them. She took them gently from his face and folded them into the palm of one hand.

Those eyelids never to open again—though I imagined they suddenly might. The mouth pulled down by gravity, covering the fine, straight teeth—though it could perhaps move a final time with the words "Don't cry."

Not much later, *Butch Cassidy and the Sundance Kid* played at the Orpheum Theatre on Central Avenue in PA and in that masking dark I thought I witnessed John's presence in the two leading men. The shape of Newman's face, his forehead, cheekbones, chin. How he carries himself in that film, rides a bike even, everything lost at the end. And Redford's teeth and magnetic smile. I imagined them as carefree, heroic versions of John, what my grandfather could've been but never was, not for me.

But at that point I knew zilch about John's history. At the service, I saw tears streaming down the face of his second son, Marvin, sitting in the pew across the aisle over my left shoulder. He was shorter than my father and Arnold but could walk on his hands and beat them in an arm wrestle. Under the ceiling fan's slow turn he looked straight ahead, his cheeks glistening.

I'd never seen a man cry: what a thing! More shocking, to me, than the box of flesh at the front of the room. I couldn't see then the four-year-old boy standing in darkness at the foot of John's bed, asking where his mother had gone. I didn't know.

Digger was traumatized too at the funeral of our grandpa. I'd entered the church by a side door and approached the coffin at an angle but Digger arrived through the foyer and saw John's casket at the end of the long centre aisle. Sitting at the back with his father and then pushed forward to view the body, his view was different. The longest walk of his life.

John had taken him into the mysteries of honey and beekeeping, placed the veil on Digger's head, prodded him to look into an open Langstroth box humming with twenty thousand bees. Had even shown him the queen herself, marvelous and waxy.

Digger approached the stillness that was John thinking, *This is a dream, not real!* And no one comforted him or told him what had happened. He was expected to figure it out, be a man, not cry.

Afterwards Edith held a reception in her kitchen and living room, with sandwiches and pickles and tarts. Stuart, Arnold's oldest and the oldest of all the cousins, sat at the piano and brought his fist down on the keys, breaking the tick-tock silence of that house. Crunchy peppernut cookies in a bowl, spiced with nutmeg, cinnamon, anise, and ginger, spun out across the floor like small wooden wheels.

It was almost Christmas. Santa would leave me a figure-eight racetrack secured to a regular sheet of plywood painted green. It lay beneath a sheet in the basement of the King Koin, the cars waiting to run right off the black grooves if I didn't control them on the tight turns.

35

Into the twenty-first century, the Boschman farmhouse near Aberdeen still holds. It even has a new foundation for the young family living there. Posted where the driveway meets the grid road that John built with draft horses named Buster and Curly, a sign advises passersby to keep going. It's adorned by a portrait of Oscar the Grouch.

No more than a few miles off, the Peters house stands too, but as a granary criss-crossed inside with taut wires meant to keep the weathered wooden shell from exploding when filled with grain. Its head removed, the staircase juts into space and bluebottle light. Two or three tarnished brass coat hooks curve from the supports beneath the stairs.

Like other abandoned settler homes, the Peters place continued to exist for years in another capacity after its people had departed. Its interior when empty has become an echo chamber for birds and insects, but with the aura of lives lived that no unequivocal grain bin can equal. When full even by half, the old house transforms to a plush sink of grain and a weir for small animals. Over the shifting mass, a dull flutter quilts the air and pigeons mouth their seedy gobble and coo in the rafters and coils of wire.

It was one of Margaret Peters's youngest brothers, Daniel, who strung the wires that have kept the house intact. He moved it from where it once stood beside the garden, with its lilacs and blood-red peonies (her favourite) to stand by the other bins. He made each wire whir like a bug as he tightened, knowing it would hold just fine: wall to wall to wall the weight of seed, those tons pressing on cedar and fir.

All that weight.

A pelvic interior, old by settler standards, with its strict cords that hold it together as long as can be.

Reading the letters, I know that John arrived within the same walls on Christmas Day 1931 with nowhere to stay but the Nickel place nearby. There she was—this cheerful young woman who would write to him faithfully for the next two years. Black-haired like her mother but taller and with her dad's broad forehead and strong brow but not his blue eyes. Helena's eyes instead, of the Buhlers of Manitoba, a tall, dark, bird-like people with bad knees and dark-chocolate eyes set wide apart. The diastema there in the smile.

36 It was family tradition to refer to relatives by the name of the male head. Marvin's meant the Marvin Boschman family, Wayne's the Wayne Funk family. So when my parents told me that Arnold's were moving in to the basement at the back of the launderette, I knew it meant all six of them. I also knew we were in for it. Willard's would live above Arnold's while my grandparents, Jake and Marie, stayed in the white house across the back alley. It was our job to make change.

The Guess Who's "American Woman" growled from the bedroom where all four of my cousins slept immediately below my room—the one with the peephole I now shared with my siblings. Under our feet, Shelly and Sherry slept in one bunk, Digger and Stuart in another, with a curtain strung across the centre. Stuart's Columbia House record collection played all day and night. Eleven records for as many cents brought Janis Joplin and Woodstock into all our lives.

Long, vicious fights broke out: Stuart pounded on Digger and Digger pounded in return but Stuart was stronger and sat on his brother's lower spine and pounded and pounded though Digger never succumbed. Fighting him was futile. Digger was like the Hulk: the more he was opposed the greater he became. THUNK THUNK THUNK. The sound carried through the floor and up the stairs.

Sometimes when the two households slept, Digger had nightmares about the Golden Moose, a fantastic dream animal who slowly clomped down those same stairs from the main floor in order to eat him alive. CLOMP CLOMP CLOMP. BOOM BOOM BOOM. Why it was golden and a carnivore were mysteries to me, but Digger was adamant the creature was real and would devour him soon enough. He lived in terror of the night, dreaming of massive antlers hovering over him so vivid and golden Stuart started to dream them too.

Both boys walked in their sleep. In their individual terrors, sleep and wakefulness clutching at their minds, they'd leave the basement by the separate entrance, climb up from the deep cement stairwell into the night, and shuffle around to our new aluminum storm door sheathing the wood one with its five upper-case letters— F - U - N - K - S —glued above at adult eye level. Even in winter, most fearfully in winter because of the possible consequences, one or the other came to our step in the night. My parents would rise to find a boy, wide-eyed, shivering, and incoherent, and whisk him by the inner stairs, down and down past the furnace and into the basement and into his bunk.

Why were Arnold's even there and not back in Langham living in one of a succession of rental homes— like the green one on the eastern edge of the town? It wasn't to help us in the launderette. Arnold and his sons were adept at sweeping the earthen aisles of a horse barn; they hadn't come to PA to sweep cement in the King Koin. They could expertly brush and curry a horse, not wipe down Philco Bendix washers and dry cleaners. My cousins mucked out stalls with professional ease; that didn't mean helping Willard my father clean a sump or get rid of old perc. Giving a horse its measure of oats didn't amount to change for a five.

Or did it?

When I asked, my father said that Arnold would look after Grandpa Funk's car wash across 2nd Avenue while the grandparents took a winter holiday, driving south to Kansas, where the Funk clan had originally immigrated before some moved north to Canada.

"Will Arnold shovel out sumps, then, and load them in the wheelbarrow?"

"Yeah."

"Make change and spray down the bays?"

"Yep."

But there were other plans afoot as well, things I wasn't privy to but saw. For years already Arnold had followed the Standardbred race circuit in Saskatchewan, racing his and others' horses in small cities like Melfort, North Battleford, Weyburn, Moose Jaw, Prince Albert, and Estevan. These meets usually lasted a few days and were topped off by one-day affairs in smaller places such as Beechey. Then all the harness horse people met for two weeks in Saskatoon and Regina.

Arnold's stable consisted of three horses—Senga Babe, Richelone Todd, and Guy B. Pointer. They, too, moved to PA, kept in the barns at the Exhibition Grounds down on the East Flat. Arnold was the trainer for a man named Fred Gartner, who owned Babe and Todd; Guy B. Pointer was another matter. My father and Arnold co-owned this horse, a nine-year-old maiden with knocked knees, purchased for a hundred and fifty dollars.

Pointer was to be the first in a series of acquisitions by the newly formed Boschman Bros. Racing Stable, which now also owned a second-hand International box hauler decked out in the stable's colours, brown and gold. A laundry customer painted the cab while the brothers took care of the box, which would carry horses and livery gear.

My father bought a pair of books, hefty hardcover editions, one black, the other green. The former was a detailed record of sires and dams, going all the way back to the foundational Standardbred sire, Hamble-tonian (1849), and back even farther to the primordial Messenger, who died in 1808 but not before mating with mares of every kind throughout America. The other volume, the green one, was a collection of essays published in 1968, *Care & Training of the Trotter & Pacer*.

If the black book was a kind of sacred genealogy of the modern Standardbred horse, the green one explained its history and rituals. It related major trotting families, the Morgans, the Clays, the Messengers. It fleshed out the names listed in the black book: Bellfounder, Mambrino, Abdallah; Old Shales, son of Blaze; the immortal Dexter; George Wilkes, Axtell, Electioneer; Adios, Volomite, and Chimes; Billy Direct and Tar Heels. These names were underlined in the pages of the green book, and I heard them come up in conversations.

A horse's speed and gait, whether hobbled pacer or free-legged trotter, were matters of great concern to my uncle and father. Guy B. Pointer, a pacer, knocked his front knees so hard you could hear him being jogged around the PA track. Painful to witness, it got downright pathetic when Al Oeming brought his cheetah to the track to run behind his car at sixty miles an hour. The only thing Arnold and my father could do to alleviate the Pointer problem was to let his front hooves grow out and re-shoe. Arnold, a skilled farrier, correctly surmised that the extended toe would cause the knees to miss each other, albeit narrowly.

In his maiden race at PA, Guy B. Pointer took first place in a time of 2:28. Even in 1890, the world record for a pacer was 2:06$^{1/4}$. By 1967, on a fast track somewhere in the East, a pacer ran in 1:53$^{3/5}$. But a win was a win, and in the swept alley and tack room of the Boschman Bros. Stable down on the East Flat my dad and uncle celebrated with stubby bottles of Boh lager. Thereafter Guy B. Pointer might place or show but never again stood in the Winner's Circle.

Eventually one of Pointer's previous owners talked Arnold into letting the gelding go. "Arn," he said, "that horse is dangerous. Those knees. You get boxed in along the rail and that sonofabitch panics and trips, you'll bring half the track down, including yourself."

With that, Guy was quietly shipped to a meat packer in Edmonton for nine cents on the pound.

37

Justina Nickel stands before the Boschman house near Aberdeen circa 1929. Her dark-framed round spectacles hardly hide her attractiveness. Even as a child, when I first saw her in this photo, I thought she was beautiful. I could see why John's younger brother Jake wanted to marry her. Before they left for the north in 1930, the Boschman boys spent much of their time with the eight Nickel kids. Both sets hung out in the Peters house, gathered around the piano singing gospel and having what they called a "swell time."

Sixty years later, one of Margaret's brothers recalled, "I knew that Johnny Boschman was going with Margaret and Jake [Boschman with] Justina Nickel. And there was a '27 Chev Johnny's dad had. I remember they were all off in the yard a ways and I could overhear them laughing but I don't know what it was about. I didn't want to eavesdrop."

Jake and Justina married on June 29, 1930, and set up their first household in an empty outbuilding on the vacant Boschman farm while they—along with Anna, Bill, Herman, and Art—waited for construction to be completed far to the north. Once the whole move was complete, Jake and Justina transported their household to a granary on the homestead.

It was the tragedy of Justina Nickel that added to John's heavy gloom during his first year of school at Rosthern. The general good times of the mid- to late 1920s had turned to widespread economic catastrophe and mayhem; and out of that mayhem the Boschmans had lost their farm and been dislocated from the community in which they'd lived since 1903; then, after being forced to relocate to wilderness conditions, Justina was killed.

Although from childhood onwards I had heard the story of her death several times, of its tremendous impact on the Boschmans and Nickels, it took decades before I realized that its timing on the new homestead at Carrot River in October 1931 coincided with my grandfather's decision to return to high school. The family storytellers had focused on the intense drama without making this connection.

Eventually it came clear to me that John, in addition to seeing his family lose the farm on which he'd grown up—and on top of the deaths of his sister, plus the separation from Margaret Peters, whom he loved intensely but without any prospects beyond courting—had also witnessed the direct aftermath of Justina's accidental death by strychnine poisoning on October 13, 1931.

In John's mind, his brother Jake, then twenty-four years old, had found true happiness in the midst of much turmoil, but even that had been ripped away.

In the Boschman house near Aberdeen, Cornelius and Anna had kept poisons under strict lock and key in a cabinet in their bedroom. During the chaos of moving, the cabinet was opened and the contents packed and subsequently unpacked in one of the new sheds built on the homestead property.

Into this shed Justina, in the early stages of her first pregnancy, went one morning in search of Epsom salts for her stomach. She inadvertently opened the strychnine container, obviously still unsecured as well as unlabelled, and took the lethal crystals thinking them innocuous.

Although these substances can look alike, the chemical properties and actions of strychnine and Epsom could hardly be more different. The latter is magnesium sulfate ($MgSO_4$), a benign salt with wide uses, including medical. Magnesium relaxes the musculature of the stomach and soothes gastric disturbance. Strychnine, on the other hand, completely disrupts normal muscular control. In a poisonous dose, this alkaloid product of the *Strychnos nux-vomica* tree native to India and Australia, and historically used to kill rodents, causes all the muscles to spasm violently until finally asphyxiation occurs.

With a half-life of ten hours, strychnine does not bring death quickly. In Justina's case, she lay on her mother-in-law's bed in the newly constructed log house for an entire day, while the Boschmans looked on in unspeakable anguish and helplessness, especially after Anna realized what had happened. The youngest boys, Bill and Herman, watched the agonizing process unfold.

After her heart stopped, one of the older boys walked into town fifteen miles to report the death to the Royal Canadian Mounted Police. Soon an officer and the coroner appeared on horseback to survey the scene and interview family members.

Although the subsequent inquest found no one responsible, Anna Heide Boschman blamed herself. She was the one who'd directed Justina to look for Epsom in the unsecured cabinet in the outbuilding. More to the point for Anna herself, the terrible accident took place because Jake and Justina were living in a granary and not in the main house. Anna had not allowed the newlyweds to move in as a matter of principle drawn from her own experience of living with Cornelius's widowed mother during the first months of their marriage. As her son Bill would say more than once, the death of Cornelius's father created a situation in which Anna found it impossible for two women to live together.

A photo shows Cornelius and his ten sons standing across a beaver dam surrounded by forest. This was either just before or after the funeral itself. All wear suits and smile except Jake, his face a tight mask, aged beyond his years. John stands just behind him, almost as though ready to catch or follow.

From childhood on, my eyes scanned their faces hundreds of times and I knew all their names, these ancestors who started from scratch with their fifty-seven-year-old dad and obeyed their fiery little mom always.

It was here in late fall 1931, after the train from Aberdeen and a long walk into the forest from the new town of Carrot River, that John found a gathering of family in the aftermath of Justina Nickel's death. There might be identity and consolation for grievous losses but scant prospects for John, who turned right around to attend school in Rosthern. He'd take with him a love for Margaret Peters that caused him no end of anxiety.

38 Long before my childhood in PA, white coal was going to come from the river and make certain Prince Albertans rich. Thus dreamed the city fathers. Hydro power would be drawn from the water and sold, driving up the value of real estate. The river would be a real money-maker.

"This'll put PA on the map," they said, congratulating each other, and the 1911 White Coal City Band struck up a tune. Its thirty-odd members, sporting all-white marching band uniforms, were outfitted with a complete array of Old World brass and drums, anchored in the centre by a big black bass drum. It's all there in the old postcard.

kistapinânihk, the sitting pretty place, had already been supposedly erased and forgotten when the electric dream bubble popped and PA went bankrupt.

My father and Arnold took Digger and me out to La Colle Falls to see the ruins of the failed dam. My cousin and I raced across a ploughed field toward the crumbling cement hulk lying across the North Saskatchewan, then abruptly reversed course when my father and uncle hollered on finding an arrowhead turned up in a furrow.

We yelled with pleasure to see the tool some hand had crafted ages before La Colle Falls.

The dam was a decomposing digit stuck out in the river. I stood at the end of it and peered into the rushing water, saw how it had been constructed so that half the North Saskatchewan was forced through it while the remaining water beyond flowed past as though nothing had happened.

La Colle was designed so half a river ran through it, endlessly trolling for white coal. Lichen festooned the yellowed cement. Rust crawled from the rebar oxidizing deep within, oozed down the damp sides. Pits gaped everywhere. Our fathers warned us not to fall. Behind stood the bank of the river thick with forest—scratchy poplar, birch, conifers—from which the cement appendage had apparently sprung or grown, a gruesome and uncanny thing covered even then with years of graffiti, old campfires, tin cans, and broken beer and mickey bottles.

The place made me shudder. Its name rang with gloom, an epic flunk.

The river kept its white coal to itself and joined the South Saskatchewan a few miles east. When we stopped there to see the watery convergence before heading home to the little city with its razor-wired gothic incarceration units filled with Indigenous men and women, its church steeples and its oily streets, its sanitarium and its slaughterhouse, I forgot La Colle Falls and became mesmerized by the Forks.

Following our dads, Digger and I stood at the chevron of earth where the rivers met and merged. I looked over each shoulder—the North on our left, the South on our right—and watched the waters join and churn eastward. Those waters lay empty of people and vessels, unlike the small lakes just to the north, with English names like Emma and Christopher, where motorboats of every kind roared up and down, each leaving a patina of rainbow-coloured gas.

Here the Forks were silent except for the sounds of birds, wind drifts, and water. On the surface of the waters flowing from the North, I saw the usual ridges of brown foam.

Our dads claimed through their Uncle Bill (Grandpa's younger brother) that this place had teemed once with people each and every spring because in that season, for centuries and more, First Nations had traditionally met here. I thought about that and about how many fish were meeting and meeting and meeting down below even as we stood there. When they were kids, our dads caught goldeye in the North Saskatchewan as it passed Langham. Digger would catch sturgeon on draglines spanning the river as it passed beneath the Borden Bridge.

All the while, the putrid brown foam spoke to me of people in Edmonton flushing their toilets, of the new pulp mill, opened for business in 1968, releasing chemical torrents into the water.

In this the year 1970 you couldn't eat the fish anymore.

This all stuck like glue inside my head, congealed and shimmering like the sweet green Jell-O thick with suspended bits of awful cabbage and carrots that appeared at every family gathering.

39 What good could come from playing on a PA hockey team with Digger?

No sooner had he and his family moved into our basement than it quickly became apparent that his stated intention to join my team, the West Hill Black-hawks, would cause bad blood. For one thing, he made short work of every bigger boy in our two-block territory between the launderette and Bryant Park, which held the only indoor rink in the area.

Part of me wanted Digger to say later he never meant to be violent. I thought he only went wild when pushed or challenged; imagined his mind going all snowy as he tore into his foe; saw him come to in the aftermath, survey his handiwork, and feel guilt for what he'd done and fear for what he might be capable of.

Another part of me loved him with all my heart, including his crazy violence.

I wondered why these things happened whenever Digger was around. Where had this will to break things come from? I didn't yet know to ask out loud but Digger never once laid a finger on me, or even threatened to, but instead quietly said, "Robbie, no one will touch you while I'm here."

I wasn't sure how to feel about that. It's true, I was getting threatened and beaten up. One kid had come after me with a wooden knife and I'd fought another in an alley while swarms of kids looked on. I'd been roughed up by a third boy, and later two boys joined forces and gave me a thrashing on the car wash pad until Louis Henry intervened, saving me from what was already a drawn-out beating. This was before my steady diet of being bullied as a lowly member of the West Hill Panthers Optimist Hockey Club. By that time Digger had already moved on, left PA and resettled in Langham— just when part of me thought I needed him most.

But during that one winter when he and his family lived in the basement of the King Koin, Digger was adamant he'd play on my team. There wasn't much I could do to stop him—and a part of me was quietly thrilled. I knew shit would happen.

He wasn't the best skater. Had he been better on blades, maybe things could've been different, or so I thought. He could have been a hero, celebrated even, like the great figures of hockey whom Prince Albertans looked up to and fantasized about. Indeed, within a year the Prince Albert Raiders (with a pirate logo) would come into existence as one of the pre-eminent junior hockey clubs in Canada.

But our coach, working with what he had, placed Digger on a grinders line and no one criticized that decision. Part of the problem was that his equipment was from the 1940s. His skates were primitive hunks of worn leather and old steel, entirely lacking support. His ancient red shin pads were made of wooden reeds sheathed in cotton and lined with felt, the kneecaps shielded by hard leather ovals.

Did he even have a "can," the protective cup I dreaded to forget, that was so fraught with potential shame? Because the can went on first in the elaborate ritual of dressing for a practice or game, forgetting to include it meant having to leave the ice, return to the dressing room, remove all one's equipment, and start over. Others noticed such things. If Digger did have a cup, it was vintage—unwashed and mildewed.

I at least had been lucky enough to get some newer stuff. I wore a garter to hold up my socks—like the other boys in the dressing room—not worrying that women wore garters. I did what I had to, what I saw the other boys do, and was relieved to produce just enough decent gear to avoid being singled out.

But Digger could not. Everything from his helmet to his pants and skates made him a target on and off the ice.

In the PA universe, he looked and moved and smelled all wrong.

Even the coach's decision to put him in goal backfired. The original goalie dazzled us in his new position at centre, quickly becoming the team's top scorer. But for every extra goal he produced, Digger allowed two. He was doomed.

But so was anyone who said anything.

One night a fight broke out in the Texaco parking lot outside my window. It was dark outside but I knew from the voices that Digger was in a brawl.

"C'mon Bushman faggot. You can blow me."

"Yeah blow him."

"No guff! Suck him off, Bushgopher!"

"Look, his gauche!"

"Pull it!"

"Aw haw, feckin' hilarious! Tiny!"

"Dubeck!"

"Eew, don' letim hit ya! Watch it!"

"Fuck you Boschman!"

Years passed before I realized how lonely and under siege Digger was. Arnold never attended our games. He was down on the East Flat at the Exhibition Grounds, busy with horses. My dad attended games, though, and maybe that explains how Digger came to see him as a kind of second father.

40 I noticed Gabe's hands as soon as he was born, squirming and bawling on his mother's chest. First the dark hair and furious face, with dimples like Kerby's and thick lips; and then the hands—so big they seemed to me out of proportion to the rest of his body. His hands hung down from the wrists, fleshy and powerful like the mitts of a grappler, as I cut the umbilical cord that had tethered him to Sari until this moment.

Those hands don't come from me.

Eight years later, because he still wants to hold hands when we walk to school each day, I'm reminded of this fact often. My hands are proportionally smaller and they tremor. The shaking is getting worse, and I know with a grim certainty that if it weren't for the SSRI and other anti-anxiety medications I take, my condition would be pressing. I'm open about this condition of mine and the fact that I've been taking medications for almost twenty years. I don't hide it. I say what I know to be true: that I wouldn't likely be here with my family, my wife and children, if it weren't for these new medications that have stabilized my nerve-wracked mind and allowed me to function as a relatively happy person.

Although Gabe and I have much in common, I don't see in him a tormented mind like John's, and for this I am thankful beyond words. The hands are connected to the mind by a direct route and are often, for me, a tell. Gabe's hands are spear-throwers, inherited from some other part of his lineage, one that will require love and education, like the kind he receives at the Montessori school he attends. Once, when we hiked in the snowy hills alongside a small mountain in British Columbia, he threw a long, straight branch at me. I happened to be holding a camera at the ready in that moment and happened to collect a startling image of the javelin leaving his extended right hand and flying directly toward my open lens. Fragments of snow fly off in multiple directions. The expression on my son's face is of indomitable confidence and joy.

41

John's depression, what he called his "melancholy," in that winter of 1931–32 always strikes me as though I've just found it for the first time. I can feel it gnawing at his guts.

He was a young man with a churning stomach, despondent for reasons beyond his powers but still responsible to his punishing God, or so he believed. The financial catastrophe of 1929 had, for one, completely rearranged his and everyone else's future prospects. It'd separated the Boschmans from their farm at Aberdeen; then Justina Nickel, his sister-in-law, died a grievous and completely unnecessary death by strychnine poisoning not long after the Boschmans had resettled up north. And now here he was back in school, surrounded by kids with whom he had little in common. He hoped to complete his exams before the summer and then start in at Normal School in the big city in the fall. That was the plan. But his confidence was shaky. He seemed haunted by more than the catastrophic failure of capitalism.

And then there was Margaret Peters, gorgeous and kind. He sometimes had trouble believing she was interested in him, even though—or perhaps because—they'd known each other all their lives. This new relationship was solidified by their secret engagement on Armistice Day 1931. But rather than bringing confidence, it caused him tremendous anxiety.

Margaret's disposition, on the other hand, was sunny, as John himself noted. Her family was younger and they'd only moved to their farm a few years before, a farm where they remained intact and where Helena, her mother, held occasional "hospitals" in which she worked on various bone, muscle, and even psychological problems experienced by folks in the area.

One of these was Margaret's second cousin, who "once jumped from a car when it was going twenty-five miles an hour and dislocated his back, but never got it fixed, and now he is getting a hunched back from that. So now he wants mother to fix it up for him."

The Boschmans had lived nearby for almost thirty years—just to the side of the only hill in the region, on top of which was an ancient buffalo rubbing rock—before everything crumbled for them in a flurry of deaths, dislocation, and financial ruin.

42 There was a snake that threw up a frog in a deep white pail. Earthworms rose from the ground when it rained, lying in still patterns in the mud around the King Koin. Leopard frogs were still plentiful then in green streaks across my sight. Tiger salamanders clung to a wall; they seemed to lie vertically and glistened like obsidian. Small, delicate tree frogs with brown backs and bulbous eyes popped along in the quack grass at the edge of the alley or under the caragana that lined Bryant Park. I saw a brown moth the size of a small bird sail with powdery wings over the pebbled, flat roof of the launderette. It disappeared and I never found out what it was.

One time a pike jumped right into my lap. It chased my lure over the gunnel of the family's aluminum boat and landed on me in a gelatinous spasm of sheer gluttony. It had the greenest gills I ever saw. My cousins and I stared at it, unable to suspend our disbelief, and our parents laughed when we told them the story. Not even the unbloodied creature held up before them for dinner that night could convince them that it had actually jumped into the boat after my lure.

In my school notebook in 1969, I'd written, "A nature detective is a man who looks after nature." At night I lay awake worrying about pollution, a buzzword then for environmental degradation. I had this chronic ill feeling, an instinct that told me something was wrong. Used oil tins were scattered around the Texaco station. Pop cans, worth nothing then as empties, littered the vacant lots where I played and rode my bike. Wrappers and newsprint rustled in the wind, partially trapped in ridges of dried mud. I saw wads of pink gum and Pud comics; long empty tubes of white paper that once held flavoured sugar; crumpled gold foil smeared with chocolate; shattered bottles in green and brown. The odd unbroken one held a shrivelled carcass (a mousey brown tuft, legs, a looped tail)—the musty smell of decomposition emanating faintly from the shadowy interior.

The thought that all this mess couldn't continue without consequences made me anxious. I worried about the small lake where we'd purchased a cabin. The water of Christopher Lake held the rainbow sheen of gasoline throughout the spring and summer months, and sometimes bathers cut their feet on the broken bottles lying beneath the water at Bell's Beach.

Across 2nd Avenue from the launderette a shopping mall was built where, for as long as I could remember, the marsh had always been, with its chorus of frogs, insects, and blackbirds. The sounds and smells of that wild place were covered over with pavement for PA's first mall. I'd never heard of a mall. A man approached Grandpa Funk to buy his car wash but refused to say why he wanted it so Jacob refused to sell; only later did my grandfather find out that the man was the developer of this thing called a mall, which was built despite Jacob's stubborn refusal to sell, the pavement stretching around the weedy lot where the King Koin car wash stood.

Our incinerator burned all day and late into the evening, when it smoldered and petered out for the night. In the morning, it chucked up smoke again. It was my job to feed the fire, collect the tall garbage bins strategically placed around and inside the launderette and empty their contents into the hot mouth. Fires in green and blue and yellow grew together and merged. Everything burned in its own time, or burst or popped. The circle of heat was unbearable by the time I emptied the last bin, slammed the heavy door, and scurried to a safe distance to watch the fire burn. A black ring mottled with exploded cans and shards of melted glass surrounded the charred structure. Farther off, behind the Nor-Lite, a Dalmatian dragged itself feebly, its hindquarters disabled by age.

I was so used to the acrid odours of things on fire, I didn't always notice them though they clung to everything, part of every waking moment. When a northeast wind blew, it brought the combined smells of the Burns slaughterhouse down on the Flat and, farther off and across the river but no less intense, the Prince Albert pulp and paper mill. Like braids in a yellow rope, the odours of animal death, excrement, and sulphur entwined and descended on the neighborhood. Not even the lilacs in June, growing everywhere in purple, lavender, and white, could counter those stinks that combined with each other along with the smoke from the incinerator.

43 They were children of the new grid, living in a time of tremendous changes to the environment. At the outset of the 1930s, when they began their correspondence, the work of the government surveyors who had measured and quantified the land into units was complete. Seeing land in terms of sections allowed for private holdings and use. It was all about possession. Fences, roads, telephone, and rail had by this time supplanted the travel routes of the Cree and other First Nations. Their ancient paths had already started to disappear beneath the colonizers' recent and continually expanding network. The third meridian ran west of Prince Albert in a long arc that almost intersected the PA Pen and outlying places like Rosthern. Although the electric grid was still to come, some farmers, like Margaret's father, Jacob Peters, had found a way to supply enough electricity to light a single primitive bulb by way of a small windmill perched atop the house.

As a boy, John helped maintain the eight hundred acres at Aberdeen owned by his father. Cornelius and Anna took possession of their farm two years before John's birth. The land flowed in a steady decline from the buffalo rubbing rock perched on a hill close to the home yard to the banks of the South Saskatchewan. John literally grew into the land, emerging into young adulthood only to see his parents lose it. The rail ran next to the Boschman property in an east–west line connecting the nearby town of Aberdeen to the surrounding lands with their villages and townships that had sprung up almost overnight.

The entire region was being farmed now, or used as pasture.

The soil of the Aberdeen area had already become famous. It was so dense that in soggy weather carts and buggies bogged down. The cloying earth was called gumbo, a term applied to the soil of other parts of North America as well. The gumbo here, however, was heavily interspersed with good-sized rocks and boulders protruding from the ground. The earth heaved up the large, worn rocks in an imperceptible but continuous ejection that complicated farming, fencing, and road building. All these activities required implements to pierce the terrain, even as it resisted cultivation with a double whammy of gumbo and boulders. The landscape in the area seemed to be in a slow boil of dirt and rock left by the South Saskatchewan flowing north to meet its partner at the Forks east of PA.

In the twenty-seven years during which the Boschmans held this piece of land and John and his siblings were growing up, the entire region was in transition—more so than it had ever been in any comparable period in its history. Using the Boschmans' pair of Percherons, eighteen-hundred pound heavy draft horses named Buster and Curly, John constructed the roads intersecting near the farm. One ran parallel with the rail line between Aberdeen and Clarkboro, where his older sister Margaret lived with her husband, David Dyck, who operated the ferry.

During this period, when the automobile was beginning to overtake the horse, John was instrumental in constructing the very roads on which this drama took place, using horses his father had lovingly bred.

Cornelius Boschman preferred the Percheron breed over its main rivals, the Clydesdale and Belgian. The massive Curly, a stud, had an especially close relationship with John. John could walk ahead with a red bandana sticking out from his hip and on command

Curly would take the bandana and pass it gently over John's shoulder. Descended from the warhorses of medieval France, the impregnable Curly, like his mate Buster, had strong feet and was often crossed with smaller horses to create a lighter draft animal. Cornelius and his sons—as well as others in the area who brought their mares to the Boschman place—favoured offspring they could both ride and work.

John loved to ride. He had a fine but nervous saddle horse, a mare he sometimes rode bareback. Once she got out of control and ran toward a three-strand fence as though to jump it, then changed her mind at the last second and dug in. John flew over the mare's head as well as the fence, landing in the ditch beside the new road—somehow still on his feet and with the lines in one hand.

The same mare was terrified of motor cars, increasingly seen on the back roads. Her fear was so bad she became overwhelmed at the mere sound of a combustion engine. So John placed her in heavy harness out in a field, well away from fences or anything by which she might, in her panic, become injured. Then he had one of his brothers drive a car slowly, across the field, toward her. It approached gradually till she could smell it. He let her stand and examine the vehicle, walk around it.

That was the end of her fear.

* * *

Beside the open casket lid in the photo's foreground, children gaze at her. One boy wears a cap with a bill and appears dazed. Two of Margaret's brothers look down on her over the top of the lid. They have disbelief on

their faces and in their eyes. One of them grips the lid
as though he will keep it open a while longer.

Whenever I visit Saskatoon, I think of how the city
scared her, almost like she knew it would kill her.

44

My father underwent another surgery
during the winter of 1970 when Digger
lived in our basement. He'd developed
ulcers that made life unbearable. He drank whole milk
constantly, gained weight. I saw his face as a taut mask
while I watched him go about his chores: sweeping floors,
hauling mud, fixing machines, handling perc. When the
doctor severed the nerve connecting my dad's stomach
to his brain, his ulcers disappeared; but now he had a
new livid scar additional to the one he received during
his emergency appendectomy. As though in sympathy,
my mother had the identical surgery. Once again the
big vagus nerve that ambles down from the brain was
disconnected, at which point my mother's own gastric
rumbling fell silent.

Then chaos ensued and all of us associated with the
launderette, it seemed, were sick.

Grandpa Funk's gallbladder almost exploded and had
to be removed. My mother's thyroid suddenly stopped
working; she became lethargic and swollen until the
doctor put her on thyroxin, which she'd have to take
for the rest of her life. Garth's thyroid became dysfunc-
tional too—slowed, sped, slowed again. My sister's
immune system cranked up: she could barely tolerate a
mosquito bite. My little brother, hyperactive and prone
to sleepwalking, was prescribed a drug called Phenergan,
flavoured to taste like orange Fanta. I took it too, for

those sleepless nights when I lay awake worrying about pollution or because a breakout occurred at the PA Pen down on the far side of the West Flat.

What better place for an escapee to find refuge, I reasoned, than the King Koin Launderette that never locked its doors? Even on Christmas Day, it was open, lit, and warm—and someone was there for sure, and the dryers were humming and beaming heat, and the place smelled like fresh sheets.

Uncle Kerby was at Rosthern Junior College during this time but appeared on weekends to help with the stream of requests from customers. They needed change day and night.

So began a time when Kerby was the guardian of my siblings and me whenever our parents needed to escape the pressures of the launderette. Cool and cynical, he drove a battered white Vauxhall and brought the Beatles' *Abbey Road* into both the white house and the King Koin living quarters. In the white house, it played on his parents' GE system till I knew all the lyrics. The heavy wooden Dutch doors with brass knockers opened and the soft crimson platter slid out, turning in three speeds on dark-red metal. "Mean Mr. Mustard" was funny at forty-five and manic at seventy-eight. Except for this one album, Kerby professed a loathing for all music. Three years later, though, his collection of LPs doubled when he bought *Dark Side of the Moon*. By 1975 the slender collection became a triptych of rock-n-roll irony as he embraced Steely Dan's *Katy Lied*. After "Throw Back the Little Ones," the last song on that album, the GE needle had nowhere else to go for Kerby.

My father's taste in music exposed the generational gap with his brother-in-law. The Beatles were another universe, their alien qualities and funny hair trumped only by the Rolling Stones' even more disturbing features and hair—but Kerby didn't care about the Stones. If *Abbey Road* blasted from the white house, my father in his own way blasted back with the Chuck Wagon Gang, Jim Reeves, Anne Murray, and the triple beats of German polka. "Snowbird" alternated with the oompahpah of polka and the old-time gospel of Reeves's "I'll Fly Away." Our family would return from Calvary United Church's Sunday service still humming "Lord of the Dance" and "Put Your Hand in the Hand" only to find Kerby making change for customers to the irreverent strains of "Polythene Pam" and "Carry that Weight" on our new one-piece stereo system purchased at the Hudson's Bay Company store at the new mall. Canada's oldest retailer, in operation since the late seventeenth century, had maintained a trading post along the river in downtown PA, but now it had expanded its presence with a department store where the marsh had been.

My father was outraged by Kerby's disrespect for his mom, Marie. John Boschman had taught my dad to see women, and moms in particular, as hallowed. He'd beaten that ethic into his sons, and those same sons, when I pressed them repeatedly, testified that they never saw John hit a woman or a girl, or speak unkindly to either. All his violence was reserved for his boys. For Kerby Funk, though, there was no beating but Ringo's on the drums. In full view, Kerby was smoking as furiously as his dad, Jacob, but with his own style of brandishing a cigarette. He pulled hard and squeezed the filter, eyes squinting, like his life was on the line—then exhaled just as hard, second-hand smoke tunnelling up, separating the Lennon bangs from his forehead. When the cigarette—at first Craven "A" King, then moving to his brand of choice, Du Maurier—was half gone, he snuffed it, blowing gale-force smoke a last time while the cigarette was folded in the ponderous brass ashtray. He did this thirty times a day till the tray filled. When I asked why he didn't smoke more of each one—and save money at least—he said the second half contained a deadly buildup of nicotine and other toxins. He was too clever to smoke that second half like all the dummy smokers in the rest of our family.

Debates emerged about the wisdom of smoking down to the filter. When I started at thirteen, sneaking out to Bryant Park with a smoke filched from my dad or grandpa, I thought about this but decided I didn't have the luxury of tossing half a smoke. In fact, as the craving grew I embraced smoking *everything* but the scorched filter. I became an anti-Kerby, a chronic secret dummy smoker of my uncle's butts.

With Kerby around, my parents escaped to our cabin at Bell's Beach. They went to the Flame Room every night to listen to Llew Bell and the Cotton Pickers. They drank the standbys: Canadian rye whisky and coke, Boh lager or Lethbridge pilsner. Louis Henry smoked his Export Plain, my dad his Sweet Caps according to schedule— one cigarette at the following times: 10:00 a.m., noon, 3:00 p.m., then 5, 7, and 9. Maybe one at 11 on an especially late night. After last call, the shindig moved to our cabin. More polka, this time on a tinny old record player. Louis's high singsong voice above the oompahpah. My father laughing and crying at the same time.

45 Soon Digger would move back to Langham, taking with him the golden moose of his nocturnal terrors, the glowing yellow dream animal clomping down the stairs to stalk his very life—as though he unconsciously knew the moose was, in fact, the most dangerous animal in Canada. He and his siblings vacated their jam-packed basement bedroom with its curtain divider, and I moved in with my little brother. The divider was gone but the spirit of the room where so many spine-pounding brawls and bad dreams took place remained. Ben and I slept together in a double bed but there was a strict yet unmarked line down its middle: if even one pinky toenail crossed that line I hit him as hard as I could.

Before Digger returned to Langham he walked with Barry Henry and me to Vincent Massey every spring morning, past the old jail. Behind its cruel facade, I imagined, festered resentments and anger. I knew most of the inmates were First Nations or Métis. By 1977, the festering became so bad the whole place erupted in an unforgettable riot. The prisoners led a coup and took guards hostage. Waves of grief rippled down the street to the King Koin. All of Saskatchewan watched as the drama unfolded on television and in the papers.

At school one morning, my classmate Jimmy, whose dad was a guard and would be taken hostage in the riot, mocked Adolf Hitler. I knew little about who Hitler was; but my friend made me laugh, and when our teacher overheard and discovered the cause of our guffaws he made us stay after school and write lines on the board.

"Adolf Hitler was a great man and did great things for the German people." When we were finally allowed to go home, the blackboards were completely covered in that sentence. Soon enough, parent-teacher interviews were scheduled and my parents were informed that I was having trouble concentrating.

When, later in my youth, I learned in detail about the unspeakable actions of Hitler's criminal regime, especially the Holocaust, I remembered writing this sentence over and over on the blackboard at Vincent Massey. Through the authors I've since read on this subject—from William Shirer and Hannah Arendt to Alice Miller and Benjamin Carter Hett—I've come to see my childhood experience of writing this sentence as a kind of hazing.

My Prince Albert.

Our teacher had black hair slicked back with Brylcreem; wore thick-rimmed black glasses and had a black mole on the tip of his long, sharp nose. He threw a kid named Joffer over a row of desks once because Joffer spoke disrespectfully, an incident that terrified us and was discussed for years. The same teacher made us laugh with jokes about his wife; compelled an errant boy to stand at the front of class as a wallflower, his face trimmed with yellow and orange petals made with paper and crayon; and we always knew when this teacher approached in the hall because he wore loafers that went clackclackclack, unlike the military thump of Mr. Reed's black boots.

When Wilfred Stanley Robertson, a Métis man, shot and killed two RCMP officers in nearby MacDowall in October 1970, the same teacher provided commentary every morning as the police searched for Robertson. As weeks became months everyone in PA and area was nervous and afraid. The police set up roadblocks and stopped vehicles out on the highways. People remembered where their rifles were. My dad had a single-shot bolt-action .303 stashed in the dugout basement of the white house. I went there to take it from the old floor-boards where it hung, down in that cat-pee-smelling brick-and-earthen cellar. I held his rifle and slid the bolt back and forth, wondering where Wilfred Stanley Robertson, described in the papers as a trapper and farmer with eight kids, was at that moment. I studied the gun and its ammo, long golden missiles of death, and knew better than to place a bullet in the chamber. My dad had already given me lessons in gun safety and I'd soon take the Fish and Game League's gun safety course.

The police looked for Wilfred Stanley Robertson for months. The people of MacDowall had long been coming to wash their clothes in our launderette. My dad knew the Robertson family; Wilfred and his wife and children were regulars in the King Koin. He also knew of the families of the slain officers and was deeply grieved and horrified by their murders. Newspaper articles across Canada urged Robertson to surrender. In November, an anonymous report of Robertson's death by suicide couldn't be corroborated; meanwhile, the shooting by police of an Indigenous teen driving a stolen car at Onion Lake was said to be without connection to Robertson, whose name had been added to Canada's most wanted along with members of the FLQ. While the RCMP hunted for Robertson, the FLQ were terrorizing Quebec with bombs, kidnapping, and murder, provoking Pierre Elliot Trudeau to say his famous three words—"Just watch me"—as he declared martial law in Quebec. By January various reported sightings of Wilfred Stanley Robertson throughout the country were discounted. The newspapers began to wonder if he was dead. Our teacher forgot about him and talked about his wife again.

Robertson's body was finally located in spring, deep in the Nisbet Forest, where he'd fled after shooting the two police officers, Sergeant R.J. Schrader and Constable D.B. Anson, when they came to investigate a reported domestic dispute. Occasionally during that winter, the RCMP surmised that the vast forest named after PA's founding missionary preacher was where Robertson had gone, although really they didn't know and said as much until his body was discovered. He could have grown a beard, they said, and been living in Saskatoon. An article filed in PA by the Canadian Press in early January 1971 quoted the police as saying, "It would take 2,000 men to cover that area inch by inch." After the thaw, he was found hanging from a tree. He'd been dead all winter and had most likely killed himself right after the shooting.

* * *

In school during that time, I studied Europe and its satellites—their histories, geographies, rainfall, economic outputs. Though my parents were sympathetic to First Nations and Métis people, and saw and spoke to them each and every day in the King Koin, they were running on experience, intuition, compassion, and the few books they'd read. No one at Vincent Massey ever mentioned the five Indigenous languages spoken in the PA area: Dene and Dakota and three dialects of Cree—Swampy Cree, Plains Cree, and Woodland Cree. I knew next to nothing regarding the histories and traditions of the Métis people who lived on my block next to the park and the jail, even though I played with some of their kids and certainly knew their names: the Henrys, the Corrigals, the Primeaus. Instead, I drew maps of Europe and Australia and made notes in immature cursive.

I knew that 570 miles lay between the north coast of Scotland and the south coast of England, while the length of Saskatchewan, which had entered the Confederation of Canada in 1905, was 750 miles. I knew of the colonies of Africa circa 1953 and the population distribution of Australia. According to one of my notebooks, I knew, too, that "if I were to stand on a tall building in Basel I would be able to see France, Germany, and Switzerland."

I also knew that the mayor of PA was Frank Dunn, the premier of the province Allan Blakeney, and the prime minister of the country Pierre Elliot Trudeau—who said "fuddle duddle" and made my dad angry when he gave someone the finger as his train passed through Salmon Arm later on in the decade.

At the behest of a teacher in 1972, I drew a careful map of PA on an eight-by-eleven-inch sheet of paper coded in four colours: light green, dark green, yellow, and brown. The colours corresponded to land designated, respectively, as undeveloped, developed, residential, and commercial/industrial. Traversed by the Diefenbaker Bridge, the North Saskatchewan constituted a mighty royal blue flowing across the map. To the east of my address at the launderette, I drew a long, slender rectangle in dark green ("developed" being defined as "parks, school grounds, etc.") that represented Bryant Park and the lands of the old jail for men. To the west, I drew another patch of dark green with the letters "S.R." for "student residence," meaning All Saints. Off to the west, light green took over, following the railway tracks into the "undeveloped" lands—"mainly farmland, woodlots"—and then the dense muskeg and forest where Wilfred Stanley Robertson had died by his own hand.

46 My parents began to think about adopting a child of Indigenous ancestry. My mom later wrote, "Will and I felt we had 'room for one more' in our family of 3 children. In the years leading up to our youngest going off to school, we saw an ad in the *P.A. Herald* for A.I.M., a program to Adopt Indian & Métis children." Part of the Sixties Scoop—the large-scale forced adoptions of First Nations children by white families—AIM was not to be confused with the initials of the American Indian Movement just south of the border, where, in South Dakota in 1972, armed conflict erupted at Wounded Knee between US government agents and Native Americans. AIM in this instance meant something very different.

My parents were still young when they phoned the number given in the newspaper ad and changed our lives forever. "We had thought," wrote my mother, "of a child that was already here as opposed to having a baby of our own." There were foster homes throughout Prince Albert at that time. My mom had been in some of them and had seen "5 or 6 in a bedroom." Some of these homes, the Henrys' for instance, were not overcrowded; they were loving and warm and proved an inspiration to my parents. Others were not. So my parents "felt we could give one such baby a better chance at life, other than being in the system."

Soon a social worker appeared at our door at the back of the launderette to carry out a home assessment.

* * *

The system *was* the Scoop, described by the Truth and Reconciliation Commission in 2015 as "the wide-scale national apprehension of Aboriginal children by child-welfare agencies . . . without taking steps to preserve their culture and identity." This practice continued until the 1980s. But the crisis is ongoing and its effects run deep in Canada. Today, the foster-home system still assimilates a disproportionate percentage of First Nations children. The Truth and Reconciliation Commission has extensively documented this fact. In the words "of Old Crow Chief Norma Kassi . . . 'The doors are closed at the residential schools but the foster homes are still existing and our children are still being taken away.' "

47 Jacques Lemaire wound up for a thunderous slapshot from centre ice. He scored. The crowd in Chicago roared with pain. It was game seven of the Stanley Cup final, 1971, broadcast live from the Mad House on Madison. Sitting in front of our television next to my father, I hung my head even though the Blackhawks were still up 2–1. I wanted Bobby Hull to win the glorious trophy but knew how this would go now. The Montreal Canadiens would, as usual, claw and finesse their way to the championship. The Habs' captain, Jean Béliveau, lifted the shining silver chalice for the tenth time in his career and the next day retired at the age of thirty-nine.

My father blamed it all on CBC's Danny Gallivan, whose voice—along with that of Dick Irvin—filled our living room throughout that spring. Gallivan called the play and Irvin analyzed; and whenever the former used the word *scintillating* in conjunction with the Habs and their glorious brand of hockey, my father caught fire. His beloved Leafs were already in free fall from their pinnacle of 1967, and all my dad could do was rail against the horrible Canadiens and half-heartedly admire the Boston Bruins.

During one evening's telecast, Gallivan paraphrased the poet John Keats to describe the Canadiens' hockey. It was, he ejaculated, "a thing of beauty and a joy forever." Willard my father went ballistic.

The poem is called "Endymion." Keats, who because of tuberculosis wouldn't live beyond his twenty-fifth birthday, starts out with this line: "A thing of beauty is a joy for ever."

In a long career spent teaching poetry in Canadian universities, I often remembered Gallivan's passionate declaration transmitted into our boxy, cramped quarters at the rear of the King Koin. And I noted, with some chagrin for my dad, Keats's second and third lines, in which the thing of beauty becomes more powerful with time.

"Its loveliness," Keats wrote, "increases; it will never / Pass into nothingness."

48 In the fall of 1932, when my dad's dad was living in Saskatoon, Saskatoon was in deep trouble. John had been admitted to Normal School for the nine-month training program for teachers. He'd never in his twenty-seven years lived in a city. Looking out from his attic room a few blocks from the school, he described in his letters how he'd barely made it into this little spot in life—one with a glimmer of hope. The brunt of the Great Depression was, in this very autumn, hitting the city with force. He called it "the Great Goliath." The magnificent CP Bessborough

Hotel, completed the year before, stood empty, a palatial unfurnished shell overlooking the South Saskatchewan. It remained shuttered until December 1935.

The streets were, by contrast, filled with people, out of work and without prospects, many of them homeless. Evictions were on the rise. Relief came available to married men with families but first they had to sign a form promising that any funding received would be repaid. Rations of milk for kids showing signs of malnutrition were also available but these were far from adequate for families in deep distress. Protesters in the hundreds gathered. Marches and parades were everywhere and frequent. Activism was on the rise. The city's administration responded by creating what they called a "concentration camp" on the grounds of the summer Exhibition, where shiftless troublemakers would be incarcerated under the watchful eye of the Canadian Legion.

Without financial aid from his older brother Martin, John, too, would likely be wandering, destitute, and without a future. He knew this and it frightened him. It could all be taken away. He'd learned this as a hard truth that would, like so many others of his generation, hound him for the rest of his life. He half expected to lose everything at any moment, day or night.

The towering Bessborough kept its empty vigil by the river; and, below the hotel, throngs of men, women, and children simply tried to survive.

John had a roommate now, a happy-go-lucky young man with curly blond hair named Cornelius Epp, who would feature twice in John's life in the years to come: the first time in finding John the teacher's post at Neuhoffnung; the second in identifying Margaret in the Saskatoon morgue. Like John, Cornelius came from a humble rural home. Together they explored the city on foot and by streetcar.

In that fall of 1932, Saskatoon's population was just over 40,000. The vast majority—nearly 90 percent—of the people living in Saskatchewan then were rural. The wheat economy was dominant, with a farming population of over 800,000. There were over 2,500 grain elevators by 1925, measured against 298 in 1905. By 1931, more than 27,000 threshing machines were being pulled by teams of draft horses, and Saskatchewan people maintained a total of about a million horses. That number would plummet with the steady rise of the tractor, combine, farm truck, and family car.

When Margaret tells John in one letter that the city is a mystery to her, it isn't because she's a naive and isolated twenty-something stuck on the farm: it's because human community in this time exists apart from the metropolitan reality that will take over in the late twentieth century.

John urges her to take a job opening in Saskatoon but she can't, she says, because her family needs her. She's the oldest of many, all crammed miraculously into a smallish two-storey farmhouse built from cedar and never given a coat of paint. The Peters barn, house, blacksmith shop, and various sheds on the ramshackle yard will stay brown and iron grey, in a long tilting decline, for the next seven decades.

49 The intersection of the alleyways behind the King Koin Launderette was a place of daily meetings. Two alleys came together there like a big upside-down T—at a right angle, one strand joined the large cement pad where we played shinny in every season but summer (and sometimes even then). There was the incinerator, lit and smoking and too hot to touch, Dole banana boxes stacked alongside. Also the Nor-Lite store with its aged Dalmatian and its candy bags for a nickel. We were white settler, Métis, and foster kids playing next to the launderette where everyone except the well-to-do and early adopters (with their own washers and dryers) came to get their stuff clean.

The launderette was a hub. Its patrons came from all over the city as well as from the farmlands and park-lands, the bush and the reserves, that surrounded Prince Albert. Vehicles of every shape and kind nosed up to the lit facade, behind which were the chronic odours of detergent, perc, and hot fabrics wrested fresh from pale turquoise dryers. All those smells, borne on a hot wind, hit you in the face as you opened the door.

Customers too restless to wait on a bench for their loads to run through the cycles visited the Nor-Lite or, on the other side of the King Koin, the Texaco gas station. Or drank hot coffee across the avenue in the café of the Flamingo Motel—or, farther south by a few blocks and right on the edge of town, rye whisky and cold beer at the Coronet Motor Hotel.

The neighbourhood behind the launderette was a mix of old and older homes, and many of my friends there were Métis. There was the white house with the red roof, built during the Great War, where I lived now and then; and next to the white house the Henry home, with its thick horizontal red stripe, the product of the Second World War, a wartime bungalow.

At the other corner of the alley, directly across from the white house, was the Corrigal place, a small ramshackle structure packed with kids, whose mother

Ann worked part-time for my father and grandfather. When they had to step away, Mrs. Corrigal walked over to make change for customers. She was the white wartime bride of a Métis man. Together they had six kids and theirs was the third-smallest house on the block. Cars and trucks—some of them on blocks, with hoods and trunks standing open or chassis revealed—filled the Corrigals' undeveloped, unfenced backyard, which but for the alley blended with our equally undeveloped lot behind the King Koin.

Deep ruts created by vehicles lined both lots. Quack grass and thistles grew in profusion.

A Corrigal boy named Greg went barefoot each summer, spent much of his time in the trees. Many times during a barbeque with the Henry family, Greg was spotted hiding in a nearby lilac bush, a regular stopover for all the kids who played in that area—it was quartered like a hot cross bun and in the middle was a small open area the size of two children. That's where Greg would hide, watching the Boschmans and the Henrys eat burgers cooked over charcoal that smelled like diesel.

Louis would call him over in that haze of smoke and charred meat, his high-pitched laughing voice cutting through.

"Greg my boy. Are you hungry? Come and join us."

Everyone would laugh as he ambled over with his head down and either my mom or Mrs. Henry handed him a hard white Corelle plate fringed by tiny blue flowers. He was my brother's best friend. He was also Métis, and Louis—whose family had fought in the Riel Resistance—understood hunger, fear, and loneliness.

* * *

Into this we bring my new sister Crystal in June 1972. This happens after Digger has left and I miss him and am constantly bugging my dad to go to Langham. I know nothing about the Scoop or where Crystal is from exactly. I'm ten and love her instantly.

50 Travelling home that day in June when I see her for the first time in the social services offices in downtown Saskatoon, I hang over the front seat to keep my eyes on her small form: she is five months old, adorned in a small pink gauzy dress.

All within my gaze on the scarlet seat.

It's hot that day and there is no air conditioning in the wine-red Bel Air, so I take off my T-shirt and fan her with it. Tiny, perfect beads of sweat have formed on her nose. I've never seen a human perspire there. You can see her perfect skin through the translucent bubbles of sweat.

And she doesn't stop crying during the entire hour and a half it takes to return to PA. Crying in that red car as it hurtles across the land, her people's land since long before time could be written down. I worry and worry—we all do in that scarlet rocket—as we pass the familiar landmarks on Highway 11: Warman, Hague, Rosthern (where I was born); Duck Lake (Gabriel Dumont lived here!); Beardy's Reserve; then the Nisbet Forest, parkland, MacDowall, Red Deer Hill. I know all the landmarks and every bend in the highway. Till my mom lays her on my parents' bed and we older kids surround her, seeing as we change her diaper for the first time that there's a pin sticking in her side, in her hip. It hadn't been removed from the dress and the dress is store-bought new. That pin will always be remembered and spoken of.

Photos are taken. She has a tuft of dark hair that sticks straight up. Bonding sets in.

My parents in the years that follow refuse to say what they know about her, which is the name she had been given by her mother, and we older children eventually stop asking. They say perhaps we can know when she's old enough to know for herself and decide for herself.

"When will that be?"

"When she asks. But by then it'll be her business, not yours, you *oola näs*."

They say she is Cree. Born December 28, 1971.

One more thing, they say: when the time comes and she asks, they will help her find her people, but that, too, will be up to her, and none of our business. And my parents hold to their word.

* * *

"Why can't they be like the rest of us?"

I grew up hearing that question posed in various ways by white settlers. Seeing the pursed lips. The glittering, resentful eyes. Or listening to talk of taxes unpaid and houses built by the government, of laziness and handouts, funny accents, and rez wagons. As though aliens lived in our midst and this ground was always all ours; that, or the alternative, the celebrated green man represented in the person of Grey Owl, who once lived in a cabin on the north shore of Kingsmere Lake in the PA National Park. A Prince Albert street is named after him. Only Grey Owl was really a boozy Englishman named Archie, headdress and all, posing romantically as a First Nations wise man.

To the settler conversations that categorized Indige-nous persons, my father learned to cut in early.

"You know my daughter is Cree, right?"

They knew all right, but they said it all anyhow.

Living between All Saints and the old jail built after 1885, my parents considered the state-run foster home system from which they adopted my sister to be inhuman. They responded instinctively and with anger. They were opposed to assimilation and believed strongly that status was crucial and that someday Crystal would choose to find out about and reunite with her biological and cultural kinship network.

I talk to people about Prince Albert and they look at me.

"You're from PA?"

I tell them I breathed in its air and was part of it. If I couldn't find a way to fit in, I paid. Woe to the kid who had a cleft palate or "buck" teeth or was fat or poor or had zits or who stood out in any way, skin colour aside.

One woman advised my mom to scrub Crystal's face hard every single day and thereby whiten it. No one should stand out beyond the pale of White Coal City.

I myself wasn't immune to meanness and prejudice born of fear. There were Indigenous boys with red hair who lived in an old two-storey along 28th Street just past the jail. I passed their house two times a day, five days a week, through the school year. They didn't go to my school, Vincent Massey. I feared them.

There were also two white boys living in the smallest, poorest house on our block who wanted to be my friends. They came over to see me and say hello, friendly but stunted and they also smelled. Living in a cloud of perpetual soap vapour, I was unacquainted with the sour smell of poverty, how it got right into the fibres of clothing, hair, skin. I looked at their house—it was covered in tired brown asphalt tiles and would soon enough be replaced by a Credit Union, also brown—and knew I'd never enter there. I could go to the Corrigals with my brother Ben and stand at the back door and look in and call for Greg. But at this other house I'd never do that. The pair of boys, brothers, was probably hungry—something told me they were—but they also made me gag. The smell struck terror. When they asked to come over to my house, I ran away and we never spoke again even though I saw them daily at Vincent Massey.

51 Part of me wanted to watch pain unfold. See impaled bluebottle flies in the buzzing, overheated porch of the big white house. Blow up ant colonies with firecrackers on Dominion Day. Witness woolly bear caterpillars seared under the eye of a magnifying glass beneath the summer sun. Wait for the soft mosquito to alight on my arm and insert her proboscis, then gently pinch the surrounding skin so that she couldn't withdraw but was stuck there, destined to fill till her ruby sac burst.

I learned repeatedly that doom isn't one event but repeats many times. You may move toward it incrementally, unaware of where it is you're going; or, perhaps worse, you move away from the point of pain or rupture and it follows you. Time doesn't heal everything.

I punched a friend on his abscessed tooth once just to see what would happen. He told me he had an abscess (I had never heard that word before) so I hit him there. I wanted to see what would happen. He cried, tore into me with his fists and knocked me backwards. His parents were horse people who had lived hard lives already and recently moved to our block from a town called Cudworth. The dad had come to work in the new pulp mill. One day the dad got metal shavings in one eye and he'd go on to lose that eye. One day a crop duster would fly overhead while my friend walked across a field. He'd get caught in the pesticidal drift, then be hospitalized for a long time afterwards in PA's Victoria Union Hospital.

"Robbie, you little fucker."

When I stood up, we both gasped at the rat I'd apparently fallen on. Had it been there all along lying dead with its sawtoothed mouth opened wide? Or was it living in the tall grass when I, receiving a blow I richly deserved, fell on it? I studied that rat for a long time.

* * *

Ethnic jokes in PA seemed like the only jokes worth telling. They derided everyone except northern Europeans, with special mockery reserved for Ukrainians. That community had already suffered plenty in the Old World, though the PA kids who traded in such jokes could say they knew so little. Could we have known, despite our narrow formal education, that the cruelties of Europe were being played out through our words, words we'd heard others use and which shaped our perceptions, sometimes for life?

QUESTION: What's the most dangerous
                      job in the world?
ANSWER: Riding shotgun on a garbage truck
                      passing through a Ukrainian town.
QUESTION: What's black and hangs
                      from the ceiling?

ANSWER: A Ukrainian electrician.
QUESTION: If a nuclear bomb were
                 dropped on Ukraine, what
                 would the repairs cost?
ANSWER: Three bucks.

PA's version of "Eeny Meeny" was the Americanized one from the previous century, with its reference to runaway slaves and the *Fugitive Slave Act* of 1850. Yet here it was in my Prince Albert. It'd migrated north and been adopted and widely used without question. Could PA have known that "fugitive slaves" who were apprehended often paid with a toe?

"My mother said to pick the very best one and you are NOT it!"

Rituals of exclusion also fed hockey games on the ice and in the street. The captains of the opposing sides called out names. You waited for yours, dreading to hear it said dead last.

At Vincent Massey School, though, such rituals were sidestepped by designated mandatory membership for all students in one of four houses: Huron, Ojibway, Algonquin, and Iroquois.

I was made a member of the House of Ojibway.

52 My father's leg could suddenly twitch and shake if you were walking beside him, let's say up the back alley toward Bryant Park. The leg farthest away spiked out unexpectedly at forty-five degrees, accompanied by a loud fart. Then it shook slightly to indicate residue in the pant leg. Alternatively, if a ready emission couldn't be found, the same leg surreptitiously crossed behind to clip you in the ass. This occurred mid-stride in one smooth move without pause. Eyes straight ahead, demeanour serious.

Dad and his brothers strode in tandem at gatherings at Edith's house in Langham, either in her basement or in the spacious yard backing onto the parking lot of Zoar Mennonite Church. As in a moving picture they walked as one. There were five men: three by Margaret, two Edith. In order of birth, Arnold, Marvin, Willard— then James and Randy. Lola Margaret, also Edith's, sat and watched this flawless unison, her brothers' faces grotesque masks: eyes crossed, teeth bared, lips contorted. Once James donned a fur bonnet filched from an auntie.

Then there was the annual tart eating contest, which James always won. Digger could challenge but was physically unable to contain more than two dozen butter or mincemeat tarts dabbed with whipped cream. One year they were cherry. James won anyhow, his stomach distended like Paul Newman's in *Cool Hand Luke*.

At one of these gatherings, Christmas 1972, I met Margaret's mother, Helena, for the first time. Edith had invited her. This was the start of a long friendship with my great-grandmother, ending with her death in 1988.

I'd recently injured my right elbow playing hockey for the West Hill Bruins. Although the team was B league— its players considered second tier—I'd risen in PA's hockey universe. I was the captain and wore the Bruins' colours, brown and yellow, with pride. Like my hero Bobby Orr, I played defence and was a leading scorer. Despite my poor depth perception, I played with confidence, encouraged by teammates and our coach, Mr. Hegland. I could see and carry the puck and was unafraid of going into corners or blocking an opponent's path.

This would be the pinnacle of my career, the happiest I'd ever be playing the game of hockey. I was a leader. I felt that what I did on and off the ice mattered. Unfortunately for me, the West Hill Bruins were noticed by a coach with A league ambitions, and in time both Coach Hegland and I (as well as a couple of other players) were adopted into a new super team on the West Hill, the Prince Albert Optimist Club Panthers.

One night at the Kinsmen Arena, I fell on my elbow. The pad failed when I hit the ice and a piece of cartilage broke inside the joint. Afterwards I felt a crunching sensation when I flexed my arm and soon began to flex the arm just to hear that sound. That only aggravated the injury. Rotating the wrist caused a flaring pain, and then finally I couldn't straighten my arm. When my mother, the nurse, had me lay it out on our kitchen table, we could see that the hand, wrist, and forearm tilted upward. Soon I was visiting a physiotherapist at a clinic down on the Flat, where I was forced to straighten the injured arm, now an immense problem, bending it flush with a flat surface over and over. It resisted with a sensation like a fiery needle inserted into the joint itself.

It was with this recent injury that I was presented to the great-grandmother I'd never met. She sat at Edith's dining-room table, the same table where the box had previously been opened, and I was introduced as her great-grandson Robbie, whose elbow was injured. I learned in that moment that she was a bone doctor, an orthopedic craftswoman. With an uncanny ability to set fractures and dislocations, she'd gained a reputation in the rural communities surrounding Saskatoon. Meeting her, I had a strange sensation of pride. I also detected humble love and power. Where those things originated I couldn't tell, whether from her or from the adult reverence for her filling that room or from, most likely, a combination. But it bowled me over.

There I was standing in front of this wizened woman with nut-brown skin, her long grey hair gathered in a bun and covered with a small black cap, when her thumb and finger dove into the joint of my right elbow as though it were water. She wore glasses and across her shoulders a white shawl knitted finely. She was tiny. Her voice quivered with age and was high. As though of iron, her digits probed the interior spaces while I looked into her eyes and almost broke down. In my mind's eye I seemed to see the sun, which hurt with a weird joy. I'd feel that happy pain again in the years to come whenever I saw her; and again, almost as intensely, when I said goodbye to Edith in the hospital in 2000.

Everyone watched this operation—the frail woman inserting her gnarled finger and thumb into the arm of an eleven-year-old boy. Someone thought to ask Helena, as I swiftly deduced she'd been asked many times before, where she thought she had gotten this gift.

In her high, trembling voice, she said she didn't know but attributed it to God.

Since her childhood in Manitoba, where in the late nineteenth century Mennonites settled large tracts of land on either side of the Red River just to the south of Winnipeg, she'd demonstrated a way with bones. During Helena's teens, her father had been gored by a bull, trapping him for several hours in a corral. Although she was quick to credit the family terrier for sinking its teeth into the bull's nose and not letting go even in death, it was Helena who set her father's ribs and verte-brae after he was removed from harm's way. By 1909, when she married Jacob Peters and moved west to the new province of Saskatchewan, she was a practising bone doctor who both received and visited her patients without charge. Driving her black carriage pulled by a horse named Charlie, Mrs. Peters was a familiar sight in and around Aberdeen. After the goring, her father, a tall man, would forever stoop, his chest concave.

Occasionally it was whispered that "dark blood," supposedly uncharacteristic of most Mennonites, had entered the Peters line before their migration from Europe, in some distant era when a Mennonite boy had copulated with someone from the Roma community. Such stories are common in Mennonite families. Some of the Boschmans were also spoken of as proving an exotic admixture of lineages between Mennonites and "wild folk." David Boschman, an older brother to John, was said to be swarthy when he shouldn't be. In almost all the fifteen children born to Helena and Jacob, who was a fair-skinned, blue-eyed man of stocky build, the mark of the putative Roma made itself known to one degree or another. Margaret, the oldest, born in 1911, was as dark as her mother, though taller and with some of her father's big-boned features.

As a young teen, Margaret helped her mother receive and tend to the patients who came from miles around: Ukrainians from Vonda, German Catholics from the Humboldt area, the French from St. Denis, and, of course, people from all backgrounds in the Aberdeen region, all of whom knew about Mrs. Peters's gifted hands.

Strangers routinely knocked on the farmhouse door and asked her to accompany them, sometimes in the dead of night in mid-winter. Jacob and the children would watch Helena go, and—depending on the weather—not know when they'd see her again. Sometimes they resented these intrusions but they also knew Helena couldn't say no. They understood the reality of living in the country. Rapid access to a doctor wasn't possible, broken bones improperly set meant being disabled for life. Bad breaks could result in death if a splintered bone punctured an artery or vital organs like the liver or lungs.

The stories about Mrs. Peters as well as her children were legion, much to the annoyance of the medical establishment, who regularly threatened Helena with legal action. Two Aberdeen-area physicians, Holmes and Jackson, quietly supported her, having seen first-hand the quality of her work. Most of the Peters kids knew from their mother how to make splints using cloth and sticks and, under her direction, were precise in their ability to restrain new patients, placing pressure on key areas as Helena manipulated bones and joints back into place.

For breaks that were especially critical, she went off alone to pray, meditating on a verse from Isaiah. In the years of our relationship until her death, whenever I visited her in the home for seniors in Rosthern where she lived out her final years, I saw a small plaque on a wall in her room that bore the words by which she'd always conducted herself: "The hands of the Lord are strong and mighty."

As for my elbow, Helena entered the joint from either side and found a loose piece of cartilage the size of a quarter.

"There," she said, "I've nudged it back."

In time the arm healed, and I could almost straighten it.

A few years after Helena's death, the cartilage broke again. My arm seized and swelled. I couldn't lift a fork or spoon or use a pen. And I thought of her. I sought out a surgeon, who took X-rays, spied the fragment, operated, and removed it.

The scar from the incision across my elbow remains clearly visible. I've explained it to my children: how it reminds me of the West Hill Bruins and of the season I was happiest playing hockey in the PA Minor Hockey League, B Division; and of Helena, the mother of Margaret, both of whom were introduced to me by Edith.

53 One night in 1932 John has a dream about Margaret. It presses on his mind all the next day. When he arrives home from Normal School, he checks the bannister for a letter. There isn't one. So he bolts upstairs and writes a letter in which he recounts his dream: "I dreamt I was at Aberdeen and you were at home. There was a party or some gathering at your place. I was rather shy and so were you, neither speaking to the other, but all the time we wanted to talk. I suppose you thought at last everybody was gone and you went to sleep. I knew where you were and I slowly crept up in the dark to see if you were sleeping. There was a side frame on your bed like on a child's bed and I came up and peered through between the bars. As I looked, you stretched your hand through the bars and stroked my hair."

* * *

They were married in Aberdeen on July 12, 1934. Reverend J.J. Nickel, father to their late friend Justina, officiated. That the bride wore white made a few tongues wag because a Mennonite girl should really wear black on her wedding day. Only the Bride of Christ wears white, as stated clearly in Revelation. Margaret is standing in her mother's garden in a couple of candids with John. In these, the younger Peters children stand close to their sister, the eldest, her brown eyes large and liquid. She wears an artificial wreath of small white budding flowers clasping a long veil that descends to her heels. This John left in the box along with fragments of real flowers. Also a four-inch kewpie doll adorned in wedding garb, an avatar with eyes looking off to the side and slightly down. One can see on closer inspection that her neck is broken just below her chin and to the right, so that the head tilts with her eyes cast to the side. There are no cards with wedding wishes but instead tiny signed slips of paper that read, "With Best Wishes," "Glückwunsch," "Wishing you the best of happiness," and so on. Around Margaret's wreath the top of the veil protrudes like a crown. One thinks of *Song of Solomon*, "My sweetheart, my bride, is a secret garden, a walled garden, a private spring."

54 Four successive Langham houses containing the Arnold Boschman family were held fast in the field of Edith's gravity. Two were green and stood on the outskirts of town. In each green house, the front door took you onto the last street while the back looked out on the prairie; which now in the case of the second one on the west side rolled down imperceptibly to the North Saskatchewan River, interrupted by the Yellowhead Highway, grid roads, and barbed wire.

You can hear the semis coursing along the highway late at night. Coyotes yip and cry, and in the morning you wake to the raucous, pining laughter of a black-billed magpie right outside the window.

When I walked on the prairie in any season with my dad and cousins and Uncle Arnold, I felt caught between different types of birdsong. In winter it was the chickadee pitted against the raven. In spring I heard the robin and the red-tailed hawk. Summer brought a one-sided sing-off between the chipping sparrow and the magpie. (I loved the sorrow of the chipping sparrow's simple song.) In early fall the crow took over and the meadowlark sang a lonely sendoff.

My father talked crow. He'd call to the crow. He'd cup his hands to his mouth and cry out, sounding infinitesimally human, the rest crow. We marvelled and asked him to do it again and asked him how he did that. He didn't know and couldn't say. I tried and failed. We all tried and failed.

Willard my father laughed and his gold-capped diastema reflected a gleaming of sun. CAW CAW CAW. Perfect guttural crow, produced only on seeing one or more of the familiar black forms. They often called back or flew over to look, and sometimes my father and they conferred. But only if you didn't carry a long gun, he said. Crow, raven, and especially magpie know full well what a rifle is. If you carry one out on the prairie, forget it—the corvids leave.

Year after year, out on the edge of town, Digger tried to raise magpies. I wandered along behind him in the spring to raid nests in the scruffy poplar bluffs. We spotted their domed twiggy shapes from a distance. Ten, fifteen feet off the ground, as high as possible in the stunted, twisted aspen that whispered all season.

Digger climbed up while I looked up.

"What is there? What do you see?"

An egg fell on the lower trunk.

Sometimes he brought one down for careful evisceration, preserving the shells. While the wind rustled through the grove making a sound like thousands of tiny feet, Digger produced a needle and made a hole at both ends. Then carefully placed his lips at one of the holes and blew the contents onto the ground, leaving the shell intact.

He wanted young birds to take home and put in a cage, to feed them white bread soaked in milk. I saw them being fed, how they gobbled the white dripping gobs. The hungry heads and black beaks opening wide and snapping. Annually the fledglings failed and died. Our dads laughed and told Digger what he was doing wrong. "Dog killer," they said, "that Digger! He's feeding them dog killer! Can you believe that?" And they laughed and laughed and the tears streamed down my dad's face.

"Dog killer" was John's term for refined white bread. My dad and his brothers along with Lola Margaret grew up in the open spaces south of Langham, where John taught in a school called Neuhoffnung, German for "new hope." John swore by the old heavy breads of Europe. Mealy and dense and dark brown, a slice slathered in pig fat kept you going all morning. He despised the soft white breads that began to appear everywhere during the 1950s, all doughy and insubstantial: big city bread. To support his contempt, he referred to a study in which scientists fed dogs nothing but white bread and all of them died.

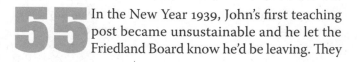 In the New Year 1939, John's first teaching post became unsustainable and he let the Friedland Board know he'd be leaving. They

were spiteful. They demanded notice and he gave them thirty days. Then they quickly hired a replacement and required the family to leave the teacherage immediately even though it was -40 degrees Fahrenheit with stiff winds. The house stood beside the grid road John himself had helped build with his father's draft horses during the 1920s. The old Boschman place was just down the way. His first son, John Arnold, had been born here, and quickly became a lover of the horse, spying the best-looking equine toys and accessories in the Eaton's catalogue.

John was delighted with the boy and said so in his and Margaret's journal. At first, during those early years at Friedland, John was happy. He was teaching at long last—and then Arnold was born in August 1935, "a real live genuine he-boy, looking about with wide-open wondering eyes, as if to fathom the meaning of light, coloured objects, and the people around him." In quick succession, Marvin and my father came along as well.

During that time when summers saw grasshoppers and much smoke and dust in the air, the couple and their boys did things just to while away the hours. They also had no car. On Sundays, Margaret's father would arrive with the old Ford and take them home, back to the Peters place. Then she and Helena might sew a dress for Margaret while John worked the garden. Margaret's father had a pair of draft horses named Myrt and Marj that caught Arnold's eye. Once a week in the evening John rode a bike into Aberdeen to sing in the choir at the Aberdeen Mennonite Church. There were also many visitors at Friedland and sometimes he went away with them to attend political meetings, looking for an answer, anything, from the government over its neglect of teachers.

Margaret washed and ironed clothes and scrubbed floors and looked after the boys. Once she bought two dresses for herself in the city. Once they all caught a touch of diphtheria after the booster and were sick with a fever for many days and John had a backache. Many times John's stomach was sore when his ulcers flared so he worked in the garden to get his mind elsewhere.

On November 11, 1938, Armistice Day, they celebrated the anniversary of their secret engagement. "Armistice! Remembrance Day! Seven years ago (1931)—Oh, yes!, we Remember that night—don't we Margaret!"

A few nights later, John was rousted out of bed by the phone and then walked to a neighbour's to tell them to go to another farm where a child, a son, had just been born. He walked for miles in the darkness under a star-studded sky.

On the day after Boxing Day, they left the boys with Helena and travelled into Saskatoon. They stayed that night at John's cousin's house on Avenue A on the northern edge of the city. This was Jake Heide, a nephew to John's mother and a lover of automobiles, always tinkering. The two men started to talk about a car for John.

The Friedland School Board called to announce that the school wouldn't open as planned on January 3; and on the twenty-first, at a meeting of the ratepayers at which "all were against everything," John's annual salary was cut to six hundred dollars. He resigned on the spot and began looking for a new position when his old roommate, Cornelius Epp, phoned serendipitously from Neuhoffnung to say he was leaving his post and would John consider coming there to teach.

And hence the move was made.

Margaret goes from her mother this once, having lived all her life in the Aberdeen area.

When she and the boys take the train that day in January 1939, they cross the South Saskatchewan River within eyeshot of the ferry. The trestle bridge is high at the crossing and can be seen from a long way off. Once they cross—the three boys and their mother looking at the frozen river stretching in both directions at right angles from the train—they are between the arms of the North and South Saskatchewan Rivers, which turn northward in unison like tendrils reaching for the sun and meet at the Forks and become one river flowing east.

56 East of the Forks where the North and South Saskatchewan Rivers combine, white coal was finally drawn with the 1963 construction of a hydroelectric dam, at first called Squaw Rapids. The name stuck for twenty-five years. In 1988 the dam was renamed for the SaskPower man who built it, an engineer named E.B. Campbell; and the following year, the utility paid fifteen million dollars in environmental damages to those who would otherwise have made a living along this stretch of river.

For at least thirteen thousand years Indigenous Peoples had lived here, in the basin stretching west—like the branches of a tree—to the Continental Divide and the Columbia Icefields; and east to Cedar Lake and the Saskatchewan River Delta and then Lake Winnipeg.

My parents took me as a boy, well before the name change, to see the dam and the lake it had created, shaped like a distended human stomach. Tobin Lake drowned the river itself, displacing people, fish, and animals. I watched my parents, then young and dark-haired, scramble along the shore to pick up pieces of driftwood that caught their notice. Three stayed in our family for decades. My mother sanded and lacquered the wood the river had sculpted. Their flowing shapes spoke of the relations between waters from many places on the continent and the forests once flourishing beside them: one was the remains of a small trunk; another was the worn intersection of branch and trunk that resembled a hatchet; the third and smallest was shaped like a boomerang. These pieces, perennially "wet" with varnish as though just pulled from the river, decorated my parents' house in PA into the twenty-first century.

My father had already told me that the Boschmans, Cornelius and Anna and their children, put up their log house in the old-growth forest just to the south of Tobin Lake at a place called Petaigan. By 1963, when the dam came online and caused the water to rise, the forest was gone—erased—and Petaigan was merely another section of arable land under the Dominion Land Survey. On Google Maps today, Petaigan appears as a name in a field south of the lake.

One of the Boschman brothers, Henry, was shot in a field at Petaigan in 1954. The field where he was murdered (by a bachelor named Jake Froese) is close by the cemetery where Cornelius and Anna, and Henry himself, are buried. It was July and Henry wound up being interred on his parents' sixtieth wedding anniversary. He was the biggest and strongest of all the Boschman brothers. His son, also named John, would move to northern British Columbia and become a lumberjack and never return to Petaigan. If there was a hero to worship among the brothers, it was Henry. Bill Boschman, one of the youngest boys, who happened to write everything down, remembered his older brother's immense physical power. This came in handy after their 1930 move from the wide spaces of the prairies to the thick old forest around the new town of Carrot River. Henry was twenty when the move occurred, Bill fourteen. Bill called these their golden days. "Having a creek where we could swim every day. Berries. Fireflies flitting among the dense trees at night. A clock ticking in a rotten log, and when we approached to investigate, it stopped ticking."

My father loved Henry. He was already a teen when Henry was killed but he remembered in earlier years sneaking up to Jake Froese's sod hut at night. From their cousins, Henry's kids and others, Willard and Marvin and Arnold had heard it said that Jake talked to himself, so they figured on getting up close in the dark and listening.

"Sure enough," said Willard, "he was jabbering away while we sat outside under a window. He'd read too many westerns; talking like a cowboy, 'Draw, you coward, or I'll shoot you.'"

Then in 1954, the shot in the field. My father and Marv on the way to Petaigan that very day, a hot one, hoping to go fishing with Henry and the two Johnnies, their dad and their cousin. Arriving to find gloom and doom and Aunt Netha beside herself. Their uncle's John Deere idling for hours out in a field till someone went to investigate and found Henry lying by the machine, a wound to the back of his head.

Froese had used a .22 bolt-action; then went straight to Nipawin to turn himself in.

Henry had been easygoing, the family all agreed, and took care of his horses, so naturally Arnold liked it there too. Henry and Netha had seven kids. Whenever

Willard and his brothers arrived, they slept in the attic where the mosquitoes hummed at the small screen all night long.

Henry's killer spent the rest of his life in the asylum at North Battleford. I found his gravestone there in the fall of 1980, in the old hospital's cemetery chock full of the shell-shocked and traumatized. I remember large planted conifers and the north bank of the North Saskatchewan and a few islands. The largest island is called Finlayson—and beyond, south of that, there's an arm of water you can't see flowing eastward.

57 Outside our living room window, a true picture in three panes, the incinerator burned on and on. Often the Nor-Lite store, which sold groceries and meats and did its own butchering, burned the large bones of animals. The offal collected behind the great door, with boxes and garbage tipped in from the King Koin till the bin was full to the brim and someone, like me for instance, decided to light a match.

The animal ash and fat fell to the bottom beneath the heavy cast-iron grate. You had to pull it all out when it overflowed, using a short-handled shovel with a square blade. You opened the smaller door level with the ground and a thick black tongue emerged and you scooped it out to be taken away to the nuisance grounds north of Prince Albert, a place where the jack pines grow in profusion and gulls rule the day.

One day my mom saw a man, bedraggled and thin, rifling through the bin. He'd opened it before the burn and found the bones with raw meat clinging to them and started to eat without delay. My mom was in her early thirties when this happened, when she witnessed real hunger in another human being. She was seventy-six years old when she told it to us, her family, sitting around the table in Saskatoon remembering PA.

* * *

Where the prairie landscape and silence and winds can undo you, hockey saves the day as well as the night. How many grey-faced lonely men, wearing trucker caps or toques, have I seen in rinks all over Saskatchewan? I couldn't count them. They eat rink burgers and drink from Styrofoam cups. Their breath freezes on the air as they watch the game through flat eyes. Going out into the cold for a smoke between periods.

In Langham, the town drunk was such a man. Every day he stopped in at the Langham Hotel. Every day the lady who ran the pub there gave him a sandwich wrapped in wax paper. Every day that man took the sandwich and in winter stopped by the hockey rink, enclosed and warm, and held that sandwich and watched the play. He lived next to the fourth and final Arnold Boschman house, a grey house on a corner. When they found him— the town drunk that is, not Arnold—dead and decomposing in his home, someone opened the big freezer and it was full almost to the lid with sandwiches wrapped in wax paper.

Where I played hockey in the early 1970s, in the Kinsmen Arena down the back alley from the King Koin Launderette, I saw men just like him, and a few women, and a few of them were parents of kids on the ice. They watched their kids and yelled at the refs. Facing the Kinsmen was the Prince Albert Jail for men, mostly

Indigenous, who apparently didn't constitute Kinsmen of the right kind. I walked the gauntlet between the two places every school day to and from Vincent Massey. All of this up on the Hill overlooking the flood plain below, the Flat, and in between the steep incline along which big homes and a courthouse and a hospital sat erect and clenched and impregnable.

Hockey is enclosed now for the most part. The NHL televises an outdoor game once a year to commemorate the past and millions watch, which in itself points to hockey's outdoor origins, a time before it was brought inside on artificial ice. Domesticated, as it were. Cities struggle with plans to build a new arena sponsored by a bank or some other titan of business. I'm not much interested in hockey nostalgia, although there are moments and individuals I remember. What interests me is the relationship between the game and the environment and the past. Northern humans in a place called Canada created an outdoor ice surface, whether on a lake or river or in someone's backyard, and donned blades attached to leather boots and carried sticks cut from trees and skated as fast as they could while shooting a black disc called a puck. The puck, in unnumbered stories, was originally a frozen turd of some animal. Trees and shit and ice and leather. In hockey, the land is repurposed and mythologized in a narrative of heroic proportions.

On another level, though, hockey fends off panic and passes the time during the worst weather of the year. It probably has prevented numerous shootings, like the one that befell Uncle Henry at Petaigan or the one that took place thirty years later at MacDowall involving Wilfred Stanley Robertson and two RCMP officers, both of whom were killed. It's better to go to the rink and just shoot a puck. And when the rink is enclosed it not only keeps you warm and dry, it also means you don't have to look at the indefinite horizon. The game gives you focus, like any good story, and it keeps your mind from falling apart or going bad. It seems like a no-brainer, especially with a helmet on.

This was precisely the case made in November 1972 when my parents received a letter from an ambitious coach on PA's West Hill. The letter, a long one, concluded with this: "On one point we can be sure; these boys pass this age but once in their life time. To let the opportunity of working with them escape us is to lose it forever. On the ice is off the street, and during those hours both you and I know where they are and what they are doing."

The helmet, in this case, was a CCM one. Brick red, with a hand-painted panther's head on either lobe. A black panther, mouth open in a snarl. On the back of the helmet, my number, 11, also hand painted in white. A white leather chin strap wrapped in white hockey tape.

For the next year and half, until the middle part of the 1973–4 season when I was demoted to the B league, I would be a member of the Prince Albert Optimist Club Panthers.

58 Exactly when Harry D. Reid started to head west from Toronto is unknown—as is the make and model of his car. The newspapers and coroner's report don't identify the vehicle, though the *Saskatoon Star-Phoenix* indicates that Constable Gilfred Greggain tested the brakes and found them in good condition. The remaining information concerning the Reid vehicle is lost. At some point in June 1940, when the good weather had reliably arrived in Ontario,

Reid got in his motor car and started out on a long drive. The *Star-Phoenix* called his vehicle "the death auto" in its articles printed on July 3 and 6, 1940.

Look at a 1940 road map of Canada and you won't find much of anything in the province of Ontario north of Lake Superior. One lonely road takes you to North Bay and then it comes to an abrupt end at Ryland. By 1940, the Canadian government had already spent tens of millions on road expansion, even during the worst of the Great Depression, when it announced a project called the Trans-Canada Highway. A hard cement highway connected Toronto to Hamilton. The road from the Niagara Escarpment to Detroit, all part of the King's Highway, was fair; and beyond that the American highway system positively flourished. Harry D. Reid had choices once he crossed the Ambassador Bridge at Windsor: he could drive up into the Mackinaw region or, more likely, go straight west to Chicago and from there to Minneapolis–Saint Paul and onward north by west. Either way, there were plenty of good roads and he had things to sell along the way— women's hosiery and other undergarments; pesticides; Genuine Klasolem Haarlem Oil Drops prepared by the Harry D. Reid Agencies Limited.

* * *

On their first road trip in their own family car, the green 1929 Plymouth, with wooden spokes and a wooden steering wheel, John and Margaret and the three boys arrived at the Peters farm and the threshers were out. Spelt dust, suspended in the air, filtered the light.

* * *

There is no present moment naked and singular and pure. Whatever the present is occurs in the context of what has gone before and is processing that continually and circling back—pulling what has gone before and taking part of it with it in the nonstop formation that is now.

The past is always now.

"June 26th/40: Out of money, food, and gas," notes John. "Had milk and bread and butter for breakfast. Luckily our neighbours brought us a pail of milk last night, or it would have been water, bread, and butter."

At a school picnic on June 28, a Friday, he was handed a long-awaited cheque for ninety dollars. This wasn't something he could predict. The arbitrary but welcome appearance of a few dollars meant this trip into the city the next day.

THE
BUMPER
BREAK

59 In the late 1990s, I tracked down the last living person to see the death of my grandmother. Her name was Elsie Heide and she was a teenaged girl when she witnessed the accident, standing beside her mother Susie on their front yard at 1619 Avenue A North, only a few blocks from Normal School and the house where John had stayed as a student. Uncle Johnny and Aunt Margaret had just stopped to say hello quickly at Elsie's family's home.

Elsie was living in a trailer park in British Columbia when I reached her on the phone and she told me about seeing her Aunt Margaret die as well as the one thing that really embedded itself in her memory. And that was the sight of a black Oxford shoe, Margaret's shoe, sailing through the air in the same direction as Margaret herself.

Most people, fortunately, never experience first-hand the death even of a stranger, let alone that of someone they love. Witnessing a death such as Margaret's does its own peculiar damage, most of which has only recently been acknowledged in the literature on psychic injury;

but the true extent of such trauma, inflicted in a split second on the mind and memory, depends on a wide range of individual factors such as physical constitution, genetic disposition, temperament, religious belief, and emotional involvement with the victim.

All these were crucial for John. Since childhood, he had suffered from stomach ulcers, which came and went several times a year and frequently flared up during times of stress—of which there had already been plenty in the 1930s. Otherwise physically powerful, he had this one weakness, like the hole in the dike that holds everything. Besides this, he was intelligent, well-read, romantic, but with an emotional life at times so forceful it needed frequent checks and balances. Control was essential; indeed, he was so good at it really that no one except Margaret knew what she called "the real Johnny Boschman": charming, mercurial, flamboyant, volatile. His outlets lay in the journal he kept with her, in the voluminous letters that formed the bedrock of their life together, in their three beautiful "he-boys," and in his dedication to the land and to horses, dogs, and honey bees. And God played His inextricable role, of course, for it was God who had created all things and ordained everything down to the smallest detail. In my grandfather's mind for the rest of his life, the God who had made Margaret and brought her into his life had also taken her back again.

Margaret was not bleeding externally when John reached her. That's the thing. Nor were there any broken bones. Nothing at all, except a welt forming on the left side of her face and head.

A voice behind John.

A man's voice.

"Knocked out cold."

My grandfather turns his head for the second time in less than half a minute.

He looks up at the man but can't see his face because of the sun.

"She's been knocked out," the man says again. "She'll come to. Salts will bring her around."

"She's dead," says John.

The man looks at her and returns to the big car, make and model all a blur to this day.

He gets in.

He drives away.

Canada's *Criminal Code* first addresses failure to stop at the scene of an accident in 1919: "Whenever, owing to the presence of a motor car on the highway, an accident has occurred to any person or to any horse or vehicle in charge of any person, any person driving the motor car shall be liable on summary conviction to a fine not exceeding fifty dollars and costs or to imprisonment for a term not exceeding thirty days if he fails to stop his car and, with intent to escape liability either criminal or civil, drives on without tendering assistance and giving his name and address."

Failure to remain is added sixty-six years later in the 1985 amendment to the *Code*; the penalty then, as now, is imprisonment for life for failure to stop or remain when the driver knows a death may have occurred.

My family has always maintained that alcohol played a role. We will never know for sure. The phrase "driving while intoxicated" entered the *Criminal Code* in 1921, but there is no record of Harry D. Reid being asked to perform a roadside test for intoxication once he was apprehended north of Saskatoon and brought back to the city. (The Breathalyzer was first used by police in 1952.) In Alberta in 1920 in *R v Nickle*, a case of drunk driving was judged unlawful and supported a manslaughter conviction, but there is no indication in any of the legal documents or newspapers that Reid was impaired.

The Peterses and Boschmans could be fair and forgiving, gentle even, and had Reid ever shown a sign of remorse or horror, said he was sorry or written to them, I'd have heard. In the late 1990s, those still alive who were connected to John and Margaret and could recall June 29, 1940, all said the same things. That Reid, a travelling salesman from Toronto, was drinking that day and that he left the scene and was stopped by the police at Thirteen Mile Corner. Yet his name wasn't even brought into the inquest; it was left to the press to publish it.

Harry D. Reid was exonerated, though his insurance policy and lawyer in the East kicked into gear to negotiate a settlement with John through his lawyer. Jacob Peters was angry and said, "If I just had the money, I would make that man pay." But, of course, Jacob, Margaret's father, had no money. At this time, his fifteenth and youngest child was five years old, the same age as Margaret's oldest boy.

After the autopsy, the coroner's inquest, and the final preparations at McKague's Funeral Home, Margaret was taken to Aberdeen by train. John asked that she be outfitted in her wedding dress, the white one that had raised a few eyebrows. And so I continue to see her dressed in white in the photograph that stunned my childhood mind and continues to grip my adult one. Her eyes are closed, her face lovely and young, hair corvid black against the white satin. Someone in the family—likely Helena or John—took the picture. The casket is open in the parking lot of the Aberdeen Mennonite Church. The lot is crowded with men and women and children, and off in the distance I can see vehicles of that era as well as the Aberdeen Grain Terminal. The men wear hats of various kinds and one boy wears a ball cap; the women wear hats with floral arrangements, and one woman looks on at the open casket with hands clasped at her bosom. I can't detect my father or his brothers in this photo, though they are there. My father remembers nothing of this day—indeed, nothing of Margaret—but according to some who were there, my two-year-old father walked around matter-of-factly informing people, "My mommy is dead."

I was living in Winnipeg in the autumn of 1995 and thinking, as usual, about all this when I received by post an hour-long audio cassette tape from Arnold in which he details what he could recall of the events of and around June 29, 1940. This small parcel from my uncle came as a complete surprise to me. The harvest moon was out and I was watching it every evening, thinking about John. I was always so intimidated by Arnold and never expected him to reach out to me. He has a fierceness about him even in his old age, like the heat of a white coal lying in a recently used firepit: looking at it, you can't tell its temperature, but you know to be careful all the same. One time, he brought a horse whip down on my father's head, stropping Willard with a hot slash that angled across his face from forehead to jaw. My father told me about this event one time only, when I was very young. Many years later, I asked the boys who were born to Margaret to tell me about this incident, but they refused to discuss it. "No, we won't talk about that." But here was Arnold in 1995, and when you listen to the tape you can feel his heat. His voice like one of those midcentury movie idols—a forceful and rich projection of sound. Very masculine, like what I imagine John's voice was like, since I can't remember it at all.

"This is stuff for me that was buried. Bear in mind that I did not know that I knew all these things for a long, long time; but in my research into my own life . . . I have found out so many things, with the help of an awful lot of good people. . . .

"My understanding of the story is that Harry Reid was drinking on the day he ran over Margaret. This was a hit-and-run accident. Reid struck her and kept on driving. He was caught by the police at what they now call the Thirteen Mile Corner, which is straight north of Saskatoon. That's the story I remember. Of course, the resulting court case and all that exonerated Reid and there were, uh, some pretty powerful people that went to bat for him. Back then a travelling salesman from a city like Toronto was a big man, respected.

"I remember the circumstances of that day almost like it was only last week. I was four, Marv three, and Willard two. And we were to stay at the Nickels' that day while our folks went to Saskatoon. However, late that afternoon I sensed something was wrong. I don't remember that Willard and Marvin did; but I sensed something was wrong because it was announced that we'd have to stay there for the night. Now that really upset me, and I was—I was wild then. That upset me because of several things. First of all, we had intended to go home; we had expected our parents to pick us up. And secondly, I did not like Reverend Nickel. No sir! I didn't like him then and I didn't like him later. I have to be candid and honest about that. He represented the old style of finger-pointing, fear-mongering, making-you-feel-guilty kind of a preacher, which was prevalent in those days and I understand that and it's not personal. I just didn't like him. But when we were forced to stay there I raised quite a bit of hell. I can remember being upstairs in a bedroom lying in bed with Will and Marvin, but I couldn't sleep. And I plotted. I knew in my little heart of hearts that there was something desperately, desperately wrong. And I guess it was a natural thing for a kid to want to be at home, the safe place. And I remember that I got those two boys dressed and we commenced going downstairs to sneak outside.

"Now my plan was, and this is ridiculous for a four-year-old to think he could pull off, but I know what the plan was. The plan was to walk home. Now that was seven miles. And I kinda think we could have made it. I kinda believe that. However, we were caught even before we got out the door. And like it was yesterday I can remember the adult hand of Reverend Nickel squeezing my arm and making me go back up them stairs—firm and unrelenting and with no sympathy whatsoever.

"You gotta remember, though, at this time I didn't know what had happened. It was just an idea that something was dreadfully wrong. Something was going to change my life, and I was very fearful.

"Anyways, we spent that night there. I don't remember if I slept or not. My next memory is Dad being there in the morning and walking us three boys down a board-walk, and that boardwalk—the slats were all an inch apart, I can remember that just as plain as day, and the three of us walking down in a line with our little hard leather shoes."

What had happened was beyond anything Arnold could ever imagine, then or since. Though he wasn't there and didn't see it, he suffered from it for the rest of his life. We all did. It ripped us apart, from the past and from each other.

The evening before, while he and his brothers ate supper with the Nickel family, John and Margaret were wrapping up a day of shopping. They were on their way home—driving north on Avenue A at 6:10 p.m., having spent the afternoon sauntering around the downtown core of Saskatoon, stopping to make purchases at Eaton's and the Army & Navy—when John impulsively pulled over at the corner of 38th Street, across from the home of his cousin Jake Heide. It was on the way.

Jake and his wife, Susie, lived with their seven children in a small bungalow numbered 1619, right on the edge of the city. Although the house stood by itself on the paved avenue, the Heides constantly admonished their kids, who liked to play in the surrounding lots and the field across the way, to watch for traffic. There was a lot of traffic. And there were no sidewalks, just a band of gravel on either side of the road.

Like Margaret, Susie Heide was pregnant. The two women enjoyed each other's company and had been supporting one another through this time. In fact, Susie was expecting any day, and my grandparents, knowing this, had already stopped to check on the Heides that morning on their way in. There was so much news to share and discuss that Jake and Susie persuaded them to stay for lunch, especially after John and Jake began making adjustments to the Plymouth. Because the mechanically minded Jake had been so instrumental in helping John and Margaret find their first motor car the summer before, now whenever the Boschmans stopped in to touch base the two cousins inevitably wound up discussing, if not working on, the car. It was eleven years old and needed frequent repairs. Jake's oldest sons, Eddie, Walter, and Norman, enjoyed watching their dad fix cars.

As John pulled up across the avenue from Jake and Susie's, he told Margaret he was just going to run in quickly to ask Jake a question about the Plymouth. Margaret replied that she would wait for him. Her legs were sore and she wanted to get home; the boys would be missing her. Leaving the car idling, John jumped out and crossed the avenue.

It wouldn't take long.

The avenue then wasn't nearly as wide as it would become by the early twenty-first century, when a boulevard was constructed down the centre and its name was altered for the third time. In addition to becoming Idylwyld Drive, it would also at last be called the Louis Riel Trail. But in that summer of 1940, the place where Margaret was killed wasn't even really a part of the city—or perhaps I should say that Saskatoon proper began to peter out by the time one got to 1619 Avenue A, as it was then known. Small bungalows like the Heide place appeared intermittently and were both in and out of the city.

So Margaret watched John knock on the door and saw Elsie, the oldest Heide child, then fourteen years old, come out on the step, pleased to see her Uncle John again. She turned and said something through the doorway. Jake and Susie both appeared, said hello to John, who in turn pointed in the direction of his wife.

Susie looked at Margaret and waved, then stepped from the porch toward the avenue and beckoned to her. Margaret returned the wave and decided at least to get out of the car and visit with her friend across the avenue while the men talked. She climbed from the running vehicle and walked around to the front, standing by the bumper on the busy thoroughfare, facing the yard where Susie, Elsie, John, and Jake were.

"Hiya, Margaret!"

"Hello again, Susie! Hello, Elsie! Gee, didn't think you'd see us again, I bet!"

Elsie waved too. She liked her Aunt Margaret, who teased and tickled her. Above the roof of the Heide bungalow, the early evening sun remained high in the sky, shining obliquely on Margaret's face. She had to shade her eyes with one hand, though the sun certainly didn't blind her.

Susie: "Why don't you come over here?"

A light delivery truck with a man riding in the back passed right in front of Susie, heading south. Fifty feet behind the truck was a car driven by the Reverend Henry Rempel.

In a hurry now to cross but seeing Rempel's car, the only vehicle approaching as far as she could see, Margaret stepped out, smiling at Susie, whose face was already contorting in fear. Susie Heide screamed and John, still on the porch, turned around just in time to see Margaret hit by a bulky car coming from the south. There was a liquid thud as she was struck from the side and began to pitch, thrown by the force of the impact up through the air and ten feet away from the Plymouth. The Oxford sailed on and landed in the empty lot well beyond Margaret.

Time dilates here and bad dreams intrude. There is the running toward Margaret but not, it appears to him, ever getting to where she lies. Athletic, graceful man who can move quickly and walk on his hands. Space and time conspire against him as though swimming through hot animal fat. Or honey, brown and pungent, like that which comes from the jimson weed found across Western Canada. About this moment he dreams for years afterward. The fruit-like thump, a once-in-a-lifetime sound, Margaret pitching upward, twisting and instantly lifeless. He runs over all the time in useless dreams fixed on the instant. "Last night I dreamt Margaret was badly hurt, and when I knelt at her side she raised her arm, put it around my neck, and said, 'Johnny'—the way she always said it."

Susie Heide's mouth forms the letter O. A howl follows while behind her Jake stands stock still. Elsie will remember this all across the decades right to the end of the century. The freezing panic, disbelief washing over like a drought or dust storm, the kind made by men. Margaret lying at the side of the road, beyond the gravel fringe. The Oxford turning stupidly through the air. In the middle of the avenue several yards ahead of the Plymouth a big northbound car at long last becoming motionless.

Audio of Arnold, 1995:

"We went out behind a shed there [behind the Nickel house], and that's where he told us . . . that Mom had been killed. I can't remember what Dad was like, what he looked like or anything. I can remember looking at the ground. And I can remember Marvin starting to cry.

I don't know if Willard knew what was going on, he was just a little blond-headed, round-faced boy of two; and I don't know if he knew what was happening, but Marv started to cry.

"I did not cry. And I never in my adult life ever cried again. There was a tremendous decision made by that four-year-old boy that day which ruled the rest of his life. The only time I ever cried during the rest of my life was when I was hurt, physically, physically hurt. Otherwise, I did not cry [*taps his knuckles on a tabletop for every emphasized word*].

"Incidentally the time came when through some counselling and some research I wrote a letter to Margaret trying to explain to her, as a four-year-old boy would, how I felt and what had happened, and then I cried. That was a major breakthrough for me. I had to start that letter over two or three times because I cried the ink right out of the pages. And since then I have been able to, you know, uh, express that emotion. Not often, but I can and I know I can and that's—that's what's important. But the rest of the time I did not cry.

"But anyhow, imagine that—now I think that what happened there was that four-year-old boy made some decisions to live and be in a certain way and those decisions ran his life till one day he finally started to take a look at the way things really were and what had really happened.

"So I guess [*laughing harshly*] you pretty well know what happened."

When John phoned the Peters family on the evening of June 29 to tell them that Margaret was dead, he was still at the police station. He had just given a statement along with the other eyewitnesses and the driver of the car, the man from Toronto. Convinced that the woman he had hit was not dead but merely injured, the man had returned to his car and driven away. The police had had to retrieve him north of the city and return to the scene with his car.

The Reverend Henry Rempel's vehicle, coming from the north, was almost precisely opposite Margaret when the car struck her. As he drove past, Reverend Rempel saw her body projected up and ahead of the Plymouth as well as toward the east. He estimated the driver's speed at fifteen to twenty miles per hour; the driver, he said, came to a stop seventeen feet past the point of impact. Looking for southbound traffic, Margaret Boschman hadn't seen him coming.

Just ahead of Rempel on a return trip from the airport was a light delivery truck with a young man named Gilbert Mooney riding in the back, leaning against the cab. As the truck passed, he saw the two pregnant women chatting across the avenue, and thereafter Mooney witnessed the entire accident unfold as he telescopically pulled away and the car that would strike her approached. Like Rempel, Mooney could see that Margaret was in a hurry to cross the avenue and wasn't watching for traffic from the south; she didn't appear to notice the oncoming car's horn either.

Mooney's co-worker, David Penner, riding in the cab, also heard the horn; turning around to look behind him through the rear window, he saw a body flying through the air.

Susie Heide disagreed with this account. She hadn't heard a horn at all and estimated the driver's speed at thirty-five to forty miles per hour. She'd noticed him driving somewhat erratically and for a moment thought he would hit John's Plymouth. Margaret, she maintained, had hardly taken her hand from the Boschman car when the other car struck her, tossing her like a green leaf scudding across the ground.

These various and conflicting statements were documented by Constable Greggain, who had tested the car's brakes and found them in good working condition. Hitting the binders at twenty miles per hour, Greggain brought the vehicle to a full stop within nine feet; hitting them again at thirty required an additional seven feet before the big machine ground to a halt. There was no evidence of skid marks.

Margaret, meanwhile, was taken by ambulance to the City Hospital, a red brick edifice one block from the river, where Cornelius Epp, John's old friend and fellow teacher, identified her on John's behalf. In the emergency ward, a young intern, Dr. Alexander Danylchuk, pronounced her dead, and another physician, Dr. W.S. Lindsay, established cause of death as shock and internal hemorrhage of the brain. Lindsay verified that Margaret's death had likely been instant, and that she was in her sixth month of pregnancy.

By the time her family arrived, Margaret had been transferred down to the morgue in the basement of the hospital. None who saw her that night—neither Jacob nor Helena, with all her experience, nor the two boys, Jim and Bill, who had come along with their parents and, like them, descended the stairs dreading what they'd see—none of these was quite prepared for the sight of Margaret laid out on her back on the coroner's table, her head resting on a split block of wood. Fifty-eight years later, Jim recalled most vividly the block of wood. He was dying when he said this, cancer all over: "It seemed so cruel, you know, that block of wood for a pillow."

When young Bill Peters had taken the phone call from his brother-in-law earlier that evening, he'd been unable to tell Helena, standing by the kitchen table, that Margaret was dead. His face as white as could be, all Bill could say was that she'd been hit by a car in Saskatoon.

Now the unbelievable news was so real they could reach out and touch it, touch her, down there in the basement of the old City Hospital, all red brick and gloom, the South Saskatchewan River flowing silently past only a block away.

* * *

Among the Boschman and Peters families, no one had ever witnessed one of their dead processed by the system in place in the city. They were used to taking care of their own—putting them to bed, they called it. John was the only member of the two families who had actually lived in Saskatoon, and that was during the school term at Normal School eight years before, when all he could think of, really, was Margaret—when he might see her again or at least find a letter from her at the foot of the stairs leading up to his rooms over on Avenue B, and that dream of his, Margaret reaching between the bars of her bed to touch his hair.

Two days later in the pre-dawn, July 3, 1940, the day of the funeral.

When he opened his eyes Arnold saw nothing, it was so dark. He was at Grandpa and Grandma Peters's house on the farm at Aberdeen. He lay on his back and sucked his thumb while his free hand rested on the edge of the bed in the inky black. Beyond this point was his father and beside him were his brothers, and the only sound in the heavy silence was the sound of their breathing. He turned his head toward his father but his eyes saw nothing; he heard his father's breathing and knew he was still asleep.

Arnold didn't want his dad. All he wanted now was his mother though he knew he couldn't have her. He could never have her again. He had seen her at McKague's Funeral Home in Saskatoon, and then his father said they would see her once more tomorrow.

Now it was almost tomorrow, and they, the boys and their father and many other people Arnold didn't know, were getting prepared for the funeral. Grandma had been there with Arnold earlier, held him and laid him on his stomach. Her hands had stroked his back and he'd fallen asleep. He could still hear the murmur of her voice. Or was that his mother speaking up above his head? Arnold. Go to sleep. You're talking in your sleep. It's too early. Little boys should be asleep yet. Your brothers are sleeping.

When he opened his eyes again there was a shimmering patch of light on the wall. His eyes rested on the light and the light grew brighter. He could see the outlines of the patch become distinct and then he saw a square, like one of Willard's blocks, and the colour of the square was changing. First it was grey and then it was dark blue and then another kind of blue, like the sky. It was the sky.

He'd seen Margaret yesterday afternoon in the brown brick funeral parlour on the corner of the busy street. He and Marvin had followed their father inside that building—John carrying Willard—and like the trip along the boardwalk two days earlier it'd seemingly taken forever.

Decisions were being arrived at for Arnold. He was caught, it appeared, between his brothers and his father, and this seemed especially true as they walked up to Margaret inside McKague's.

She had a purple bruise like a bunch of grapes on one side of her face and head. Someone had tried to cover it up but hadn't quite succeeded. The face didn't look like hers. That wasn't her mouth, it hung down too much. It was too wide now.

A man approached and shook John's hand and gave John a card. Yesterday, he explained in a quiet voice, Margaret had been transferred from the coroner's. But the inquest was still going on. They should know the verdict by the end of the week. The man was whispering now, and as he did Marvin began to wail, and then Willard began to wail with him.

Arnold looked up at his dad, who was listening to the man but also busy reading both sides of a pale, cream-coloured business card. The proprietor, Mr. Harold McKague, had written in pencil on the back side, "Mrs. Boschman, $65 complete."

"The autopsy was yesterday morning," the man whispered. "Dr. Armitage. A very good man."

John was tense and rigid, contained, the opposite of Marvin and now of Willard too, who could see his mother and know that all was not well. Arnold followed his dad emotionally. Perhaps his decision had already begun to take shape when he'd heard Reverend Nickel take John's phone call on the Saturday evening before. Even then, Arnold had felt angry; and the next morning, out behind the garden shed, with Marvin crying his eyes out, he'd felt it again. He wouldn't cry. He'd never cry.

In the funeral home, he dug fiercely in on that decision, and when the four of them left there, that was it for Arnold. He was done.

Today, however, July 3, was the funeral, when he'd test his decision one more time. To be sure, this was a process, organic and hidden, not an overt thought in a four-year-old mind. In the parking lot outside the Aberdeen Mennonite Church that afternoon, a large crowd gathered. There were more people there than Arnold had ever seen in one place. It was hot, and the people were standing around in knots and clusters talking to one another, waiting for Margaret's remains to arrive. The train from Saskatoon was late and folks were looking for the "hearse," an open-back half-ton truck, to appear coming from the station along Main Street.

Through the crowd a rumour circulated that the results of the autopsy had been disclosed. Apparently, Helena's daughter had been carrying another boy.

"Imagine," someone said in the sweltering heat, "the fourth son taken like that. A double loss. Stolen."

When Arnold and his brothers arrived with their father and the Peters family, many of the strangers placed their hands on Arnold's head as though in benediction but also to admonish him, "You're the oldest, you've got to be strong now. You've got to help your father and your little brothers!" He hated hearing this; it made him angry and sullen.

Some among the crowd brought along hand-picked bouquets and, if they could afford them, sympathy cards, while others simply wrote their condolences in German and English on bits of paper. They approached John and the Peters family, now joined also by the Boschmans, and offered their gifts and words of sympathy. They meant well, and more than well, sprinkling their thoughts with Bible verses, some in German, that had endured the tests of experience and time. "God is faithful, who will not suffer you to be tempted above that ye are able." Still others employed more modern forms of consolation professionally printed in Ontario on small single sheets of stiff white paper.

> Oh no, not dead, but past all fear of dying,
> And with all suffering o'er;
> Say not that I am dead when JESUS calls me
> To live for evermore.

One uncle wondered how the church would hold them all. They were still pulling up in motor cars and horse-drawn carriages from all over. Mourners and the curious were arriving from as far away as Carrot River, where many former Aberdonians, including the Boschmans, had gone ten years before. There were also people from the city, as well as attendees from Langham, Hague, Rosthern, Waldheim, and many other smaller Mennonite towns in the region, arriving by train.

A few had read about the death of Mrs. Peters's oldest daughter in the *Saskatoon Star-Phoenix* only that morning. They'd seen the headline at the top of the third page beside the photo of Margaret—"INQUEST IS ADJOURNED. The funeral will be at Aberdeen in the Mennonite church at 2 o'clock this afternoon"—and started out on the spot, even without their good clothes pressed and ready. Others stayed home and wrote letters that John would see later: "When the news reached me of the tragic death of your companion my heart was sore, and I am praying for you John." There were letters, too, from fellow teachers, and from Sunday school children, and from total strangers who had heard the news of the young pregnant woman struck down by a car from the East. And on the backside of one of these letters, John wrote the name of a Saskatoon lawyer, Henry Rees.

The casket arrived on the train accompanied by Jake and Susie Heide, who insisted on keeping Margaret company rather than drive out from the city. Since the accident four days before, the Heides had neither slept nor eaten properly, and Susie was increasingly worried that all the turmoil would affect the health of her unborn child.

In the crowded parking lot outside the church, where J.J. Nickel performed the funeral service, Helena Peters opened the casket for viewing, only to discover a stain spreading across her daughter's white dress. Six years after the wedding, Mennonites still weren't accustomed to brides in white. Black, rather, was the rule, and the sight of young Margaret Peters all decked out in white in 1934 had sure caused a ruckus; that is, until Reverend Nickel calmed everyone by citing a verse from the Revelation of St. John the Divine, "Let us be glad and rejoice, and give honour to him: for the marriage of the Lamb is come, and his wife has made herself ready. And to her was granted that she should be arrayed in fine linen, clean and white: for the fine linen is the righteousness of saints." Back in '34, Nickel had cleverly taken the verse typically used to object to a white wedding dress and employed it in defence thereof. Now, however, with the ride from the city jimmying open Margaret's torso, the dress was discoloured. Helena quickly covered the spreading stain with a bouquet of peonies, her daughter's favourite.

In the moments following the end of the service, someone—quite possibly John—snapped the three-by-five photo that has haunted my life, found in the box in an envelope with the word *coffin* written across the front in pencil in John's hand.

July 3, 1940.

Margaret Peters Boschman, Aberdeen, Saskatchewan.
COURTESY OF THE BOSCHMAN FAMILY

Audio of Arnold, 1995:

"The funeral itself is a bit of a blur. I can remember Marv went nearly hysterical. When they started to throw dirt on the coffin in the old way that they did it in those days with everybody standing there, he went wild. Was just gathered up and taken away. I stood there looking down at that hole, dry-eyed. And, uh, you know, the big anger was already setting in. I didn't know it then, but I can see that now.

"Now something else happened there that was also a turning point for me. I can remember that after that day I got a lot of hands on the shoulder, hands on the head, from adults who said, 'You're the oldest, you're gonna have to look after your little brothers; they've got no mother. You're gonna have to be a big boy now. You're gonna have to be a man.'

"Now what a helluva thing to lay on a four-year-old kid! If you detect a little bit of self-pity here, uh, you're probably right. I may have suffered from self-pity for the rest of my life, and I really only got in touch with that little aspect of things here eight or nine or ten years ago.

"Of all the females in my life, Grandma Peters was the only one, the absolute only one, whom I ever trusted implicitly and can say I loved. Because from the time of Margaret's death, I don't really believe (from what I know of myself and my life and my actions and my reactions) that I ever really knew about love. But Grandma Peters I believe I loved. I can feel her hand on my bare shoulder—that is, when I was going shirtless as a boy—I can feel her hand on my shoulder right today, still a source of comfort. She was there for us, you know, in what ways she could be.

"When you think of Grandma Peters during this tragic summer, you have to remember that she still had a whole houseful of kids of her own, Margaret being her oldest daughter. She was as busy as a healer could be, with the work that she did setting bones and fixing people up, plus running a household and the farm.

"And yet I always knew without a shadow of a doubt that she was there. That was maybe, just maybe, the only source of consolation I had."

* * *

Fall 1940.

"Big full moon in the southeastern sky" where John feels God's presence and calls the moon a shepherd.

The hiss of the lamp, a rude dog barking somewhere.

The little poplars scratch and whisper all around the house and yard. One of the boys is restless.

"The longing for her has worn me down."

This moon of John's has been a real problem for me. Since I first read the green notebook, I've felt the weight of it. Placed my shoulder against its serious mass, most of the time without knowing it.

I've probably never seen a harvest moon on my own terms. I don't feel resentful. It is for and through and with and because of my damaged grandfather. This continues even though I don't believe in his God, the one whose awful presence he felt under the Saskatchewan night sky—a sight that can really get inside your head. Just as much as, if not more than, any shepherd, the harvest moon can appear as a hot orange ball burning the horizon.

In the teacherage next to the grid road on the table by the window where the gas lamp hisses, he keeps scratching away in that notebook of theirs. Looks out at the barn where the horses are stamping for feed.

If I was born into his questions beneath that amber body, bone to his bone, I have come to conclusions with which he wouldn't agree. We might argue, though I wouldn't want to. I might simply try gently to nudge him three degrees.

Don't box her up.

Don't suck it up quite so much. It's okay to cry. Maybe have a beer or three with one of the Hutterites. Sure, get on with things. But leave her picture there in the open where you and the boys can see it.

Of course, I can't do any of that. It probably isn't fair. Trauma wasn't understood in John's time, and is only beginning to be acknowledged now.

Still.

One afternoon in the late 1990s, I interviewed one of Margaret's brothers, a dark-haired gentle man named Bill. I always thought that Bill Peters and my dad could be twins. Except that Bill was older and had only one eye. One day as a young boy playing on the home farm he shot an arrow into the sky and the arrow returned exactly into his right eye, the very one with which he had taken aim. I saw that sightless orb weep when we talked about Margaret. Even close to sixty years after her death, Bill—the same boy who took the phone call from John—could feel the whole thing coming down again. I saw this response from the other siblings I spoke to as well. Abe, for instance, couldn't even talk about it. He just broke down in his living room in Langham the moment I spoke her name.

When I asked Bill if he thought that John perhaps didn't handle things as well as he might have, Bill's response was sharp: "He did things his way; I would have done them another."

Bill also told me a story, one that I heard repeated by the other Peters siblings. This story seemed apocryphal at first, the kind of thing families hold as true and maybe even embellish over time; but it became apparent to me that there might be something to it when I heard it repeated as I talked to Margaret's brothers and sisters, some of them quite different from one another in temperament and world view, during the late 1990s. They are almost all dead now. But here's the story—an anecdote—as relayed to me by Bill:

The three boys were seen standing beside a street in Langham and one of the boys said, "If we sit in the middle of the road, a car will come and run us over and then we can be with mom."

Audio of Arnold, 1995:

"Another thing that stands out most in my mind is that Marv cried a helluva lot. Marv and I slept together in a double bed and Marv would cry every night . . . and I couldn't cry and I couldn't feel and it made me mad. He'd cry and keep me awake. Poor Marv, he got pounded on on a regular basis. I would beat on him, I would pound him, till he quit crying so we could go to sleep. Uh, I think in those years Willard was a little scared of me. I was already playing that role of running things, you know, making some rules, I suppose trying to be that older brother looking after things, I don't really know. But I just know that poor Marv took a licking on a regular basis because he was crying; he was very, very upset by this thing. I know he talked to Dad about it. He went to Dad a lot as a small child, but cried mostly."

John saw Marvin from his own perspective.

Of the three boys, his second-born was both the most muscular and perhaps the most sensitive. He was also the shortest. Even at four years old, his powerful physique was readily apparent. He would become in stature the most like his father and, like John, become a teacher. But as 1940 passed darkly into 1941, Marvin clung to John for dear life and almost every night wound up standing by John's bedside, a small, white-haired apparition.

On December 29, when John marked the six-month anniversary of Margaret's death, Marvin was nearly inconsolable. "He cried about everything. It seemed he just could not get a hold of himself. During one of these spells, he told me he wished the men would dig a grave for him so that he could go to heaven to Mamma. He said Mamma liked it so much up there that she didn't want to come back anymore. It was a rather pathetic scene to watch him. I know how he felt."

When spring came, Marvin was still in the grip of grief.

"April 11, 1941. Often at night when I put the boys to bed, Arnold & Willard go to sleep quietly; but Marvin cries for his mother. Last night he cried so hard. I tried to calm him, but he kept right on, saying that Jesus could take Mamma's wings off so she could come back to us. I explained that she could never come back. Then he insisted on getting a new mamma. I said Jesus could give us another mamma if he wanted to, but we would have to pray for one. With his eyes full of tears, and crying so he could hardly speak, he immediately said, lifting up his hands, Jesus give us a new mamma. It was such a pitiful sight. I know I could never take the place of a mother in the hearts of my boys. We would have been so glad to keep Margaret, but apparently the Lord had better plans. He makes no mistakes, so I can only believe even though I don't pretend to understand His riddles."

By the time June 29 rolled around again, and John was marking that day in the green notebook, Marvin remained deeply grieved (as he would for the rest of his long life). He not only continued to mourn the loss of his mother; if anything, his state of mind was worsening. The crisis simply refused to pass.

"At dawn I woke and found him standing at the window talking to me. He asked, with tears in his eyes, why I had not brought Edith back, because he wanted a mamma. I explained that it would not be long till she came to stay, and then our troubles would be over. They would have a real fine mamma again, and we would all be very happy. I quietened him finally by allowing him to sleep with me."

That day, June 29, a Sunday, John had been to Saskatoon to meet with a young woman named Edith Ewert, with whom he had been corresponding since Christmas. He left the boys in the care of his parents, Cornelius and Anna, who had come to live with them the previous fall. Without their company, John and his sons would have fallen even further into loneliness, the house into chaos and disrepair. He called his mother a "good manager" and, because of her steady attention, the boys were cared for properly throughout that winter. Before Anna's arrival, Margaret's brother Abe lived with them but Abe never pretended he knew how to keep house.

So said John. "The boys are dirty, their clothes are dirty, the house is dirty, bedding is all dirty; everything gets dirty & soiled so quickly." John held God to account for all this, his anger barely concealed. "Things look a bit blue these days, when everything seems to go wrong. However, I am quite well used to adversities. Nothing has ever really gone according to our plans. Yes, one thing; the love and happiness between Margaret & me. But it didn't last very long. Only the disappointments and the worries and the miscarried plans last. God sees, and God knows it all."

This was November 10, 1940, the day before the anniversary of their secret engagement. That evening he went through everything pertaining to Margaret and boxed most of it up in a sturdy wooden container that said "Champion Chemicals" along one side.

During this period, John corresponded with the lawyer, Henry Rees, known to his friends as Hal.

Rees practised out of the Birks Building in downtown Saskatoon and was honoured and respected by all who knew him. Since John was a steadfast Mennonite, and therefore non-adversarial, his retaining a lawyer at all was close to improbable. Retribution was the Lord's, revenge *verboten*. But because Margaret's father in particular did not share John's principled reluctance to pursue remedy, and because the Teachers' Federation could provide some monetary support for a legal action against Harry D. Reid, John allowed for the possibility. Hal Rees was a lawyer with a reputation for integrity, and so the now-single parent retained his services.

Almost immediately there was a misunderstanding. Rees wrote to John on September 13, 1940 to correct

John's mistaken notion that an action could be started without suing. "Starting action is suing for damages and it is, furthermore, necessary in order to demand a jury to claim a specific amount of damages. The only safe thing is to claim enough to allow for all contingencies and that is why I have named the sum of $20,000.00."

The prospect of a civil suit and a trial with a jury was more than John could bear. It went against his religious grain, against all his thinking regarding the sovereignty of God. Besides, a trial would put his boys through further grief. And, most significant, as my father would tell me in conversations seventy-five years later, John really felt strongly that no sum of money could compensate for the loss of Margaret. He couldn't put a price tag on her. He couldn't accept that this or that amount, whatever it was, constituted, or might be seen as equal to, Margaret's value as a human being, friend, wife, mother.

I'm sure that Margaret's father, Jacob Peters, disagreed. Jacob wasn't a fervent Mennonite, unlike some of his children, and he fumed and boiled over the fact that Reid had been exonerated by the coroner's inquest. He wanted to make "that man pay" for the wrongful death of his first-born child. Who was pregnant, no less. Then there was Helena, Margaret's mother, the famous bonesetter. She couldn't bring herself to want any kind of revenge on Reid. It wasn't in her makeup to carry around big heat or hold a grudge, even though the loss of Margaret was almost unbearable. Legal action wouldn't bring her back and she doubted that Margaret would want them to pursue it. Forgiveness, instead, was warranted, was her duty as a child of the God who imbued her hands with healing power.

So a legal action through the courts did not take place. Instead John pursued a middle course—the one he was likely thinking about when he came across as confused in his initial contact with Hal Rees. John would proceed carefully between the poles set by Margaret's parents, both of whom he loved very much. His relationship with them would continue for the rest of his life, and he would comport himself toward them insofar as he could as if Margaret weren't in fact dead. The boys were the main beneficiaries of this decision, a good but difficult one: to maintain contact, to continue to visit the Peters farm often and for extended stays, especially in summer.

On his client's instruction, Hal Rees corresponded with Reid's Toronto lawyer, a man named McIntyre, in securing an out-of-court settlement. Reid's insurance policy would cover everything. Over that long winter, Rees checked in with John from time to time in order to communicate his progress. He phoned and he wrote letters, and his letters were always the same: brief, type-written, respectful—also businesslike, professional, his letterhead making clear his good standing and central location in Saskatoon and area.

In other words, he wasn't what John would call a *scheisser*. Far from it.

Audio of Arnold, 1995:

"Now here's another thing. In spite of the fact that Edith came into our life not very much later and was, without a shadow of a doubt, the absolute best mother she could be to us boys, and pretty well devoted the rest of her life to the raising of us, plus three more of her own—in spite of that, I can also remember—and boy, this is not something that Edith should take wrong, and I don't think she would—I considered myself motherless. And I think I remained aloof. Edith tells me now that I was a hard guy to get a hold of, I wouldn't let anybody touch me. If she reached for me, I was gone."

A voice in the background asks a question: "Did your father ever hit you or beat you before Margaret died? Or was it only afterwards?"

"That's part of my life that's completely blocked out. I only have one memory from before the time Margaret died, and that has to do with loading a hayrack with furniture that was going from Friedland School at Aberdeen to Neuhoffnung School at Langham. In fact, I remember the horses—a pair of sorrel mares of Grandpa's called Myrt and Marj. And I have absolutely no other memories [*taps his knuckles with each word*] before Margaret's death. None. So I would venture to say that being almost five years old there should have been more but I don't remember. I venture to say that was a block."

"And no beatings?"

"I don't remember a hand being laid on me. No, for me the lickings and the beatings came after Margaret died and, uh, there was a certain confusion. Dad could be real light-hearted and when he was that way and full of fun then what he would do was what was termed in those days as being foolish . . . yeah, it was pure foolishness. Nothing serious, we would do the damnedest things and he'd be a boy, and we'd laugh and talk and wrestle, stuff like that. But he seemed to be either one or the other—either very stern and removed or we'd be jacking around. And, uh, okay, God the lickings were terrible! I've got that sorta straightened out in my mind, and it's taken me a long time to realize that it didn't happen because I was a bad kid. But people would often say, 'Take that frown off your face, boy, you're gonna have a crease right in your forehead. You're too young to be worrying.' Well, I can remember that. And I also remember exactly what booze did to me; it relieved me of all that anxiety. I became easygoing and entertaining and I think comical and put on a show. I loved doing that. I became the guy I wanted to be when I'd had a few drinks.

"Dad really never did talk about Margaret's death, not to me. He had a heck of a time. I can remember being a grown man and asking about some things and he just kinda turned away, and if he had anything to say it was just a few words, nothing informative. He had no explanations. But I definitely got the idea that he had been so very much in love with her, that he had been deeply hurt, traumatized you might say. These things I realized later in life—that it was, uh, it was a heck of a thing for him to go through [*voice gets lower*]. And, uh, you know, I can see now the reasons why he became like he was, together with all the religious stuff based on fear and guilt and those things. I can understand exactly why he was like he was."

Edith Ewert was a year younger than Margaret. She was already twenty-eight years old in 1940 when she wrote a brief letter to John Boschman at Christmas. In those days, a single twenty-eight-year-old woman was considered a spinster, though I highly doubt my grandmother saw herself that way. Edith attended Normal School during the 1930–31 year—two years before John. By Christmas 1940, she'd been a professional for almost a decade and had shown little inclination to marry, spending most of her free time with her parents at the huge Ewert farm near Drake, Saskatchewan. My father told me that there were times when John would, with a wink and nudge, quietly remark, "Your mother is more intelligent than I am." He meant it.

And John never allowed anyone to refer to Edith as the boys' step-mother. She was their mother, grafted onto Margaret's place. Edith herself went along with this—was often heard to say that she was standing in for Margaret. The Peterses appreciated this but there was also some dissent. When I asked Jim Peters about it, his response came quickly: "She wasn't my sister." I think he meant this not in a negative way but to make clear that there was only so much anyone could do. Edith always visited the Peters farm with John and the kids and would sit in for the missing Margaret at dinner tables and for photographs. In her mind, she had Margaret's back. It was an act of love and solidarity.

She was the sixth-born child of Edward and Katie Ewert, who, by the time Edith wrote to John, had had thirteen children in all and lived on a prosperous farm close to Drake, where it so happened that the Funks lived. Like the Funks, the Ewerts had come to Canada from Kansas; and together with the Funks, the Ewerts spoke no Low German. They seemed to pride themselves on that score, at least that's what my father thought. Low German, from a certain perspective within the hugely diverse Mennonite community that exists across North America (including Mexico and Central America), was considered, as its name indicates, a language of the low-born. Common, earthy, oral, the old tongue could betray your status. Not knowing it at all was a mark of a different, more elite pedigree. The Boschmans and the Peterses—indeed, even the well-to-do Friesens—all spoke the old language; and they paid for it in some-times being looked down upon.

All thirteen Ewert kids attended Rosthern Junior College—a point of pride and a financial feat in itself—and the first seven became teachers. In the fall of 1940 Edith was appointed teacher for the Mierau School District, which bordered the Neuhoffnung one where John taught. She'd heard right away about the Boschman teacher with three little boys and decided to send a card and parcel during the Christmas season. Later, in the spring of 1941, one of J.J. Nickel's sons, Frank, also a teacher in the area, arranged to introduce the two.

The letter was addressed to "John Boschman and His Three Little Boys" and arrived just as the holidays were drawing to a close. Coming upon this letter was, for me, the first of two major discoveries made during my mid-thirties, when I was the same age John had been in 1940–41. Edith's letter, needless to say, wasn't in the box. It was with her. Before her death in 2000 she gave it to my father, along with all her correspondence with John. Seeing her hand at work in this family history for the first time constituted an emotional shift for me. A paradigm came into view. It was like coupling two equal sections of a miles-long prairie train, or at least seeing where, exactly, the coupling had taken place.

The second find was perhaps even more momentous. Here it wasn't a paradigm but a day that came into view.

John's final entry in the green notebook is dated June 29, 1941. It was a rainy Sunday; exactly a year had passed since the accident. I have read this passage dozens of times throughout my life, at its different stages, poring over the words—the last words John would ever write in what had begun as his "mood book" almost a decade before—precisely because there was nothing but blank pages afterwards.

As a reader connected by blood and genes and tissue to the drama of my paternal grandfather's narrative, I was hungry for more—but there was nothing after this. Here the story abruptly ended and I was left dissatisfied, even though his last words were "I am happy." I doubted their veracity. But Edith's correspondence, which amounts to a thick bundle of letters between her and John, written throughout the 1940s while John travelled the province of Saskatchewan as a government bee inspector, generously provided the detailed sequel for which I had been longing. It amounted to a windfall.

Right after the Christmas letter, the next in terms of chronology is John's and it, too, is dated June 29, 1941. So the words had continued to flow on that rainy Sunday. It was almost as though I had known it all along, like something I myself would do: write an important journal entry to myself as well as a letter to a significant other. The writing in the letter to Edith seemed better than that found in the green notebook—writing to Ms. Ewert changed John's prose. His tone comes across as somehow more complex and nuanced. It is perhaps my favourite letter of his.

"Last night coming home the old Plym really showed she could come home in an hour. When I was about a hundred yards from the gate both lights went out. I made it into the car shed in the dark, and this morning I discovered that a wire on the switch had come off. They are not burned out as I feared, but I was glad they didn't trouble miles from home. Of course, I would have to tell you about Marvin. He couldn't go to sleep last night, and when he finally did he was very restless. At dawn he got up and asked me why I hadn't brought Edith back. I asked him to sleep with me, and he went off to sleep immediately."

* * *

From that Sunday, June 29, 1941, a new era began in the life of my family, and it began quickly. The trauma experienced by John was intergenerational and it spread in his relations, old and new. Even with a significant intervention, such as the kind available today, it could not have been otherwise. In epigenetic terms, the fracture was now at the cellular level: it would transmit to all of us, like the bumper break on Margaret's very body great with child.

Quite a while before meeting Ms. Ewert and asking her to marry him by a country tennis court south of Langham, John had already enrolled in summer school at the University of Saskatchewan; and, after a few days spent at the Peters farm, he made his way that same week to Saskatoon to settle into new digs at St. Andrew's College. On July 3, he was ensconced in his room, number 316, furnished sparely but with everything he needed. There was a rush at Convocation Hall of numerous students like himself till finally at about 2:00 p.m. everything was settled.

He wrote to Edith that evening to let her know his circumstances and to ask if she'd gotten home to Drake okay after their meeting by the tennis court when she'd agreed to marry him. He still hadn't mailed the letter of June 29 but would, along with this one.

"Our boys were quite delighted to stay at Grandma Peters'. . . . I know she is overloaded with work, but she insists on keeping the boys."

John was restless on that July 3 as he began this second stint as a student in Saskatoon writing to his beloved, not this time Margaret Peters but instead a woman named Edith Ewert. Edith Marie Ewert. Classes wouldn't start till the next day.

To kill the time, as he put it, he went uptown to find a lock for his car door and in the evening "drove out to the dam and the ski-slide." The Saskatoon weir had just been completed the year before. It traversed the South Saskatchewan a mile downstream from the university campus. Next to it was the bridge built by the Canadian Pacific Railway Company in 1908, which also acted as a pedestrian crossing. John could clamber up on the high trestle structure and look down on the river and the churning weir, then referred to as the dam since it was first used to regulate water levels on the South Saskatch-ewan. You had to be extremely careful along this part of the river, for to fall in would mean ceaseless entrapment in that long wheel of water shaped like a rolling pin and never stopping.

Later, he stopped in to chat with cousin Jake Heide at 1619 Avenue A North, the address where he'd seen Margaret killed. He stopped his car in the same spot. He opened the door and got out in the same way. He remembered his words, "I'll just be a moment." He visited with his cousin just as he had on that day, a day that sometimes—and increasingly—he couldn't recall. At night when he woke from sleep suddenly, lying there on his back in his room at St. Andrew's, there were tears running down from his eyes and his throat filled with fluid like he would choke.

Edith could bring John home that summer and the case for their expeditious marrying would be compel-ling, yet it caused some concern among her many siblings. One of these, Edwin, hadn't heard of John and didn't know of the Boschmans. He was so surprised by his sister's sudden announcement that she would marry John Boschman that summer that he stated, "You'd be surprised too, Edith, if I suddenly told you I was going to marry a person you had never even heard about."

* * *

Oh, the hellaciousness of all that silence. Big full moon hanging ponderous and orange, emerging slowly and without mercy from the horizon. Could anyone see the cross-section and make a comment perhaps? Is it juice pulp, magma, mercury, cheese inside? Maybe the moon is a woman, "bald and wild," as one poet, Sylvia Plath (also intimately acquainted with loss), would definitively state many years into John's future.

Who could really know anything when Father God decides in His infinite wisdom what is best for all?

God Alone.

So John had inscribed on her dark granite headstone standing ramrod straight in the Aberdeen cemetery, a mile from town, such a lonely place, one tree, a ring of caragana, a little rose bush here and there, a white fence with an iron gate, all of it surrounded by tracts of flat, cultivated land. No verse selection from the Old or New Testament as a part of the epitaph. Nothing much like the myriad expressions of hope and faith found on other headstones in Mennonite cemeteries across the continental heartland from Kansas to Saskatchewan, Manitoba to Alberta.

Did Edith pick up on any of this anguish of his (so different from the Ewerts, who were rational almost to the point of being perceived by some as clinical)? Wherein God knew and understood what he, John, did not and had to accept on faith while also taking responsibility for his own suffering? Because, in John's thinking, God had to correct him somehow? And if such—that is, Margaret's death—was the extent to which God had to go in order to salvage John, then things were indeed bad and this new gal, Edith, was his last chance at happiness. Did she figure this out or see any of this? Probably not immediately. She was so quickly in love, which was quite out of character for her, she'd likely absorbed John's state of mind without fully realizing it during this intense summer of 1941.

In one letter Edith almost panics, sure that something has happened. "Was there anything wrong last night, John? All night, dreaming or awake, I seemed to hear you calling me. Somehow I have been unable to escape the weird feeling all day today. I heard you calling at the washline and in the Raspberry Patch, by washing dishes and by varnishing the kitchen floor. Is it nerves, John? Or has something happened to you?"

There was no way for her to know much for certain, and she certainly didn't know that that same day, July 21, he'd tried to articulate his feelings in a letter to her but finally gave it all up: "so I'll rewrite the letter and 'live' what I feel after we are married. . . . Really, Edith, you know what I mean, that heaviness of heart, when you want to say a lot but words are so inadequate. That's the way I felt last night and this morning. You seemed so near that I could almost touch you."

On weekends John went to the Peters farm to see the boys, who were so far doing fine that summer without their dad. Even Marvin was free from longing and seemingly without care under the roof of his grandmother, Helena. One of her youngest, Mary, was in fact not much older than Arnold. They all called her Buddy. One Sunday evening before returning to the city, John took the boys for a walk along the grid road between the farm yard and the cemetery where Margaret was buried. Arnold conveyed a message for Edith: "Arnold told me to tell you that he was a real big boy who could ride horseback all alone. He is very proud of this. He says he rides awfully fast. I haven't seen him ride, but the others say he is really good for his age."

At the university, John studied adolescent development and discovered that every adult retains a vestige of their earlier and younger self. It made him see himself differently. He had little time for exercise but often measured the time it took to get to the various buildings on campus from his room in St. Andrew's: five minutes to the dining hall, ten to the engineering faculty where his classes were held. He criss-crossed the campus as necessary and as his schedule allowed. He thought about the old Boschman place at Aberdeen where he "was born and grew up and spent most of my life."

His letter to Edith, dated July 27, 1941, is one of the more handled of all the letters I have read. She wore this one almost right out so that unfolding it now is a perilous undertaking.

I imagine her reading it even up till the time she gave it to my father, who gave it to me along with all her correspondence with John just before her death in 2000.

One day at the turn of the century, Edith stepped down from a Saskatoon city bus and was promptly run over by a boy on a skateboard. She fell and was knocked out. The boy disappeared. Not much later, she had a stroke, then another, then she died in the Royal University Hospital.

In my mind, I have a picto-series of Edith unfolding and refolding this letter at various points throughout her life. In each picture, her fingers and hands have aged a bit more, as though continually morphing toward the texture of a segment of blood orange. The three-cent stamp is the colour of said fruit. It makes me long momentarily for old paper and envelopes; but in the age of Twitter such things no longer exist except as souvenirs, tokens of a longed-for but unknown settler past. Although one can purchase textured old-style paper and envelopes, one does so for the novelty, for the manufactured feeling of touching a yesterday of long ago that is largely imaginary. And I try to be careful—aware—of my own nostalgia, wanting to get the story as right and true as I can. To be truthful.

Once Edith asked me, in so many words, in a letter she wrote from the Calgary International Airport in 1997, to be true and accurate. I had requested her permission to follow her trail, and in a hand resembling the one I see in her letters from the 1940s she asked me to remember John's "love for the land . . . that he was a man of nature and the soil." She said this, I think, because she knew I suspected that he was damaged; that the experience of seeing Margaret killed in a hit-and-run had unravelled John at his core even though he'd made a strenuous attempt to keep himself together and show nothing; that this traumatic experience was shared by his sons, especially the older two but also Willard my father; and that the ripple effect had gone out through the generations and included Edith's own three children with John, born into an existential question that was never asked, let alone answered.

The woman who had first reached into their lives with a Christmas card and parcel addressed to Mr. Boschman and his three little boys, when the roads were almost impassable, would six months later be stirring their wedding cake in her mother's kitchen with two-and-a-half weeks to go.

The letter in which she indicates all this would be delivered by a neighbour going into town—"I hear the car now so I guess I must say adieu for now."

At last John reached a settlement with Harry D. Reid. He was notified in a letter from his lawyer, Hal Rees. It wasn't the $20,000 Rees had urged John to sue for during the summer and autumn of 1940. Instead John accepted the sum of $485, "which," as Rees noted, "is $250.00 for the children and $250.00 for yourself less $15.00 which has been paid to the Saskatchewan Teachers' Federation." The sum was equivalent in today's terms to almost $8,000—a pittance compared to the amount John might have received had he consented to sue for $20,000 (over $300,000 in 2017). Still John took the sum and purchased an annuity for each boy. Seventy-five years later, Arnold still received his annual cheque for $48.

Arnold doesn't remember the wedding. He doesn't remember anything of Drake from that summer of 1941, including Edith's visit to the Peters farm for his birthday party.

He does, however, remember listening to a conversation on the other side of a closed door while his father received counsel from Reverend Nickel, who was saying that this was all God's will.

Reverend Nickel, it was hoped, would officiate at the ceremony in Drake on August 16, but at the last minute he cancelled and another preacher had to be found.

After meeting the Peters clan at Aberdeen, Edith was given a small photo of the three boys cheek to cheek. Later, in the big Ewert house to the east, the picture would go missing only to be discovered crumpled up in a ball in her little brother's bedroom. Edith would try her best to smooth out the wrinkles; but she felt so guilty about this mishap that she wrote to John to apologize.

Edith then became quite unable to sleep. She told him, "You have a very magnetic quality of some kind." Coming to terms with what she called the seriousness of it all left her lying wide awake on her bed during those last few nights. This wakefulness had had its onset during the train ride back from Saskatoon, when all she could do was sit and think.

"I tried to sleep and did actually succeed in dozing off for awhile. Then of course I had to sit and think some more."

She and John had barely made it to the train station on time after saying her goodbyes to the Peters family, who would all attend the wedding. As John would recount in his next letter, his wrist watch was five minutes slow and if "we had come up one minute later, we would likely have been too late. The conductor was pulling the cord when you went up the steps."

He watched the train depart eastward and then he returned to his car—the 1929 Plymouth—and drove south on Avenue A to look in on his cousin, Jake Heide, and "have a few rattles taken out."

As he writes to her a final time during that summer of 1941, he continues to fear that something might happen. This fear will hereafter never subside. It will in fact only get worse with time. It will slowly squeeze the life right out of him.

Stamped in black on the envelope for this final letter of the season are the words JOIN THE WAR EFFORT!

He tells Edith in a brief note what he intends to do and to deal with: On the day before the wedding, a Friday, make a slow purposeful drive to Drake with the three boys. A picnic lunch by the roadside. Four or five hours in all if the car doesn't break down, the boys falling asleep along the way.

Then the wedding photo I have seen of the two standing together next to a huge automobile before the grand Ewert farmhouse. He does look magnetic; there is some charm about him that draws me even though I am older now than he was then. Old enough to be his father, yet still the grandson filled with questions.

"Till Friday, Darling, God be with you and keep you. After that the same."

* * *

Regarding that summer of 1940, the year prior, when Arnold remembers running wild on the farm at Aberdeen but nothing else, John's journal has no entries for July, and there is little immediate evidence of where he went after the funeral. His first entry is dated August 11, a Sunday night, 10:00 p.m. On this line there is also a heavily blacked-out segment as well as another on the next page.

Whenever I read here, I am a child again, discovering my father's father's trauma and identifying with it. As though it were sewn into me before I was aware. I am sitting at my dad's large oak desk in the bedroom next to the boiler room at the back of the King Koin

Launderette trying to decipher the blackened areas and bore into the clipped words and sentences with which John relates the death of Margaret. Outside my window is the Texaco gas station and the year is 1971, but in my imagination I live with my grandfather and his world is mine as he writes in the green notebook most Sunday nights at 10:00 p.m. for one complete year, one planetary cycle of grief.

"Aug. 11, 1940. This is Sunday night, 10 o clock. . . . Since my last entry much has happened. I will relate briefly. . . . June 29/40. Decided to go shopping in Saska-toon to get a few long-needed articles of clothing. Went to Langham for a bit of business. Left boys at Nickels'. Had dinner at Jake Heide's, 38th St. & Ave. A N.

"Did shopping in p.m. Going home stopped car opposite the Heides' house and ran in to tell Jake something about repair of my car. Margaret said she would stay in car. On seeing Mrs. Heide, motioning to her, she decided to cross avenue & talk to her. As she left car, a north-bound car struck her and killed her. When I ran and picked her up she was dead."

Here is the onset of memory extinction, what Arnold later would angrily call a cover-up— not knowing what one knows more intimately than anything else in life— born in the mind's need to protect itself. It had taken John six weeks to open the green notebook again. His description of the scene itself is detached and he uses the first-person "I" only one time: "I ran."

Other than this, he removes himself.

This I consider a significant tell—a foretell, in fact—a precursor to the physical and emotional suffering he would visit on those close to him.

Cathy Caruth, who interviewed those who have experienced trauma as well as those who bear witness to its effects for her 2014 book *Listening to Trauma*, found that "events, insofar as they are traumatic, may be defined, in part, by the very ways in which they are not immediately assimilated: by the manner in which their experience is delayed, split off, or subjected to social and political denial."

Those who follow, Caruth argues, "bear witness to an unconscious event."

Even as a boy, I found the date gap in the green book curious and wanted to know where John had gone during what must have been an incomprehensibly painful period right after Margaret's death. I needed to know where my grandfather had gone. They were all in shock. Arnold could never remember him during that time, and in my conversations with others who were around then I found no one who could tell me anything until I asked Uncle Bill, the younger brother who was still living around Carrot River in 1940 and had written a long letter to John and Margaret during the summer of 1938, when forest fire smoke filled the northern horizon.

Bill knew where John had gone after the accident because John was with him.

Together with a close friend, Art Nickel, Justine's brother and therefore in John's circle of confidence, Bill had taken his older brother into the forest close to Petaigan. Bill called these the Pasquia Hills. In among these hills, which stood high over the cleared fields in that region, a wilderness reserve had been established during that period—and in this reserve, before fire destroyed it, Bill held a thirty-six-square-mile trapping lease and sole guiding rights.

The hulking Henry Boschman took them to the gate, which was sometimes open and sometimes not depending on the fire situation. They walked in from there, crossing the Carrot River, and slept under a tree that first night.

Before he returned to the fields at Petaigan, Henry took photos of the three young men. In one of these a fourth individual, a child, appears. It is Arnold: small, wearing short pants, his face a frown in the bright sun. Though he doesn't remember it, he is there indeed, sitting between his father and Art Nickel on the wooden rail of a bridge spanning the Carrot River.

By the late 1990s, when Uncle Bill told me about this sojourn in the forest, he couldn't remember Arnold being there either, even though the photos demonstrate that he was. John had taken his oldest son along with him to Carrot River; Arnold had joined the four men during the drive and then gone back to Petaigan with his Uncle Henry. His grandmother, Anna Heide Boschman, would be waiting there for him.

The pictures show the three men wearing beaten fedoras, heavy denim pants held up by suspenders, and dirty white button-ups with sleeves rolled to the elbow. Bill stands, in one picture, next to Henry's farm truck, while the other two men sit on the large steel bumper. Unbelievably skinny, Bill is a tall, shambling forest animal, his head jutting forward as though ready to lope into the bush where the spruce trees were of such girth two men could reach around and only just touch each other. In one telling photo, John and Art do just that: their arms encircle a tree with their fingers touching at mid-knuckle—and here John smiles ever so slightly.

It was gorgeous and ancient forest, though even then much had been lost to clearing and wildfire. There had been so many fires in 1937, when Bill worked on the towers, that he wrote in his journal, "Visibility nil." You could hardly see the ground. One morning he saw the notorious monster later dubbed the Great Smoky Burn, a boiling wall of smoke and heat that couldn't have been more than ten miles away. Someone had thrown in a match, a deliberate act of arson.

What struck me most about discovering this lost time from July 1940 were John's own words quoted back to him by Bill in Bill's letter of 1938: "Margaret wants to come down in summer instead of winter. She wants to see the trees in summer garb, holding their arms aloft as if in constant praise for their being."

It made sense that John would want to head into that forest. He was thinking of his lost love when he decided to venture north to the Petaigan region. He needed to do this and Bill knew that he needed to. They could sleep rough under the stars and put their arms around giant trees. In this region, there were wolves, bear, cougars, moose, elk, and woodland caribou. Unusual birds and plants were here also, and Bill had knowledge of these, and he shared this knowledge and his passion for the land with his older brother. The trumpeter swan could still be seen in the area, even though it had been taken close to extinction in the early twentieth century; and once Bill "actually caught a sparrow-hawk alive. Of course, after the excitement of capturing it I found that I didn't want it and let it fly."

Few settlers ever came here, where the First Nations people from the nearby Red Earth Reserve held traditional Cree territory. They had long known what Bill was now discovering.

"It seems a pity," he added in his 1938 letter to John and Margaret, "that we humans should worry about 'jobs' and 'political pull' and such things." This seemed especially true when he encountered "a beautiful, big Bull

Elk feeding. He disappeared like a flash when he noticed me"; or when he felt the presence of timber wolves.

"I see their huge tracks in the mud and know that a pack is in the vicinity."

Bill's life was distinct from John's, and the two would proceed throughout the century in quite different directions even while they kept their affinity for each other, mainly through shared political affiliations and love of nature.

Their main point of difference was religious.

MY
PA

60 How little I realized as a child running around the tiny whitewashed Nisbet shack preserved with green shuttered windows and sealed door next to the paddling pool in Bryant Park, later renamed Kinsmen Park. I didn't know a thing about that shack, hugging its emptiness tightly. I never entered that closed dank blind space. I didn't know where or what or who I was.

What I did know soon enough was that there was an enclosed hockey rink at one end, across the street from the jail for men, and that I would play hockey, like it or not. At first, I liked it. Once I had learned to skate properly, without embarrassing anyone, and to wear the equipment, also without embarrassing anyone, I also took on puck handling and seeing the rink.

Insofar as I could see.

My father took out an ad in the *Prince Albert Daily Herald* hailing the newly formed Prince Albert Raiders hockey team of the Saskatchewan Junior Hockey League. On behalf of the King Koin Launderette, the ad read,

Willard Boschman and sons welcome the Raiders. There were our three pictures, and there I was looking out at PA with one eye turned in slightly as though trying to focus on the end of my nose.

Not knowing how much I couldn't see, I now played defence for the West Hill Bruins. I wore the colours and took the position of my gladiator hero, Bobby Orr. The way he swept around his own net and gathered speed to face his opponents was an image that almost unhinged me. When I saw him do this on our wood-panelled Electrohome television set in the living room of our apartment behind the King Koin, I felt something bordering on joy and grief. The two feelings were brought together by the sight of the great Orr, whose legs—though the knees could give way at any moment—carried him through his adversaries with superhuman agility and speed. Maybe it was partly because of this god-man who played through pain and imperfection that I believed I, too, could play the game on the B side of the Pee Wee League and do just all right.

My coach, Jube Hegland, seemed to think so. Every week the team met to practise on the open-air rink at the West Hill Community Club, surrounded by the extensive neighbourhood of newer homes adjacent to All Saints Indian Residential School. Out on that ice, where it got so cold one's toes soon lost all feeling, Mr. Hegland shot snot rockets by deftly pressing one gloved finger against his nose to close a nostril completely off and, leaning slightly, blasting a small bulb with exhilarating force. A mucosal blur. With Mr. Hegland's steady encouragement, his blue eyes looking into mine, I felt okay to play—and to play defence no less, even though my slapshot was abysmal and even though I knew just enough to realize that this B league I was part of implied an unspoken tolerance for second- and third-rate players.

A few blocks away, at All Saints, my schoolmates from our primary years at Vincent Massey, too, played hockey on an outdoor rink that I saw once when Maynard Whitehead asked me to come with him to the residence where he lived ten months of the year. That rink and the feel of that place—lonely and regimented—made me feel a keening sympathy for Maynard without my knowing exactly why. Later I would come to understand more of what my child's intuition was telling me. And all my life I would remember Maynard's wavy black hair and the shape of his face and his steady eyes.

I still have dreams of Mr. Hegland in which he wears a moss-green winter coat. He slides back the heavy dead-bolt and the gate opens and there is the dark ice. He tells me to HUSTLE like it's the last thing I might ever do on earth.

61 At about this time, I had the strangest experience. It took place when I needed it most, when things were happening to me at school that were it not for this one thing—this one person—may have been my undoing psychologically.

I'd left Vincent Massey School behind and was now attending another school named for a white man, Arthur Pechey. This school lay one block to the west of the King Koin, just a few blocks from All Saints and also from the West Hill outdoor rink where I met Mr. Hegland and played for his team. Although I no longer had to walk four blocks past the old jail twice a day, I now faced a new and nightmarish scenario in and around the rotunda where students in grades 7 and 8 gathered in cliques of cruel energy. A boy named Wags loved to fire his leg suddenly along the ground swiping my feet out from under me. I had to watch for Wags constantly after one of his felonious leg movements put me on my tailbone and I writhed in pain for what seemed like forever in the porch of that rotunda. Another boy grabbed my hand and rubbed the knuckles on the rough red brick wall till they bled. His harsh laughter and the laughter of the kids who watched. I was younger than all of them because I'd been accelerated back in grade 2, but they didn't know that, nor did they care. They saw that I was smaller and cross-eyed and had a high voice; I could claim none of the physical changes taking place around me.

I dreaded changing in the locker room, dreaded being seen. Every day at least once someone called me a fag and invited me to suck his cock. Every day when I got home, I secluded myself in a downstairs bedroom and checked to see if a pubic hair had sprouted. When one and then another appeared, I showed my little brother and felt a shred of hope. But the horror of the other kids never left me and my own physical changes couldn't happen fast enough. That year, my picture would appear in the Arthur Pechey yearbook for 1973–74, published in an orange Duo-Tang. Eyes out of sync, a blond bang slanting across my forehead, I was no match for the caption that appeared beneath my image: "Small, light and well . . . WELL? Ambition in life: to be something more than DOT DOT DOT."

One day while walking alone close to the provincial courthouse at the top of the viaduct, I saw a man coming toward me and our eyes locked. We passed one another in a turning mutual gaze and then faced each other for a split second before continuing on our separate ways without a word. He was heading downtown and I was going home. I didn't know who he was but he looked like my dead grandfather John. I thought for a moment I'd met a ghost. I was filled with both fear and relief, and a sense of recognition flooded my being.

When I got home, I informed my dad of this man I had seen who looked just like Grandpa: the same straight, strong teeth, the same smile, the same dark hazel eyes and balding head. My father told me I had seen Uncle Bill, who had just returned from world wandering with his wife Violet and who would live from now on in PA. Then I remembered seeing a man with a beard at our back door and I realized that the man I had seen on the street was this same bearded man who had greeted my father, only in the blur of routine I hadn't really paid any attention. There were so many people knocking on our door morning, noon, and night.

In a photo of the Boschmans gathered in the old forest around Carrot River, my father's finger pointed out this uncle for me, one of the younger boys surrounded by his brothers. Uncle Bill had lived differently than John had—had rejected Mennonite beliefs, fought in the last war, travelled alone to distant places. Lived for a while in northern Saskatchewan, then Mexico, then New Zealand. He wasn't afraid of going to hell and the letters he opened from fellow Mennonites warning him of his fate in the afterlife annoyed him. He'd come home, he said, because he missed the shield country and wanted to camp and canoe again. The next time I saw him, he said he'd take me with him into the forest north of PA.

62

Almost the first thing that happened to my new sister Crystal was chicken pox. Within a month of her joining our family at the back of the launderette, she was hit with the virus and hit hard. Hundreds of oozing red blisters covered her body and she lay on her stomach moaning. My mother applied calamine lotion while the rest of us took turns at her side with soothing words and love. We could all sense how the fever and burning and itching were affecting her. She was barely six months old. As the days stretched out, it began to feel to me like the worst thing I'd ever seen. If any one of us could have traded places with her, we would have.

We asked our mom why this was called chicken pox, what a chicken had to do with it.

"Nothing," she said.

The trained nurse looked it up in one of her old textbooks, which I, fascinated by the photographs of diseased humans, had already explored. The skin, eye, and mouth diseases seemed the most dramatic. Smallpox produced pustules larger than the ones we saw on Crystal's skin. Only a few years earlier, I'd stood in a long, nervous line stretching down the hall of Vincent Massey School, waiting to receive my smallpox needle, which left its indelible mark on my left shoulder.

No one knew where the chicken in this other pox (which we had all endured though not with the severity we saw in Crystal) originated. But the virus itself had come with the settlers, and we knew from our parents that the diseases whites had brought had brutally affected the people living here.

Uncle Bill was already talking to my dad and writing letters to the *Prince Albert Daily Herald*, pushing back whenever a racist letter appeared in the Letters to the

Editor section. Over the next three decades, he wrote letters and published articles under the name William Boschman. He stated in one that settler diseases had emptied the land of its First Peoples. Hence, I knew when I witnessed what chicken pox did to my sister that it could be fatal. It all depended on who you were.

63 In the Neuhoffnung School District between Langham and Saskatoon, where John and Edith taught after their wedding in August 1941, the *Englowndah*—the English—were seldom seen. Everyone was either a Mennonite or a non-colony Hutterite recently come from Minnesota or North Dakota. So many Hutterites went by the same names that they took on middle initials so that, for instance, David K. and David J. Waldner could be told apart. Nicknames helped and the Hutterites loved them. There was a man named Bush Epp, a hard man who lived close to town and rolled large cigarettes called Bush Epps. Sep Mikes, by contrast, were emaciated smokes rolled by a neighbour named Mike Waldner whom everyone called Sep Mike. Sep Mike's kids were also called Sep. Sep Bob was the junior softball coach and my father and his two older brothers played for his team. Marvin played left field and was an occasional pitcher; Arnold was the catcher. Their ace was a girl who threw deadly pitches with a small movement of the wrist, an amazing Sep Mike kind of thing, her right hand flicking like a miniscule flash of lightning on the horizon.

Where that ball diamond once was you can still see a few buildings far off in the distance, hard little black

specks drowning in the flat spaces criss-crossed by telephone lines and teeming with stands of poplar.

* * *

John they called the Scientific Farmer because he'd
absorbed the harsh lessons of the previous decade—
those Dirty Thirties—when dust and smoke gathered
in billowing, darkening walls. Too much mindless
ploughing, too much cutting and burning. John planted
trees and windbreaks where others had taken these
down in the quest for arable land that became desertifi-
cation in some places. He also ordered and tried the new
seeds being developed at the University of Saskatchewan. All these practices and protocols grew from the
near-fatal errors of the 1930s across the heartland of
North America. John wanted to learn from the past by
using new practices. The Hutterites took note and gave
him his name.

Meanwhile, however, there were other, internal things
John couldn't seem to realize. Goings-on the neighbours couldn't know. They didn't know that his insides
burned almost continuously, and not in his stomach
only. The ulcers began in his mouth and shot through
the entire alimentary canal, as if he'd consumed acid.
His mouth alone got so abscessed he'd wake up at night
with tears running into his ears and his throat choking
with mucous. He drank wine and milk, and took bile
salts, but none of these gave consistent relief, and what
he really needed was relief from fear. He could never
tell Edith where the fear started or what its object was
or why. He didn't know. He knew only that it seized
him till he was convinced that something was truly gone
wrong, that he was having a premonition of impending

catastrophe, that Edith was dead or injured, or that one of the kids had had an accident.

Their first child was born in August of 1942 and they named her Lola Margaret. She was born with a purple birthmark across her torso and another, also purple, on one eyelid.

When Edith gave birth to their second child, this time a son, John slept on a cot in the physicians' quarters at the Saskatoon City Hospital. He wouldn't leave the hospital till he was certain that Edith was well, even though he hated the place. It was winter then, and the streets were treacherous, and John was glad he had no car. To pass the time, he saw the movie *Lassie Come Home* at the Roxy. He also read Dr. Holmes's book on fractures because he couldn't sleep well at all.

All this he wrote down in a letter to Edith after he'd returned to Neuhoffnung. He said he simply didn't like Saskatoon at any time, and worse when he was alone at night in winter.

He included a note Arnold had written for Edith.

"Dear Mamma," it said in Arnold's grade-school hand. "Are you feeling fine? Here is a little verse I am going to write.

> Docter, Docter can you tell,
> what will make poor mamma well,
> she is sick and she might die,
> and that will make my family cry.
> Your son,
> Arnold"

This was January 1944. By then Arnold was called Half Horse by his father, for that was what his son, in his aloofness and horse-loving ways, seemed to him. From now on John, though he loved horses himself, would nag Arnold that the day of the horse was over and done with, and that if Arnold wanted to dedicate himself to that animal his life would be a hard one.

64

I was Old Shaky, Rotten Rob, also the *oola näs*. Old Nose.

But Kerby chewed his nails right down to the quick and my father's oily hair left a stain on the headrest of my mom's La-Z-Boy recliner. The green faux leather eventually cracked and mom knitted an Afghan cap for the headrest but it was too late. My father's haywire sebaceous glands had secreted through too many episodes of *Red Skelton*, *Carol Burnett*, *Tommy Hunter*, *Hymn Sing*, and *Hockey Night in Canada*. Between cigarettes Kerby beavered down all ten nails till there was nothing left but small nubbins and everyone wondered if they could ever grow back. That question remained forever unanswered as Kerby kept them gnawed down to bluish nubs till the night he died in 2010.

When my parents needed to step out now and then, Kerby stepped in, watched over us at the back of the King Koin, gave change to customers too, brought pretty girls by, and reminded me that my sebaceous glands were haywire as well. This new fact he posted on the fridge as a part of his "List of Child Labour Duties for the Orphans of Willard & Elaine Boschman" in uppercase letters.

It really got inside my head.

While Beatrice was to "compose masterpiece on piano about wonderful uncle . . . to be titled 'That Marvelous Uncle Kerby,' " and while Ben would be the "personal slave to Commander Funk" and as such was to "1). Pick the Commander's nose" and "2). Kiss the Commander's bum," I was ordered to "keep residence washrooms immaculate at ALL times." This included the following priority item: washing "pimple pus off mirror." Massive doses of tetracycline did little good and Kerby knew it.

He signed off in flowing script as "Commander Kerby N. Funk—by the authority of having all the muscle and most of the brains in the house." He didn't seem to know—or more likely didn't care—that I now smoked his long butt ends and sampled his White Tower, Matteus, and Royal Red. Or paged through his *Playboy* magazines and absorbed the world view of Hugh Hefner. So long as I ate his Sloppy Funk and laughed when he wrote a letter to the Campbell Soup Company because he'd found a stone in a can of vegetable soup. He boasted later how a stone in our soup got him an entire case courtesy of Campbell's.

* * *

Digger walked up when I saw him again, locked his eyes with mine. We both looked at his chest and biceps. They twitched in response.

"It's okay, Rob, we still love you, just don't ever disgrace the family by being a doctor or a mechanic."

"Or a pilot," someone chirped. "He's cross-eyed, don't forget that."

"Guess that takes care of a buncha things."

Stuart was upset because I'd called Fred Hoerdt "Fred Fart." Fred was a horseman Arnold respected who sat in the living room one night drinking beer with all the men and Stuart was there and in front of everyone I said Fred Fart.

"Well he's no good around the stables. Sneezing and shit, eyes all watery. I don't like Rob."

It's true, I was a useless dreamer, suffered from incessant hay fever, didn't like the smell of horse on my hands. And Arnold scared me. I knew he'd never strike but that was just it: Arnold in those days appeared hands off with kids and for all I knew hadn't hugged Digger in years. He barked at Digger but was a genial whisperer with a horse. No whips or brutality ever passed through Arnold, not even a smack. But he let fly with fury when he found out another horseman had beaten an animal with a chain out between the barns of the Saskatoon track.

Arnold's first horse was a gelding named Pat, brought onto the yard by John in secret while the boys were sleeping early one morning. Pat came from the Bergens at Aberdeen, a good first horse for a boy. John eased him up all glossy black to below the boys' bedroom window, then threw a pebble up against the glass and that was that.

Arnold took to riding Pat all the time, even at night. Sometimes John could hear him singing in the darkness outside the house.

65

Dip dip dip in the deep blue Cheer,
Rinse rinse rinse in the water clear.

The thing about the above couplet is that you had to say it in the voice of a weak male with a cleft palette. You were a second-rate jokester and no fun if you didn't get the voice right.

It got to be so that I was left alone sometimes to answer the door and give change at the back of the

King Koin after my siblings were asleep. Waiting for my parents to return, I would half-heartedly amuse myself with PA's jokes and riddles between knocks at the door.

One evening I watched the movie *Deliverance*, which had been to the theatres and was now being shown on one of our two television channels. When my parents returned, I couldn't sleep, kept seeing the white hand of the drowning white man coming up from the dark water. When Uncle Bill dropped by and said that the two of us were going north to a place I had already visited but he hadn't and he wanted to see it for himself, I didn't know what to think. I'd just been to Sulphide Lake on a canoe trip with all the boys in grades 7 and 8 at Arthur Pechey. On the small island where we all camped, one boy shat in a tent just for fun, for the marvelous sensation it caused. It was such a *Deliverance* thing to do. By some miracle of chance, none of the small fleet of aluminum canoes turned over as we paddled and portaged across a half dozen lakes deep in shield country north of Lac La Ronge.

Now Uncle Bill wanted to see this place for himself in a canoe much shorter than the sixteen-footer I'd been in for five days straight. Painted to look like it was made of birchbark, his canoe was four feet shy of that.

He liked a small craft, he said, because he could go off by himself and disappear for days, weeks even. He smiled when he said this, but now that I had seen *Deliverance* I felt sick. Uncle Bill was no Burt Reynolds. He wasn't like any of the men in the movie, including of course the hillbillies who seemed to glide like shadows across the cliffs above the river and through the dark forest. He didn't carry a weapon or a musical instrument or fear with him. He wasn't afraid of the wilderness, carried none of the fear of the urban white male characters in James

Dickey's novel of the same name on which the movie is based. Uncle Bill was typically calm and cheerful, especially around a small fire with a blackened pail of water coming to a boil. When he surveyed the island where I'd camped on Sulphide Lake, he immediately rejected it, said it was too low, the bugs would be bad, and if a storm came up we'd be in trouble. Instead, we paddled back the way we had come and pitched his pup tent high up on a giant rock standing over the lake. I slept in the tent and he reclined outside under a mosquito net. When it started to rain, he put up a tarp.

He was so happy.

66 That there existed another hockey universe to which I might gain admittance began to dawn on me when I was invited to join the West Hill Panthers of the A league. Mr. Hegland was invited too. I imagined I was Hegland's star player brought along in his new capacity as assistant coach. I had become his captain in the lower league, where I enjoyed pretending I was Bobby Orr. The West Hill Optimist Panthers immediately changed all that, erasing whatever playful fantasies I had had till then and altering my good relationship with Coach Hegland.

Entering the dressing room, I exchanged my moss-green Cooper SK10 helmet (like the one Butch Goring wore) for a new Bauer lid, blood-red with a grimacing black panther hand-painted on either side. My number, 11, stood upright and washing-machine white on the aeronautic ridge at the back.

I've kept this helmet all my life to remind me that accelerating, whether in school or hockey, isn't necessarily a good thing.

Gone in this dressing room was any vestige of easygoing camaraderie or fun. My life on the ice—where I no longer played defence but left wing on the fourth line—began all over in this new atmosphere like I'd been born again into another world. To me it was regimented and cold, replete with report cards and shining red jackets advertising the Optimist Club of PA. Whatever laughs took place in the Panther dressing room were, in my experience, exclusive to the boys and their dads of the well-to-do West Hill. The classiest dads entered that space with their fur hats and dark coats, emissaries from a world I didn't know at all. Without saying it even to myself, I realized I'd made a big mistake by saying yes to Coach Hegland, but there was no going back, at least not yet—not until Coach Gordon sent me back when the stress had become too much.

One boy in particular ruled this team. Mort played defence and before the arrival of Dave Tippet, who would go on to a long career in the NHL, was the best player on the Panthers. The son of a doctor, a man who seemed very nice in fact, Mort decided from the start that I was a zero, an interloper, a cross-eyed trashy kid from a launderette, and his friends on the team followed suit. I sometimes wish, looking back years later, that I had fought Mort, but at that time he was not only the leader of the team—its captain—but much bigger than me and a feared fighter. As all our stats were made public, listed on the report cards we received from Coach Gordon, I can see that in October 1973 Mort was five foot one and a half and weighed ninety-seven pounds while I was just over four foot eleven and eighty-three pounds. Mort in fact was the second-biggest kid on the roster. He had me by two inches and fifteen pounds, a lot when you're twelve. Still, standing up to a quick beating might've been better than the uninterrupted scorn I suffered during the season and a half I played for the Panthers before my return to the B league, where I finished my hockey career at the age of thirteen.

In between the Kinsmen Arena and the Prince Albert Correctional Centre for Men cars moved to and fro along 28th Street. This was PA, the hallowed home of such hockey greats as Orland Kurtenbach, Dave Balon, and Johnny Bower. The sort of world where you could live in oblivion or be a star, be contained in a cell or a dorm or else enshrined in the PA Sports Hall of Fame.

67 The thing about trauma—even a small one—is that it keeps coming. Like a nasty dog snapping at your ass and hamstrings, it follows. It's a dogged, fangy memory thing and until you turn to face it (and wise guidance is needed for this) it'll continue to nag, tear at, and hang on you.

Sometimes I think not just about my grandfather but all those around him in that moment when Margaret stepped out and was struck by Harry D. Reid's car.

From there, the event ripples across time and through relationships in ways that cannot be documented. It's created havoc in my family right into a new century, when those affected have no idea what it is anymore even though it resides as a legacy right inside their bones and dreams.

There are people who study this phenomenon; the field is called "transmissions studies." One scholar, M. Gerard Fromm, edited a book called *Lost in Transmission*, in which a researcher, Ilyany Kogan, describes "themes of joining with the damaged other, healing them, or assuaging the guilt for not doing so," as well as "the profound confusion between past and present, and inner and outer."

These researchers also speak of sequelae—those things that follow—and the damage done to the hippocampus, that part of the brain where memories are stored and where trauma is either hidden and contained or jangles and intrudes all the day long and every night throughout a lifetime.

Once I had a dream about John in which he showed me another journal additional to the several of his that I keep. Another journal unknown to me. Things contained therein that remain unknown—unconscious. In another dream, beings approach me crying, "more, more," and I wake up confused and upset.

I return to what can be teased out and known. That is all I can do. I reread the transcript of the court proceedings translated from Pitman shorthand after decades in the darkness of a stairwell at the Saskatoon City Courthouse, followed by another decade in which I search for anyone who can read the stenographer's hand from early July 1940.

And what I find there, finally, is the moment itself in fragments of writing, or as close to the moment itself as anything I will ever find. The transcriber writes, "Please be aware that this appears to be a witness statement which I believe has been taken down by someone as another person is conducting an interview. The shorthand writer is therefore writing at a very fast rate and so these outlines are almost scribbled."

Everything happens so fast. The mind strains to slow the pace of events and see the details in fragments repeated again and again.

Lawyers for the Crown and other officers of the court gather for the proceedings on July 2, 1940. Their names echo in newspaper accounts—Ross, Campbell, Wrigley, Lambton, Cassells, Simon. One puts questions aggressively to the Reverend Henry Rempel, whose vehicle passed directly opposite Margaret as she stepped out to visit with Susie Heide:

Were you alone in the car?
My wife was with me.
She was sitting in the front seat?
Yes Sir.
And how close to . . . the car and the deceased woman
. . . were you . . . in feet?
Maybe 8, yes. . . .
It happened in front of you?
Yes Sir.
Had you seen the deceased woman . . . before she was struck by the car?
Yes Sir.
What did you see her do?
I saw her coming from the car south [of me] in front of her car and past my car where the accident happened.
Was she near at the time to your knowledge in the car or was she outside on the ground? Tell me when you saw her?
I saw her coming from the car south [of me] in front of the car.

My question was do you confirm [you] saw her south in the car?

No.

And do you confirm see[ing] her when she was east [of you]?

Yes.

And from the east side . . . the car was driving away?

Yes.

Towards [the] front of the car?

Yes Sir.

And did she continue her motions? Tell me or did she [move] south?

No she did not.

Was she moving tell me? Was she moving tell me? Was there much traffic on Avenue B at that time?

Very much.

North and South?

Some south bound.

Where you were bound?

Yes Sir.

And did you . . . happen to warn her of your approach? Blow your horn or otherwise?

No I did not blow my horn. No, we screamed.

From here, pieces of memory and bits of knowledge gather and form swiftly. Released faster than I can keep up with, they coalesce and move together as one thing like shimmering small birds rising from the ground.

Digger in a green house out on the edge of town locking a mouse in a jar with a lighted candle; he watches the oxygen slowly leave before heaving the jar from the back door into the minus-forty night.

Willard my father for the first time in family history turning on the electric lights at Neuhoffnung, wondering why he's the one John selects to flip the switch.

John walking on his hands using coke bottles and one breaks and slices his palm.

Arnold bringing a horse switch down across my father's face; when I ask the brothers about it they refuse to speak—"No, we won't talk about that."

I, a teen, putting John's 1960s Philips electric razor to my nose, catching a whiff of his scent locked in old stubble, clicking the On switch to shave my three-haired chin.

Edith singing "Twilight Comes Stealing" as night blankets the teacherage newly attached to the electric grid.

68 Entering the teacherage, still standing in 1998, I see it teeming with stuffed animals. The house has been moved several miles from its original site at Neuhoffnung. The couple who live in it now are Waldners who knew John Boschman.

"David K. Waldner. That's my dad's brother," the man says as we stand in the small living room. I can't sort out all the Waldners right then because my attention is on the bobcat, fox, and deer's head that share the space with us. Everything is musty and suffocating.

The woman, Evelyn is her name, remembers my father. "All the girls loved Willard," she says.

Her husband points out a framed photograph of John standing on the school porch surrounded by students. By all accounts, students universally loved Mr. Boschman. Once in a Calgary clinic where I bring my child for immunization, a receptionist asks me if I am related to a John Boschman, the former teacher. When I tell her that, yes, I am his grandson, she says he was a great teacher, her favourite, but maybe a little distant.

My mind returns to the small house and I wonder how six kids and two adults ever slept in it. Efficient packaging must have taken place. My father tells me that he and his two older brothers slept in one bed in an upstairs bedroom that was so cold in winter the walls would be covered in a glaze of frost. Lola slept in the hallway outside their door. Lola the silent one. She will pass away in 2010, the same year as her younger brother Randolph, also silent, the youngest in the family and the first to die. James, the middle child born to Edith, in that cold winter of 1944, agrees to talk to me on camera in his living room in Saskatoon.

He has a sharp Ewert face, aquiline even, but with John's balding head. His mind is cuttingly sharp and when he smiles he looks like no one else I have met among the Boschmans or the Peterses. He has pointy canines and sometimes he sucks his teeth. I remember he tormented me at Christmas one year when I lost at Risk. And, of course, his tart consumption is legendary— he can eat anyone under the table. He offers me a glass of red wine, which I accept, and he has one too, which surprises and confuses me since for years and years James has not been drinking but now apparently he is.

I want to say, "Hey, wait a minute, you don't drink!"

In the video interview, he wears tinted glasses. The tan lenses shade his eyes as he begins to speak. He removes the glasses.

"I think from the time I was able to walk I wanted to get out there and catch Dad."

In his pursuit of John, the favoured time of day was morning, when John would rise and sit at the kitchen table wearing a sweatshirt and James could climb onto his father's lap. Then his father would shave while James watched. He loved the scent of John's shaving lotion.

"Dad was a disciplinarian. He had his warm, loving side and then there was his insane religious side. Basically everyone is guilty of everything and the one emotion you can show is fear and guilt. It was doctrinaire, paternalistic, Pauline, bastardized Christianity. . . . I think that's what killed him. He was a very intelligent man . . . but he could not reconcile what he knew in his heart to be true and what was expected of him as a person, a father, a husband, a Christian, a Mennonite . . . that it wasn't right and therefore there must be something wrong with him. He literally wore himself out with that struggle."

He smiles a little while he says this, then remembers a moment at Turtle Lake when he went there to fish with John. James was twelve by this time, and his oldest brother, Arnold, had just married.

"There was no electricity, and I took the flashlight to the outhouse and set it down beside me. It was night, it was late. And it fell in the toilet. I figured, *Oh my God, Dad is going to kill me*."

Bursts out in tears.

"But he didn't."

Laughs and cries all at once, like a relieved child, blurting out the words through tear-filled eyes. Released for a moment.

"He was just out there and happy, and there was a whole side of him. . . . If you did it at home, you could get a lickin' for it but when you were out fishing or hunting or camping he was a different person, totally different.

Good-humoured, patient, teach you anything about woodcraft or hunting."

Now James breaks down, weeping outright, but only for a second. He apologizes and composes himself.

"That would disappear. You'd get back home, back in church, and any of the things you could do when you're out on a camping trip, it was hell and damnation all over again."

* * *

From her bed in the hallway, Lola counted the strappings her younger brother James received during the autumn he entered the first grade. Witnessed and kept track of. By Christmas, there were forty-two.

69 My son is in grade 1 as I write this. I have never struck my children—to do so is unthinkable to me, as unimaginable as getting hit by a car. Sometimes when I look at the generational damage, I also have to recognize positive changes that have occurred in my lifetime. To my knowledge, none of the Boschmans of my generation strike their children. The wrath of the Black Doctor (the name given to the family strap), which terrorized my father with physical violence and always hung on a wall at home as a reminder of that violence, has been extirpated. Once, my father wrote me a letter in which he spoke of that awful talisman of power and authority, of the male-on-male violence it represents. I was thankful he'd been able to see through it, make it visible and known in a new way. It takes courage to write such things down in a letter from father to son; it meant more to me than I could really say. It gave me the chance to be different, to hope for a better future for boys and men.

When I look at my son, I see someone who loves Terry Fox, who said to me once, "When I die, the first person I want to meet is Terry Fox"; who gave a homeless man his allowance and when the man refused ("I can't take your money, kid") ran into a store and bought him a Mr. Big candy bar; and who has wrestled with the concept of homelessness—what it means, how it happens, what other terms might better represent it. What I see in Gabe, as well as in my daughters, is awareness, and my hope is that the transmission of trauma has for them activated an ability to read the past in new and improved ways.

This fresh understanding for me is inspired by a central epigenetic concept, canalization, which Susan Merrill Squier describes as "the process that enables a developing organism to withstand perturbations and continue to develop in a certain way."

The surprise isn't so much that traumas are passed on or that our offspring function at all, but that they can indeed be whole people. My children have always known about John and Margaret and what transpired in the aftermath of her death. I have not been silent about any of it.

70 What a picture of Canada it is. As Gord Downie said before he died, "Canada is not Canada." This really is all about truth and reconciliation. There's arguably no other way. To consider the Cree child, born of a far northern woman, now

crawling on the floor at the back of a launderette owned
and operated by settlers whose customers are themselves
mostly Indigenous: this is not an easy thing. Nor should
it be. Coinage and old dollar bills everywhere in our
living space. Knocks at the door throughout the day and
evening. Did we realize the situation we were in? Were
we giving her harbour or was she stolen outright, like the
land itself? Sometimes we spoke of it to one another, and
my parents' sense of justice and their love and respect
for First Peoples stepped forth. Yes, she was stolen. This
should never have happened at all. At the same time,
we would protect her with our lives. The land itself had
been appropriated, surveyed, and allotted before we—
any of us—had been born. We were the beneficiaries of a
massive theft. We argued with other settlers about things
like responsibility and accountability and justice. Great
harms had been done—were being done—and especially
for my mother it always came back to the fostered infant
children crowding bedrooms, lying largely untouched.
My parents couldn't turn away from that reality. We all
agreed on that. My mother spoke of how Crystal my
sister hadn't experienced enough one-on-one during her
first months of life in fosterage in Saskatoon. Though
we knew that our reality—our culture, language, ways—
paled against this small girl's rightful place in this land
called Saskatchewan, we also knew a far greater wrong
existed. To ignore it and do nothing was worse. Partic-
ularly as my father had himself broken away from the
religious traditions of our ancestral past, we had no wish
to impose these on anyone else.

We also knew, as one, along with our neighbours the
Henrys, who were supportive always, that Crystal would
find her way back to her people, and that we would help
her. She was in the meantime our responsibility, would

grow up in this neighbourhood, and no harsh hand would touch her. Just the thought of that happening made me fucking crazy.

71 Uncle Bill never skated or played hockey. He didn't care, knew little about the NHL or Bobby Orr. He was schooled in Aberdeen until the eighth grade and then the financial catastrophe of 1929 took place and everything was lost and he found himself living in the northern forest fifteen miles from the new settlement of Carrot River. Later he would take two further years of schooling. Of his nine brothers, his favourite, the one he felt a kinship with, was John. The two of them had attended grade 8 together, in fact, even though John was a decade older.

Of the many things Uncle Bill told me on the high rock overlooking Sulphide Lake, here was one: he and my grandfather had walked to school together every morning along the CPR tracks. And they had done that thing—walking—together many times over the years that followed. Though John went on to finish high school and attend Normal School and even earned a degree at the University of Saskatchewan, while Bill stopped formal schooling after grade 10, they took these long wilderness walks together.

Soon enough Bill was the better walker.

John, I discovered through his letters to Margaret Peters, had once walked from Aberdeen to Saskatoon. He was in his late twenties then and it was a Sunday evening. He walked back to the city past Cathedral Bluffs on the South Saskatchewan. An admirable feat, done for love.

Bill, on the other hand, finishing his youth in the forests surrounding Carrot River before the Great Smoky Burn, agricultural land clearance, and Tobin Lake swept all away, regularly walked such distances. The fifteen-mile stretch between town and the Boschman log cabin was nothing to him. Other settlers in the region saw him out walking by himself. Margaret Peters's brother Jim, who would come north from Aberdeen to see what the Boschmans were doing, exclaimed, "Man, could he walk!"

Standing beside our little fire, which he kept going through five days of rain at Sulphide, Uncle Bill said he was foolish, out in the woods everyday like that all alone.

"Older men, used to wide open spaces, were not comfortable in the forest and probably would get lost if they strayed off the trail. It fell to younger men, when rations were low, to take to the bush. Sometimes I tramped the woods for days in bitter cold and snow without success. But would try again. When there was success, the meat was distributed in the community."

He could walk twenty miles in the snow and not feel too tired, but there was risk involved. For one thing, winter clothing during those years was hardly adequate. Once when he shot a moose close to the banks of the North Saskatchewan, now all under water, he was wearing layers of denim and had no gloves or mitts. He was staying with a family who homesteaded in the area, came to them as "a skinny seventeen-year-old, poorly dressed, carrying a 30-30 rifle and a pack on my back. The pack contained food because my hosts were two days from a store. My parents were to follow by sleigh a few days later."

The deep river valley where Tobin Lake is now, he said, seemed like three miles from bank to bank, and there were islands everywhere. He was wet to the crotch in thawing snow; then the temperature dropped and a hard crust formed. "Moose could hear me a mile away on the clear, still air and left only tracks."

Where we were then when I first heard this story— by a lake someone had called Sulphide—the rain was falling steadily. We had raincoats on with our hoods up. We were eating Saskatoon berries and drinking tea. The smoke from the fire kept drifting into my face and I circled and circled trying to evade it while a nighthawk twisted and turned in the sky above our rock.

"On the fourth day the weather had changed. It was snowing and blowing. The wind rattled the frozen branches and fresh snow muffled the sound of my progress. I picked up a pair of fresh moose tracks and then topped a ridge. And there they were: a pair, feeding, unaware of me. I had been so cautious, walking slowly so as to make no sound, that I did not realize how cold I was. My fingers were numb and refused to cock the Winchester. I had to take the rifle between my knees and cock the hammer with the palm of my hand. I was shivering and had to steady my aim against a tree. The nearest moose fell. The other disappeared into the underbrush."

His mouth opened and closed and the words dropped out beside the fire like the berries we'd been picking. The whole time he spoke to me rain fell in a continual drizzle as it had for days on end. I thought I might go crazy if this rain didn't stop. I wanted to go home. Bill took bits and pieces of birch paper and sprinkled these on the fire, driving it up lightly against the drizzle, smoke rising in my nostrils while he told me all about this moose he shot when he was seventeen. The nighthawk kept darting around like a kite.

"I approached the animal from the rear. A dying moose could inflict severe injury with those sharp hooves. My usual reaction to a successful hunt was exhilaration, and then regret at having to do this thing. In this particular case, I was too cold to feel one way or another. With fumbling hands, I made a cut in the belly and plunged my hands into the warm entrails. Then I warmed the knife. As I dressed the moose, a two-year-old bull, I became quite warm from the animal and from exertion. Then I skinned it. The whole operation took about two hours. I cut a willow with several forks and impaled half the liver on it. With many a glance backward to establish landmarks so I could find my way back, I walked to the home of my hosts. My parents arrived that night."

Overnight he became ill with a high fever and delirium set in. He lay like that for two days while it snowed nonstop and his folks waited, not knowing where to go to look for the carcass. Finally Bill came around, opened his eyes, got dressed, ate and drank, and led his folks and their hosts to the place where the bull lay, buried and preserved from scavengers and the elements in a bank of snow.

His mouth opened and closed, rain and berries falling, as he told me all this, and more. We had tea and bread and butter, honey in our tea and on our bread, plus fried fish, boiled potatoes, poached eggs, and once we roasted yellow perch on sticks. His mouth was stained a deep reddish hue while he talked and told stories because we kept going back to the berry patch. Even after it was dark, as the words dropped beside the fire, I could make out his stained mouth and the dark fragments of sweet berry skin. I considered telling him but then thought mine must be stained purple too.

After the war, Bill took John on many wilderness walks. Once they saw fresh wolf tracks; the animal had been dragging something. They followed until they came upon a wolf shot through the rear quarters, dragging itself through the bush. They shot it.

Another time Bill noted his brother huffing and puffing through deep snow, struggling to keep up. They joked between them that John's legs were shorter and he wasn't used to it. That was the time Bill carried John's rifle until just before they reached camp, where some of the other Boschman boys were waiting. Bill told no one for years and years.

When he told the moose story for the last time, it was the year 2000 and Uncle Bill lived in PA near the top of a high-rise overlooking the North Saskatchewan. From here he could look out in three directions. He said he wasn't afraid to die. It was perfectly natural. He typed out the story of the moose on an electric typewriter in a letter to CBC Radio. He said it was "a world which now seems unreal."

* * *

For me, too, it seems unreal, and that is something I tangle with. It's like a dream that I was ever a child in a place called Saskatchewan. Even the lines on the map, straight as they appear, appear to come from a dream, just not mine. They are stamped indelibly as though from some Victorian cookie cutter purchased from the Dollar Store or left by a red-hot branding iron. They contained my childhood before I knew they were there, but so did the rivers of the basin that meet at the Forks and become one living thing, flowing for epochs before the sanitized, warped geopolitical lines found on a Mercator projection were adopted. They're flowing still.

Now when I walked to school, I walked into the west toward Arthur Pechey. In the morning, the sun was behind me lighting my way. I could see awaiting me out on the playground the children of grades 7 and 8. They were tying scarves around their necks and tightening the scarves till they fell unconscious. If you did this to prove your worth, which was the case, then I was worthless.

I saw the prettiest white girl do this. She had blond hair and I thought she was beautiful even as she fell backwards when the blood was cut off from her brain. That same year I saw her fight another girl in the alley where everyone met to witness such events. Her hair came out in bunches and settled onto the gravel.

The boys with whom I played hockey also attended this school. They were in grade 6 and usually gathered far off at the other end of the schoolyard. Though our worlds at school didn't intersect, though I seldom saw or spoke to them, they did attend these fights. I watched them watch this fight between two white girls. I wondered sometimes whether despite my hockey unhappiness it wouldn't be better for me to be with them, back in grade 6. More than anything, though, I missed Digger.

72 My father growing up had a friend named Donald Mierau who lived three miles west of Neuhoffnung. The Mieraus came from Minnesota. Willard my father and his friend Donald walked the grid roads together. One day they found a nice, well-kept farmer's house, completely furnished and filled, but no one seemed to live there. It was a two-storey with hardwood floors. This house contained toys, including a wind-up train. They pulled out a window to enter and played with the toys, putting them back when they finished. They replaced the window again as they left. Returning again and again to play in the unlived-in house with the wind-up toys, it seemed as though they saw a face at an upper window whenever they approached and departed.

The Mieraus attended the Zoar General Conference Mennonite Church in Langham, across the back alley from where John and Edith would later build their retirement home. Where I would see John lying in state and the German words in Gothic font taken from the Gospel of Luke were emblazoned across the nave and the ceiling fans with three tines apiece stirred the air slowly. In that earlier time, the Zoar was also called the Singing Church because it was attended by Minnesotans who all loved to sing. So Willard started to go there because he, too, loved to sing, even after his voice changed. He and Marvin sang in the choir and soon they had a bevy of friends who also wanted to sing, spurred by the old hymns composed on another continent.

"Glorious Things of Thee Are Spoken."

"Beneath the Cross of Jesus."

They visited each other on horseback and by car and on foot. His friend Donald, who was shy, had a guitar and could play, while another friend, Norman, owned a guitar as well as a gramophone. Together with Marvin, they expanded their repertoire with American folk songs like "The Eastbound Train" and songs by Gene Autry, Wilf Carter, Hank Williams Sr., and the Blackwood Brothers.

The non-colony Hutterites living in the region could also sing. Willard and Marvin attended their Emmanuel Church standing all lonely out on the flat prairie, where the sun rose and fell and rose and fell, sometimes like an orange wheel or a circular saw, and the gravestones to this day all lie prone like beds laid out in rows and covered in bright orange lichen. My father knows all the names of these people who loved to sing who lie beneath the stones there.

In their quest for song, Willard and Marvin also attended the Basement Church of the Mennonite Brethren where the emphasis was on personal salvation and altar calls. They answered the call on numerous occasions in the strange church dug out of the earth, a dank hole for praising the Lord. One night after going to the altar they returned home to find their father already in bed. Their voices carried easily in those tight spaces.

"Hey, Dad. Guess what?!"

"What?"

"We're saved."

"Yeah, Dad, we got saved tonight."

"That's good. Now go to sleep."

73 It was hard to know which was my true home—the launderette itself or the living quarters around back. I felt belonging in both places. The cement pad with its outdoor car wash and the dirt alleys and the Texaco lot sopped in oil were the surrounding land I knew best.

The memory of the smells alone spins me back into childhood—perc, dryers, hot sheets, fried onions, soap and water, cigarettes, Bohemian lager—as do the sounds of a dryer in motion or a spinner whirring down like a giant top after the chunk of its final gear.

The long, high-ceilinged public washroom of the King Koin was a desperate place, an unholy festival of the senses that could vie with any roadside jacks. We all used it when the bathrooms in back were occupied by family members.

When my father informed me that we would be moving to land west of Saskatoon, I was ecstatic. He took me to see our new forty acres of scrub poplar littered with ancient farm implements. We would leave PA and build a house to live among old wagon wheels with cast-iron rims and desiccated wooden spokes. We would keep horses and other animals, get a big dog, and—so I imagined—I'd surely come to know old brands of sensation—smoke, rain, frost, ice, old leather, and ink—in a new place. We would build our own racetrack and Arnold would come with his horses and silks and peppermint liniments, which meant Digger and Stuart would be there too. They would all walk fast across this new parcel of land and their hips would sway in unison and they would make funny faces. Arnold's deep voice would be heard. "Whoa now." Stuart would like me once more. Digger and I would push bush looking for rabbits and shoot them dead.

When my father visited me in my bedroom to inform me that we wouldn't in fact be moving to land west of Saskatoon, that instead we would purchase the King Koin Launderette, I was devastated. I wanted to take one of our Out of Order signs and put it on my door and close the door and lock it. But I could tell that my dad was sympathetic, that this hurt him too, even as he explained that Grandpa Funk's bid to have us stay in PA couldn't be ignored. It made more financial sense to stay and so we stayed. Now we would own the King Koin. It was ours, lock, stock, and barrel.

Before he sold the land, my father retrieved an entire settler wagon and brought it to PA, painted it in primary colours, and parked it next to the garage. There was also a lone wheel. My parents sanded and varnished the spokes and hub, painted the iron parts glossy black. They found a wooden barrel and cut it in half, sanded and varnished it too, painting the iron bands the same glossy black. They laid the wheel on the half barrel and on top of the wheel, finally, they placed a piece of Plexiglass cut flush with the wheel with a central hole to accept the hub. This was our coffee table for the next decade.

74 John's sons by Margaret were encouraged to go on adventures. He told them it was fine to camp in the area, build tree forts, shoot jackrabbits and gophers. Gopher tails were sold for a nickel apiece. The jackrabbits were huge rangy things that Edith cooked on the wood stove. The meat was like chicken, said John. The boys learned from their father to fire the single-shot .22 with pinpoint accuracy from an upper window in the house. In winter, they could distinguish the white bodies in the white fields.

John himself could target the eye of the rabbit. Once, when he brought one home, he invited the boys to locate the death wound. There was no blood and the boys could see nothing, no obvious trauma, till John pointed to the entry wound in the centre of one eye.

One time in summer the brothers harnessed Pat to a neighbour's cart and drove it east on Mierau Road to the Clarksboro ferry on the South Saskatchewan, then they crossed the river and carried on to the Peters farm. They spent a few days with their grandmother, Helena, and their aunts and uncles, unanimously agreeing it was a good place to visit. Arnold nuzzled into his aunties' bosoms. He felt safe and loved and could eat anything he wanted, even to the point of puking, which my father did. The peonies their mother loved were growing in the big garden. With Helena's youngest son Arthur they walked to the river. Arthur walked behind carrying a shotgun and the shotgun discharged between two of the boys. One of the boys was Willard my father; he turned to Arthur in shock and disbelief, apparently unharmed. And Arthur's face was drained of blood and he said, "An inch is as good as a mile."

John couldn't know about this. Even though most of the time lives were not lost. Arnold was nearly drowned in a water trough on the Peters farm, except an uncle was on hand to lift him out. And when James as a toddler fell in the river and my father saw his shock of hair inches below the surface being borne away, it was John who acted with electric speed to grab that shock before it disappeared and haul James back to land.

Life could go on after the close call or the saving act.

Tucked away for storytelling later.

Decades would pass, and one of the three sons of Margaret would die from old age, and the other two, Willard and Arnold, would be talking on the phone or walking on a street. A memory emerged. The life of a good horse. Cantering on a road. A song. Someone would see the two boys together and say to them, "You must be brothers." To which they would both respond at once, pointing to the other, "No, he's my dad."

* * *

When Marvin died, my father was very sad and I could see it. He visited his brother before his passing. Even at the end of his life, Marvin spoke of seeing his mother being lowered into the ground. That scene had haunted him all his life. Yet he was the one who could cry and Arnold couldn't stand it because he himself couldn't cry or speak. Marvin could feel what had happened and couldn't help but let it out. He was also the one who moved away to the west coast of Canada. For a while, he was even a teacher in Botswana.

This moving away caused some serious friction in certain quarters of the family—grumbling and resentment because we couldn't see Marvin anymore, and sometimes when he visited Saskatchewan he didn't tell us but we found out later.

When I look at my son, I think of Marvin—the powerful core, the sure hands, the passionate heart. I can't imagine what would happen to Gabe were he to lose his mother suddenly.

In 2011 the Belgian filmmaker Michaël R. Roskam made *Bullhead*, the story of Jacky, who has lived all his life on a bull farm in rural Flemish Belgium. As a young boy, Jacky is assaulted by an older boy who crushes Jacky's testes between two rocks. The film is thus divided between two Jackies, one before and one after the defining event: the young, innocent boy played beautifully by Robin Valvekens and the badly damaged man played with intense ferocity by Matthias Schoenaerts. This latter Jacky, who overdoses on testosterone supplements in a vain attempt to persuade himself that he is a real man, becomes the tragic emblem of toxic masculinity. The young, prepubescent Jacky lurks poignantly in the film's background, a horrifying reminder to the man he becomes—who like all the men before him is a bull farmer—of that which can never be.

My PA.

* * *

Then there's the brother who isn't. Uncle Unborn. He's been on my mind since I first saw the box and began to consider our relationship. It takes time to come to terms with these things, and often the negotiations are interminable. There is no final deal.

I ask my father what his thoughts were growing up regarding this brother. He tells me he had no thoughts because he didn't know. John had pointed to the box and said, "Boys, that box is about your mother," but he had also said, "Don't open it."

Who might he have been, this unborn one? Blond hair or dark? Diastema or not?

Could it have been otherwise?

Can I even ask these questions?

Surely the Tomb for the Unknown Soldier tells me I can.

Surely the *Final Report of the Truth and Reconciliation Commission of Canada*, released in 2015, tells me I must.

Or if not, if that is out of line, then surely as the oldest child of Margaret's youngest, I can represent this uncle to the living. Uncle Unborn. Uncle Never Will Be.

Taking a shower early one morning, I see the curtain pop inwards and know it's my son, a mischief-maker who takes his name from Gabriel Dumont, who was supposedly buried standing up not far from the unborn uncle. I've always revered Dumont, have visited his tomb at Batoche on the east bank of the South Saskatchewan. Even in death he stands. Against land theft and Gatling guns; and for Louis Riel and the struggle for justice for Métis and First Nations.

For what does this uncle stand? For all that cannot be and all that emerges. That there is no deal with my grandfather's God.

If there is a deal, it's with the future.

May the river that runs past Dumont and my uncle run clean and teeming with life and truth. There is so much I don't know.

Except this: Prince Albert's is the history of things left unfinished, half-completed, left to moulder, for which the future would pay. So with my family, epitomized in the child who wouldn't be, killed in Margaret's womb, buried within her and then again in stolen soil, and all of that buried yet again in a box made for chemicals, nailed shut and left in the basement pantry along with the pickles.

75 Until Dave Tippett joined the West Hill Panthers, Mort was the best hockey player I had ever played with. I waited for Mort to say a friendly word, but after a while I realized it wasn't going to happen. He wasn't going to loosen up. I got used to the scowl and tried to keep my distance, but Mort's hostility was infectious. Players who'd once been respectful and friendly turned on me in unison with Mort. No one wanted to risk being seen on friendly terms with me, the cross-eyed wannabe who lived behind a launderette. I had trouble believing it, didn't want to accept this rejection, but short of pushing back hard on the whole team, including the coaches, I was shit out of luck.

The day Dave Tippett showed up at the West Hill outdoor rink, the Panthers were practising slapshots. When I floated into the net area to retrieve a puck, the slapshots kept coming and one caught me above the knee. I doubled over and made my way to the boards while the shooters snickered.

In the first of several encounters between us, Tippett skated over. This kid from Moosomin, who had only just moved to PA and was smaller than almost all of us—who would go on to a long career in hockey, culminating in the NHL's Jack Adams Award for coaching in 2010—said three words that helped me keep it together that day.

"Just ignore them." He was obviously new to PA, but I welcomed the kindness almost as a miracle.

Tippett was the best player any of us had ever seen, and we all knew it immediately. He made us, Mort included, look ordinary—but like other talented players Tippett also raised the level of play for everyone. The entire team—kids, coaches, parents—rallied around him.

76 By 1946, John had taken a leave of absence from teaching to inspect bees for the Province of Saskatchewan. The children saw their father less and less as he bandied about the province peering into every bee box he could. He did this in a series of cars, all of which were on the verge of falling apart, though John dreamed plenty of owning a new Essex or Nash. He wore rumpled suits and slept in the hotels that thrived in every town in the province back then. He wrote to Edith on the official stationery of the Department of Agriculture, Bee Division, which he joked was completely out of keeping with his character. He commented on everything he saw, the quality of the soil, the kinds of vegetation, the wild fruit he stopped to eat. It was as though he were answering to something in himself in the only way he knew how and that to him seemed safe. Because if he was "roaming," as he called it, he was roaming with a purpose: to view each and every self-contained society of honey bees under his juris-diction. He loved their ordered society as Arnold loved horses. And John likewise hated the apian diseases, just as his oldest son loathed the equine afflictions.

But what John loved most was the focal point of bee culture, the very queen herself. He could talk about what's known as queen substance, the property uniquely possessed by the matriarch, which keeps the entire colony devoted to her alone. From the time of her weaning on bee bread and emergence from the queen cup, which droops from the frame like a peanut, she is recognized, courted, danced around, fed, preened—and all because of this substance. And because of which she lives many times longer than a worker. Superseding the previous queen, she takes a single mating flight, a tryst with all the drones at sixty feet in the air, where each male performs the only thing he was born to do: inject his semen into the royal body and fall to the ground and expire. To John, that was how it was supposed to be, but anything could happen. A skunk, a rat, a robber wasp or bear, any of these could do incalculable damage.

Then came an offer from the government in Regina, to move south and take a permanent position as the provincial apiarist. But John turned it down. Later he would decline a similar offer from the federal government. Somehow he had the feeling, he wrote to Edith, that the family would lose the good, simple, God-fearing home life they had come to enjoy. John feared that if he stayed away the children would take the path of least resistance and run with the crowd. Then the whole life made possible with this second marriage, now stable and with Edith at its centre, would fall apart.

And that could never be allowed to happen.

By sheer force of will and the strong glue of Mennonitism, John meant to keep this family together, even if against it—and against the glue—his fear collided relentlessly. The task was inhuman in its scope, both for him and for Edith. As for the children, whom he called his "Honey Children" in a note written on a piece of a brown paper bag mailed from a bus station, they never stopped dealing with the ferocity of it all, and not one went on to become a practising Mennonite. All five boys suffered as John flailed within the confines of the old edifice created from fear, brought the Black Doctor down on them, on their shoulders, backs, buttocks.

Please Dad, don't . . . I promise . . . please.

Until finally years later a pitiful end came to this particular round of violence when James, now seventeen, met his stalking father in the school barn and refused to submit to the Black Doctor, whose prescription was always the same and could indeed be administered in public, John being a public man. The older boys, Margaret's boys, had experienced this scene many times, only this time there was a sudden dramatic reversal, and Arnold, Marvin, and Willard witnessed it. Saw their raging sire beaten down by Edith's James, thrown to the ground with a sneer and a kick. And they never forgot it afterwards.

No, John would not take those government jobs as a permanent apiarist. He would stay a freelance bee man, and to heck with the money.

And so there was ever the fear behind it all that he couldn't explain. The strange, contradictory fear. Bill, in the Canadian Army, remained apart from his family for two years at once, yet John was frightened by a few weeks of solitude. He would wake up in a sweat in a hotel in Kinistino or Tisdale or PA and ring up Edith to calm himself, or else write her a letter with a new ballpoint pen.

He wasn't afraid of cars, however. The autos were under constant repair: brakes, gaskets, lights, fuses, cranks, and, once, a windshield that fell right out onto the road. Not to mention tires blowing every hundred miles or so. Once his car actually fell on its side in the ditch as the tire exploded. But he wasn't paralyzed by fear then. He coolly righted the vehicle, changed the tire, and drove out onto the road again. It was a muddy, greasy road, and later he laughed at his own soiled reflection as he walked into a café somewhere to get a bowl of soup.

Neither were bees a source of fear. John joked he could reach with his left hand around himself and scratch the sting on his left shoulder. He could also turn his head around and bite a bee stinging between the shoulder blades. Over time, he had acquired such unusual skills, he said, by defending himself repeatedly. And these bees, he wrote, were not your average ones. "Today while walking, I tripped. When I tried to discover the reason, I found that a bee had stung right through my left leg, and the sting protruded far enough to trip me when I brought the left foot forward. This is 'man's country'!"

John certainly enjoyed the company of other bee men. Not for a moment did they take second place to the teachers he and Edith knew. In fact, there were "so many more interesting personalities among the bee men (no slam on teachers), for the teachers [were] teachers only and everything [was] keyed up to teaching. But the beekeepers [were] also farmers, lawyers, teachers, doctors, cooks." They were all people who had discovered, and been entranced by, the *Apis mellifera*, the bee that bears honey, brought to North America by Europeans—hence, this insect's other name, the European honey bee.

77 I thought I saw her remember her ancestors in her body. I thought I saw her do this before she could speak. Her hazel eyes and tuft of black hair. Her slender hands reaching for food.

I thought I saw.

Years later, as a student at the University of Saskatchewan reading what was still called "Commonwealth literature," I began to understand more of what I'd experienced, what I thought I saw: you might call it the colonizer's consciousness.

In the mornings during winter when it was so cold your exposed skin began to die in minutes, we sat at the breakfast table and watched a porridge bowl slide mysteriously by inches across the dark mottled Formica banded by chrome. I could forget my troubles while laughing with Crystal and my other siblings as the bowl moved all by itself. I could feel good going out the door wearing my smoky mukluks traced with beads and trimmed with rabbit fur that my parents had purchased

at the Hudson's Bay Trading Post down on the Flat along
the river.

I wondered often in my childhood mind who her
people were and what they were doing. I thought about
that a lot. Where did they live? What did they eat? The
food at our table was so important we couldn't take it
for granted. My mother and her mother, Marie, seemed
able to make delicious meals from the air itself. Little
was thrown out. Animal bones were used for soup. Their
marrow melted and flowed with the salty broth loaded
with barley and beans. Other pieces of hog or cattle or
bird went through a pewter grinder turned by hand.
Leftover fish were reformed into cakes. Some foods we
disliked, like beef liver, but we ate it anyhow because
it was inexpensive and packed with energy and our
parents said we had no choice. Foods made with flour
compensated for such horrors. Pancakes almost as thin
as paper drizzled with sugarcane syrup or honey. Bread
and buns, homemade noodles and *vareniki* topped with
cream gravy and onions from the garden that grew next
to the white house with the red roof across the alley.
Deep-fried dough called *rollkuchen* was eaten with
syrup and watermelon in summer.

Then the cereal boxes appeared, colourful and bilin-
gual, their contents stamped in precise shapes that
looked and tasted like sawdust.

Other questions arose in my mind. Did Crystal's
people think of her, this girl I called my sister? And the
answer came swiftly: Of course they did—and then I
imagined them thinking of her and asking of the sky
and the trees and the Creator where she was and what
she was doing, eating, saying As a child, I could think
such thoughts easily. I lived as a child and thought as
a child, fluidly connecting realities that were in fact

torn. It was only later, when childhood had at last fallen away through incremental changes and painful physical and emotional experiences, that the history of North America was made more manifest to me. On the cusp of adolescence, I was reading Dee Brown, for instance, an American librarian documenting the history of some of the Indigenous Peoples in North America. I became so inflamed I could hardly manage this new knowledge. I could barely speak of it for fear I might tear at the walls. I knew where the United States was—my parents had taken me there to visit our Kansas relatives—and that Canada, where I lived, shared in the continent's history. I pored over the maps in Brown's book, saw how the Sioux had fled north into Canada, finding refuge close to PA in what would later become Little Red River Park. I knew now for certain that all this ground was the site of terrible events. Later I'd encounter a high school teacher angered by the fact that the Sioux burial ground located somewhere in Little Red River Park meant PA couldn't build a new ski hill. He was upset with me because an article had appeared in the *Prince Albert Daily Herald* written by one Bill Boschman.

At about this time a movie appeared at the local theatre called *Alien Thunder*, about a local Cree man named Almighty Voice who during the time of the Riel Resistance died in a storm of RCMP armaments while hiding, an outlaw, in a poplar bluff near Duck Lake, twenty miles from where I was born.

Like Wilfred Stanley Robertson, Almighty Voice had shot a police officer. When we drove past the town of Duck Lake on Highway 11 going to Saskatoon, we could see off in the distance the Western-style movie set. There, on the edge of the Nisbet Forest, actors—Donald Sutherland, Gordon Tootoosis, Chief Dan George—had re-enacted events that had been repeated over and over in this place called Canada.

I heard my parents and grandparents, aunts and uncles, speak Low German, the earthy oral language of my ancestors, and knew nothing of what they were saying—except that they usually laughed hard till the tears appeared in my father's eyes and he would have to walk off by himself to recover. But my subsequent language loss in this thing called Canada was easily remedied. I could choose not to attend Rosthern Junior College, adjacent to Beardy's Reserve and just down the street from the hospital where I was born. For Crystal my sister, though, as she lived under our roof at the back of the King Koin, the loss of language was immense. Like the night sky, it couldn't truthfully be described. Thirteen thousand years of language and culture were broken. As white settlers living in PA between All Saints and the old jail, we couldn't reconcile that loss, no matter how much we loved her.

78 Uncle Bill taught me what he knew about obtaining and preparing food in the wilderness. I watched him forage in the bushes and grasses along the shore of Sulphide Lake. I saw his figure from the top of the tall rock catching water for tea. If I was down by the water's edge with him it was to cast a lure where I could hear him murmuring to me. He didn't mind if I caught a small pike on a spoon but encouraged me instead to send a jig farther and deeper, let it settle to the darkest bottom and wait for a pickerel. This was the fish prized above all and it swam in schools in deep water. When you picked up a pickerel you were careful of the dorsal fin rising, for it could spike your hand. I learned patience and care from the creature we called pickerel (largely unaware of its relations with humans who had lived in these places for thousands of years) but instant gratification from the pike, the ancient predator striking torpedo-like in a silver-green flash in the shallows.

Uncle Bill watched for various berries he knew that were good to eat—blueberries, chokecherries, strawberries, raspberries, gooseberries. My favourite was the pincherry, small and fiercely red, its tiny stone enveloped by a thin layer of tartness that detonates on the tongue. I filled my pockets with these miniscule flavour bombs. Repeatedly he told me what I could and couldn't eat, what was obvious and what could be revealed. The wild rose he especially respected, saying that his mother had gathered the hips in great quantities when the family had homesteaded at Carrot River. You could eat them raw or boil them for a mash rich in vitamins, especially C. This was life-saving stuff. He showed me a small onion that grew almost in secret, unseen unless you knew what to see. He also showed me the virtues of birchbark, taught me not to strip it from a living tree but instead to pick it up from the forest floor. Long after the tree had died and decomposed, the birch shell offered itself for many uses. It was, for one thing, the best kindling on earth, would burn in any weather. I piled it white and silver and even gold next to the small fire as the idea of dependable fuel grew in my mind. Like the pincherry in my mouth, a scrap of birch sizzled dynamically.

I never once saw Uncle Bill make a big fire. He called that a white man's fire. Though he was white, he had learned something of what white meant. Though I was white and young and a male, I was absorbing as much as I could about what white meant. I didn't quite realize it then, but Uncle Bill was planting inside me the seeds of political and historical awareness. Since he had lived and worked in the North at places I had never been—Île-à-la-Crosse, Buffalo Narrows, and Patuanak—I learned about the history and peoples west of our fire. The fur trade. The Cree at Île-à-la-Crosse. The Dene at Patuanak. The Riel family and some of the events of the Resistance less than a century before. The intersecting lakes and the big river.

And I saw my great-uncle become passionate about what he knew had happened on these grounds. What was happening still. What would likely continue to happen, and on and on, until people said, *Enough!* As we drove south toward Lac La Ronge, we passed a logging site, and I remember so clearly the look on his face as he sat behind the wheel of that little green car—the look of someone who'd been assaulted. His eyes blazed in the same way I'd seen my father's do.

Once Uncle Bill and Aunt Vi went to Mexico for a long winter holiday and Uncle Bill returned tanned, his dark, thinning hair standing tall on his head as he drove his government car through the town of Île-à-la-Crosse. An RCMP officer abruptly pulled him over, wondering what he thought he was doing: ordered him out of the car, pushed him up against one quarter panel, then realized that Bill Boschman was a white civil servant. When Uncle Bill told me this true story, he was livid—not for himself but for his friends and neighbours who had welcomed him into their homes and meetings. They had given him gifts he cherished: a birchbark basket with a lid, a round beaded patch of hide for Canada's centenary, a bracelet of beads. He also had a thick Siwash coat with a heavy zipper and high collar. Aunt Vi had sewed a matching pocket into the inside of this coat.

Once he had lost his canoe, he said. It had slipped from shore when he was camping alone late in the day and he could just see it drifting a mile or so off. Life jacket still inside. The paddle and spare on the ground nearby. He had a honey pail he used to boil water, just like the one beside our fire on the rock high above Sulphide Lake. These pails were useful because they came with close-fitting metal lids, and so could double as sealed containers. He took his pail and put a hard-boiled egg and a carrot inside and pressed down on the lid till it clicked into place. Even if some water got inside, he reasoned, the egg and carrot would be okay. He looped twine through the handle and tied the ends together and put the twine around his neck and set off swimming. Breast stroke, sidestroke, backstroke, repeat, till he caught the canoe by the rope. He rested for a bit in the water, removed the twine and pail from his neck and put them in the canoe, and swam back to camp towing the craft. He arrived right at dusk and went to bed.

79 So many men living alone in soddies and shacks, remnants of migration, incursion, and land speculation.

Across the road from the Neuhoffnung teacherage was a stand of poplars and beyond that another; and on the far side of that second bluff stood a shack where a single aging male named Boehr lived. Both bluffs still exist, though the colonial dwellings—the shack, the teacherage, the barns—located at the intersection of

Mierau Road and Range Road 3072 are long gone except for traces of rubble. A granite slab attached to a wagon wheel firmly anchored just beyond the shallow ditch attests to what was once here: NEUHOFFNUNG School District No. 951, 1903–1962. That is all.

They called him Old Man Boehr (pronounced "bear"). He lay in his own filth without any food or, in winter, fire—and Edith would send over Marvin and Willard my father with lunches. In winter, in the shivering cold, the boys would walk across the road and through the two bluffs to light and feed the fire. Fearing what they might find as their boots crunched across the fields, stubble poking up like white whiskers or fish bones. Boehr's daughter had once lived there too, but since her departure the aging male lay unwashed on a bed. My father hated going there but Marv didn't mind. He'd happily feed the fire and thaw the ice in the pan.

By then Arnold had run away, never to come back except for visits, and dreading these because John would descend on him with a plague of guilt. Eschewing John's directions and advice, taking to Standardbred circuits across the country and beyond, living in stalls and tack rooms and trailers, this was for Arnold the beginning of a long life on the run. Motel rooms. Rental houses. Strung out in a long line over the years, four kids and a wife in tow.

On one return visit to Neuhoffnung, Arnold (now eighteen) found Pat the black gelding lying on his side in the school barn and knew at a glance the beloved horse (who had never suffered a split hoof and could cover sixty miles in a day) had a twisted gut and was dying. Pat lay there pounding his great head on the floor. With John's single-shot .22, Arnold placed a bullet high on the forehead, loaded Pat onto the stone boat, and dragged him over to Boehr's bluff. The body lay there till it turned to bones and Willard and Marvin could retrieve the skull. They buried it deep in the bluff beside the teacherage, along with a sealed glass jar containing a folded sheet of lined paper with the signatures of all the kids save Arnold.

Decades later, on a trip to Edith's bungalow in Langham for a family gathering, my father stopped our car in the field where the teacherage had stood. I'd never seen Neuhoffnung before. The word itself seemed as foreign as a moon rock to me. I was a new teen then (caught in one photo in a sullen pose, holding an axe for my father in a strikingly similar piece of bush north of PA that he had just purchased). I was circling our family history, partially aware of what was happening but already fixed, somewhere in my mind, on Margaret Peters. She was there always since my discovery of her, though I hadn't yet figured out that she'd left this same yard with John in the '29 Plym. On that day. June 29, 1940.

My father took his four children among the twisty poplars where he had been a child and we all began looking for the place where Pat's skull lay buried. For twenty minutes, we looked for a certain tree, next to which the dig had taken place. Then I realized I was standing on a stump and everyone laughed and our father dug till his spade tapped on glass and bone. We gazed on the artifacts—the horse head with its small hole, the jar with the signatures slightly blurred with moisture but legible still—and the past, our history, was unearthed and real. We took our finds to Langham and opened the jar for Edith to see, John now dead these five or six years, the cousins gathering to marvel at the names of parents, aunts, and uncles and brush the soil from Pat's skull.

Arnold's then lived in the second green house on the edge of Langham looking west, held there by the gravity of Edith's house: built by John and now holding her, her presence alone keeping us all intact, though we hardly realized it till she was gone too and the family split and dispersed.

Digger had a dog at this second green house, just as he'd had a German shepherd, also named Pat, at the first green house on the east side of town. Now this other dog, Angus, met his awful end and Digger grieved and nursed his anger because the dog had been poisoned with arsenic by a single old man who lived across the street, reclusive and suspicious. Angus was a basenji, an antique breed of hunting dog that originates in Africa and has no vocal chords to speak of. Angus couldn't bark. Indeed, he made no sound other than an occasional mewling. So why the old bachelor targeted Angus with his malice was a question we all asked. Arnold surmised that Angus, curious, silent, circling, and lupine, had threatened the hermit. Perhaps it was the curled tail, held erect and proud, that called for the poison of kings, in widespread use then as a pesticide. Bloated and bleeding, Angus crawled home to die—fell down the stairs leading to the basement of that second green house on the edge of Langham. Arnold and Digger took him to the town dump and Arnold shot him one time in the head.

Pat's skull was placed in the rear of our wagon to be carried hence to PA. It rested in my basement bedroom glowing pale under the black light of my then dusky teen existence. I spent many hours gazing at the small bullet hole there in Pat's forehead.

80 We met in the head coach's downtown engineering office to study charts and listen to lectures. The room was like the many classrooms and theatres I would enter as a high school and university student. The diagrams offered abstract demonstrations of how we should play the game. It all seemed to slip right by me. I couldn't retain anything.

My father was angry and went to talk to the coaches. He wanted to know why it was important to herd a group of young teen boys into a lecture hall or hand out report cards.

A photographer appeared at the new Communiplex hockey arena with its indoor heating and artificial ice. I had never seen a Zamboni before. It cruised the ice in ovals and never slipped or hit the boards, leaving in its wake a sheen of new ice. The photographer set up his equipment at one end and the Panthers lined up at the other. The arena lights were dimmed. We were to skate fast and then stop, sending a spray of new ice flying toward the camera, which flashed in the twilight. I waited for my turn and skated forward. A voice came from the boys in the darkness. It seethed with disdain as I skated forward.

"Boschman."

Looking at the photo now, when the shuffle of decades has passed, I feel it still like I felt it then, in that moment—butterflies radiating out from my gut, my legs unsteady, hands shaking and sweating inside my heavy black gloves, worrying I might fall on the new ice just as the camera flashes.

Once I saw a sports article in the *Buffalo News*, dated Saturday, June 20, 2009. It quoted Dave Tippett, only just fired as the head coach of the Dallas Stars of the NHL. "You can never go against who you really are. . . .

Players can see it. You have to trust who you are and what you're doing . . . if you are going to have any kind of credibility."

I can't summon that old faith. It's just too hard a thing to carry.

81

Arnold could walk faster than anyone I had seen. At family gatherings, he'd spring forward like he couldn't contain himself, his pelvic girdle turning to and fro, the marionette's crossbar to his flexing legs. His head lolled between the collarbones, his arms turned at the elbows. Stuart and Digger mimicked their father with the same movements and almost the same speed, as though their hip sockets contained ball bearings of exquisite manufacture, the surfaces like silk. I noticed their power, the moving sinuous curve of their backs and buttocks.

On my mother's side, Grandma Funk tried once to walk away from the King Koin. She left from the front porch of the big white house with the red roof, crossed the tarry, malodorous street, and disappeared into Bryant Park, away from the doors that were never locked and Grandpa Funk's endless engagement with machines that never stopped turning. All our days rolled and tumbled through the calendar year, including Christmas. It could get to you, cling to your personal space like the sour smell of a fried solenoid.

When at the end of her ninety-seven years she finally told this story, with its ceaseless high-pressure spray of soap and water and insulting smells of sumps and gutters that had at last breached the limits of her tolerance, I asked Grandma Funk what she'd planned to do in that moment of decision when her feet took her out the door and across 27th Street. She said she'd had no plans and realized quickly there was nowhere to go. So she turned around and walked back before anyone even noticed.

Once, at Christopher Lake, Crystal was seen holding hands with a boy her age—she was three—while they walked together through the sun-dappled trees on a hot summer day. He was a First Nations boy fostered by the Henry family, our Métis neighbours in PA. Someone in our family took a picture.

Crystal (right) and Steven, Christopher Lake, Saskatchewan.
COURTESY OF THE BOSCHMAN FAMILY

82 In those days, everyone had the wolf. *Schmayah. Schmenge.* Circles of alternating grease and pain. Like the rings of Saturn. A bath, if you had one, was weekly and everyone shared the same water in order of age beginning with the youngest. Toilet paper was *dummheit*, an unnecessary expense next to the Eaton's catalogue or the *Western Producer.* Scarlet bums were the order of the day.

Often Arnold was also black and blue from the beatings John gave when he wasn't on the road inspecting bees. So Arnold moved around a lot whenever his father was home. He danced the dance of the abused child. He learned from other men whatever he could about being a man in that world and time. P.K. Waldner taught him to smoke Dominion tobacco in Chauntecleer paper. Since P.K. had once lost a finger in a binder, Arnold rolled for him. Then there were the other men: Turninacircle Murray, Laughing Pankratz, and Singing Henry P. Mierau, who smoked Millbanks. Also Horace and Pete, Eleven O'clock Quiring, and Pete Yanchuk, who drank so much he couldn't talk and died of a seizure in jail. Johnny Reebalkin was Long Balls; Allan Krahn hung by his feet from a windmill. When Reverend Stahl married people, he said, "I now pronounce you one meat." And when Ernie Thiessen boasted of his horse, its obedience and speed, he declared, "When I say go, it went."

Arnold quizzed all these men looking for information on John, his mercurial and dangerous father, a dark blue presence flashing on Arnold's horizon. They didn't have any real answers either. Because John spoke to no one about his inner life, his fellow farmers in that region knew no more than Arnold.

With so little to go on, action was taken where needed in order to please John. The boys of course sang in church, and when Gertrude Rempel gave Arnold a Lone Ranger guitar worth seven dollars from the Eaton's catalogue, he taught himself slack key and sang the songs his father loved. The boys grew plots in the 4H Grain Club.

Arnold even joined the Calf Club, was reserve champion two years running, and won a new halter. When there was a big wind, they spread manure to hold down the topsoil. And they helped John plant breaks. Ten caragana and a maple alternating down the middle of the quarter he rented and farmed, trying with all his lore to create a new and better wheat seed.

Once in a long while John softened. One time he mentioned Margaret. He said that if she had lived, they would have had many children together. But then the memories stepped forward, like how Marvin had tried to jump in her grave but Arnold grabbed him just in time.

Increasingly Arnold took to night riding and sometimes Marvin and Willard my father also rode if a horse came available. A neighbour girl, Isabelle Wurtz, came along sometimes, riding an old white horse named Louis. They rode on the new roads and they rode across the land. Night would fall and deepen. The boys said later that there's no way to describe riding a horse at night. Sounds and sense. Night animals and wild smells adrift across the prairie. The sky.

I think Arnold knew even then—long before he finally found a measure of peace and healing through the Indigenous people he met and was taught by—that the time of the settlers into which he'd been born was like a twitch of prairie grass, though blood-spattered and real, on all the land.

83 I went to a PA hockey school one summer to improve my game and impress the Panthers but it made no difference finally. Even daily lessons from a former Raider at the

new Communiplex with its dazzling artificial ice and
Zamboni couldn't lift me to a place of respect and accep-
tance. I was entering my last stretch of play in the fall of
1974 and my final Hockey Achievement Report reflected
dismal failure. "Bob Boshman [*sic*]," wrote the head
coach, couldn't pass muster with "respect to his abilities
and attitudes as a member of the Panther Hockey Team."
I hated being called Bob, was never a Bob, yet had no
say in the matter. On the coach's "system of rating from
1–10," where "5 or lower indicates room for considerable improvement," I was found badly wanting in six of
thirteen areas. These included team leadership, agility,
snap shot, and body checking. In the latter I earned a 4;
hockey theory got me a 2. Expected to "attain a rating
above 7 by the end of the season" in all areas, I was
demoralized to see that my only two ratings above that
mark were "Attention to Instruction" and "Promptness
and Attendance."

If I wasn't having fun, what was I doing there? That
question hung from the head coach's lanyard along with
his whistle. I could be at home watching Bugs Bunny
with a peanut-butter-and-jelly sandwich. Though my
father had told me that once I started a hockey season
I had to finish, the truth is I was miserable. My dejec-
tion was like a hard kidney bean placed in water, incrementally absorbing, and expanding in, a culture where
I wasn't wanted.

I listened for the whistle.
Stops and starts.
Figure eights going backward.
Now forward.
Backward again.
More stops and starts.
Fatigue and lactic acid eating my legs.

I decided my stick should have a curve. That would help. A curved blade granted more control but, just as significant, it distinguished a player. Those who played with straight blades were boring and unimaginative next to those who used a curve. Then the general condition and look of one's equipment also became supremely important. Boys who wore Tacks or even better, Super Tacks, a top brand of skates my father couldn't afford, were amazing to behold. On the income my father earned working for Grandpa Funk, Tacks were impossible. I'd have to make do with a lesser blade.

Similarly with other pieces of equipment, talismans of status and power brandished by their owners in the dressing room and on the ice. New hockey pants, blue or black or red or even green, with an exterior stripe down the side of each thigh; shin pads that graced each leg, over which went the stocking, all of this held by thick white tape just below the knee and just above the ankle; thick cloth and foam shoulder pads with plastic plating on each shoulder; new and approved elbow pads; the red Panther helmet. Worn all together, these pieces made a statement about who you were, gave off your aura, your presence as a player. How you appeared on the ice and who you were as a person were intimately connected.

The stick, though, was all-important. Not only should it be curved, it had to be taped properly and the manufacturer prestigious. The tape couldn't be shiny electrician's tape, an automatic faux pas. In the cold it almost instantly broke and curled upward off the blade, the sure sign of an ignorant kid or parent. Dull and heavy black hockey tape was the only correct choice, to be applied in thick layers to the sawn-off butt in order to create a grip tailored to its owner. The blade as well was dressed in black, the smooth strips applied as one's own signature that strengthened the blade, gave it added weight, and called out for a pass.

A Sherwood hockey stick was glorious; a CCM less so. Any kid playing with a Koho was automatically to be admired and envied, unless he couldn't play, in which case he was held in contempt.

My dad had grown up loving hockey. On the open winter landscapes of Saskatchewan, in the various country schools where John Boschman had been the teacher, Willard and his brothers sat by the radio to listen to the play-by-play broadcast of Foster Hewitt coming over the CBC. Of the original six teams in the National Hockey League, the Toronto Maple Leafs were most revered by Western Canadian kids growing up in the 1940s and '50s. The Bentley brothers, Max and Doug, came from nearby Delisle. Gordie Howe, though he played for the Detroit Red Wings, was a Saskatoon boy. Anything was better than the reviled Habs, even if one Canadiens forward, Toe Blake, was also from the prairies.

But Willard my father couldn't help me now. Even when he visited the coaches to try to improve my situation, it did me no good. I was already sensing dismissal from the roster when an incident occurred that brought my entire hockey career to a thudding halt just before Christmas. The Panthers bus picked me up behind the King Koin late one afternoon and took us all south of the city to play in a small town called Birch Hills against another A-level team.

Through the first period, Mort chirped away at me. As usual whenever I looked his way, he scowled back and told me to smarten up, that I was no good. I'd lived in fear of Mort for eighteen months, trying desperately to win his approval, to get him to accept me on the team.

I'd even scored an 8 on my first Achievement Report in "Ability to Work with Teammates." But I couldn't take it anymore. I yelled at him on the bench and called him "Coach Man."

"Back off, Coach Man!! Leave me alone!!"

The head coach and Mr. Hegland both turned on me with looks of serious displeasure. I realized instantly they assumed I meant them, seemingly unaware that Mort was harassing me. I'll never forget Coach Hegland's face: his big eyes that had so often signalled encouragement now on fire with disapproval. I'd failed to live up to the Optimist Creed laid out in the team's literature. "Promise Yourself," it said, "to give so much time to the improvement of yourself that you have no time to criticize others." What's more, I'd made a scene, one that had finally undermined for good my "character, responsibility and moral attitude." I broke down behind the bench and was immediately sent from the ice to await further word in the dressing room.

I never played for the Optimist Panthers again.

Earlier in my career, I'd been picked up by another team, my play had been so good. I was respected then and I wanted and expected respect now, but instead whatever shred of credibility I'd ever had was completely gone and I was done. The head coach wrote to my parents: "Bob got off to a slow start and appeared to be playing under stress. We hope the move to the Black Hawks will regain confidence. Thank you for your efforts in the first half Bob and have a Merry Xmas." I played out the remainder of the season with the Black Hawks in the B Division.

Later that season a Panthers player saw me with my father at a PA Raiders game in the new Communiplex. The arena was packed as usual with upwards of three thousand fans. I was wearing my red Panthers team jacket and this prominent player spotted me. He assailed me in front of Willard my father.

"Boschman," he said, "get that jacket off! You're a disgrace!"

My father and I were so taken aback, we were speechless.

Although my parents had paid for it with money they didn't have, I stopped wearing the Panthers coat except to visit Disneyland, where no one could possibly know me.

I never again as a child played organized hockey. Even shinny, magically played outside the King Koin Launderette, lost its allure.

84 I saw a man kissing a woman, pressing her up against the mesh fence that surrounded the arena. When he kissed her, he tilted his head to one side, pushing her hard against the aluminum wires so that her clothing protruded from the diamond spaces. His head tilted and turned, driving forward like a man behind a steering wheel while he drove his mouth into hers. I'd seen people kissing on TV, what my sister Beatrice called a TV Kiss. Was this a real TV Kiss? Unsure and afraid, I pedalled away as fast as I could.

Kerby walked up to me one day with that look on his face—a whisper of a smile, eyes winking like blue dwarf stars—indicating he was about to say something unacceptable.

"Hey, Rob, have you whacked your peter yet?"

"What?"

"C'mon, Rob, you know, jerked off." Then the maniacal laugh. "Jacked off. Choked your monkey. Beat your wang. Have you jerked off? I'll bet you have! Am I right?"

Seemed only yesterday Uncle Kerby was singing "Baby Bumblebee" with me and we were eating watermelon and popcorn on Grandma Funk's bedspread and then I threw up because I had the flu but didn't know it.

I drew symbols in the air. Also in the dust on my father's car, a Ford station wagon. The Grand Marquis. I watched the symbols glow in the white paint and then wiped them away. Kerby didn't know this. No one knew. It was my secret. Mine.

My father sold the King Koin Launderette finally to his neighbour and best friend, Louis Henry. Sometimes I worked for the Henrys, making change and doing the chores that Louis knew I knew so well. After a few years, he sold the King Koin and it was torn down and a Bonanza restaurant was built there instead. The Henry family had already moved away to live in a new house that Louis built. Our family moved to the suburbs on the far east side of PA, across the river and up the hill from the pulp mill. My parents bought a new bungalow on a new street. Every morning, the smell of rotten eggs hung in the air, drifting through the treeless streets from the mill, where trees were fodder for gargantuan rolls of paper that looked like ass wipe for giants.

Crystal my sister took to calling me Red Lumps as my acne spread. She also said, "I know you are but what am I," with a take-no-shit authority I could only just match.

* * *

When she asked me to come with her, I knew our parents had kept their promise. She said it like this:

"Hey loser, Red Lumps, I need you to come down to the Co-op with me." She didn't ask my parents or any other family member—she asked me. Not an invitation either—a directive. An expectation. She wanted me to be there, she said, because I was her oldest sibling, her brother.

I didn't realize it quite then, but by requiring my presence in the Co-op cafeteria where she would be reunited with her biological family, who were all driving down from the north to meet her, Crystal was claiming me. I felt the honour and privilege of being asked to witness this moment in her life, of course, but many years would pass before I more fully realized what it meant—not only to her but to me.

It was the poet Richard Harrison who catalyzed this insight. When I told him the story of being there in 1990 to see Crystal's kin file into the Co-op cafeteria in downtown PA, he looked at me and said, "She claimed you."

In they came. Her sister. Her brother. Cousins, nieces, nephews. A brother-in-law. Her mother. Not a dry eye in that space. News of a brother who had died. Stories of her grandmother, her *kokum*, waiting to meet her and take her on her trapline.

These gentle, loving, resilient people had been searching for Crystal at the same time she'd been looking for them. Our parents had encouraged her to start the process by writing to the government; and no sooner had she done this than she was informed that her birth mother had reached out, hoping to find her daughter.

When I talked to her mother, sitting across from me at the cafeteria that day, she said, "I hear you are working hard on your PhD—Piled High and Deep. I don't need my PhD." She said this with a sly grin. "I died twice already, once in a car accident and once when my heart just stopped 'cause I had a heart attack. I saw the light twice. I met the Creator. I got educated."

85 Uncle Bill lived through a depression and went to war. Bequeathed to me a blooming Christmas cactus, the Siwash coat, some papers, a book or two, and precious stories.

Once he found a freshwater spring in the Little Red River Park north of PA. My father and I would meet him in a hidden dell surrounded by forest where water gurgled from the earth and flowed through a steel pipe he'd inserted. We'd sit and stand and sit again for hours beneath huge conifers and talk or just listen to the wind sway the treetops. He'd tell us stories then. So many stories.

It was the late 1970s. He'd only just written a long essay called "The River" for the *Prince Albert Daily Herald* detailing the known colonial history of the confluence of the South and North Saskatchewan Rivers. How before fences appeared explorers like David Thompson had surveyed the land and waters. Uncle Bill didn't mind Thompson, said of all the early explorers he was probably the best and gentlest. Peter Pond, on the other hand, he did not like—could not abide the secrets, betrayals, and murders. The greed. Thompson and Pond and many other white men—the Frobishers, Henday, Mackenzie, Franklin—had been through the area that would become PA. Uncle Bill had found in his own explorations physical evidence of their various passings: survey markers, corner stones, foundations. He remembered something Norman

Bethune said once, which he included in his essay: "I come of a race of men violent, unstable, of passionate convictions and wrong-headedness, intolerant yet with it all a vision of truth and a drive to carry them on to it even though it leads, as it has done in my family, to their destruction."

When we asked Uncle Bill about his own first memories in the years after his birth in 1916, he said there were two. The first was of crossing the South Saskatchewan River by the ferry at Clarksboro and the second was laid down during that same journey—to visit his twenty-one-year-old sister Katherine—and was of playing with a piece of a clockwork mechanism in a sandbox next to Katherine's house. The shape of the clockwork had stayed with him all his life.

The year was 1919 and the great influenza outbreak of that year was killing many children. His mother, Anna Heide, was under such tremendous stress—she'd been burying kids, including those of her brother, Martin Heide—that she had no milk for Bill. He was, he said, the only child of her fourteen who got no milk.

Of all his nine brothers, he was the weakest, the runt. Yet he could outwalk them all, and they knew it. By the time he was eighteen and living in the forest at Petaigan he was bushed, wild, and spent much of his time alone, reading books ordered through a travelling library service that occasionally stopped in Carrot River.

When he joined the Canadian Army and went overseas, he made sure he used his furloughs to walk and hitchhike throughout the UK. He saw Chester, Leeds, Birmingham, and Brighton; Glasgow, Edinburgh, and Darlington; York, Brampton-on-Swale, Richmond, Manchester; Crewe, Oswestry, Wrexham. He saw recent stones with markings like "died of wounds, age 18." And as he wrote to his brother John in the spring of 1945, the numberless dead indicated lessons unlearned. History would record these. "We quickly forgot the loss, the lesson. . . . We continued to compete with each other and to oppose each other, as individuals, as groups and as nations. We allowed children to go hungry and cold while food rotted in heaps. . . . We had not yet learned to live collectively as a brotherhood of men. And we paid; we are still paying. The price is the greatest misery the world has ever seen, more graves and more tombstones." This was before the summer of that year, when Hiroshima and Nagasaki were bombed.

At the beginning of November 1945 "Restless Bill," as he called himself, was on the move again, using his free time to see London, and writing to John from Canterbury. "Last night I had a dream and in the dream I returned to the old homestead the way it was years ago. The walk in along the cut-line was complete with all the trees still standing. In one place there was an old car stuck in the mud. Further on a deer disappeared in the woods. When I reached the homestead old Flip was there to welcome me. He greeted me in his joyful high-pitched whine. Only (strange things happen in dreams) it seemed I could understand every word he said. 'Do you remember such and such a partridge hunt, etc.' I woke up at this point and remembered that I was in ancient Canterbury. 'Strange,' I thought, 'that the ghosts of old Hengist and Horsa, Ethelbert, Thomas à Becket, and the Black Prince would thus let me wander out of their world.' "

He'd recently seen a coyote, in London of all places, where he'd visited the zoo. "He did not keep still for a moment. Up and down, back and forth he ran in his pen. He seemed oblivious of the curious crowd, his gaze lifted out over their heads, looking no doubt for the snowy spaces he was doomed to see no more. There was one heart in that crowd that beat in sympathy with his. I understood him completely and to my mind came the words, 'Don't fence me in.' 'You and me both,' I said, 'Amen.' "

* * *

Once he was hiking out of Little Red River Park, returning to his car. He was coming down a long slope through sandy soil and jack pines when he suddenly stopped in his tracks. "It was like a hand I couldn't see brought me to a firm halt and then pushed me off to the side," he said. Uncle Bill was the last person on earth you'd expect to relate a tale of the paranormal, but he was unflinchingly honest. He said he crouched down low among the trees and watched and waited. An hour passed and he saw a man walking his dog along the road below, close to where the green Comet was parked. Suddenly there were police everywhere Men had escaped from the PA Pen and taken someone hostage in the park. If Bill had continued on his way, he said, he, too, would've been taken hostage. Some force, however, had intervened. Uncle Bill told this story many times, the story of the unseen hand that saved his life.

But why had an unseen hand saved him, and not Margaret for instance? It never occurred to me to ask him why.

86

It turned out we'd been regularly visiting the place in the north where Crystal's family and their ancestors had been living for centuries. Uncle Bill and my father had taken me there to fish. During one of these stays before Crystal's reunion, when none of us knew the whereabouts of her home and her people, we saw a woman fishing in a nearby set of rapids and my father recognized her. He pointed her out and said to me, "That's Maria Campbell." He knew her from the cover of her book, *Halfbreed*, which had so informed his thinking and knowledge about the land where we lived as settlers, about some of the customers who came to the King Koin and had become his friends, the Métis folks from the area south of PA. I was drawn to Maria Campbell and wandered down to the shore to say hello. This would be one of the most formative meetings of my life to that point.

It was August of 1990, five months before Crystal met her biological family. I'd been having strange dreams that were so powerful and detailed and real to me that I recorded them in a journal. Sometimes I drew pictures of the people and things I had seen. In the most perplexing of these, an old woman tapped me on the shoulder. Her appearance was so striking that on waking I drew a rough sketch of her face. Next to the sketch I wrote, "What is her name?? Where is my cheque?" She had long black hair tied in a ponytail that hung across one shoulder. Her eyes were grey and wide set and she had a wide mouth. She wore dark-framed round glasses and dark round earrings. On her face there was a noticeable growth of whiskers, not a beard but definitely a stubble. She asked me to help her tend to the dying and the dead and began to write me a cheque, which she filled out in a beautiful script that flowed from right to left, then took a sharp U-turn and flowed in reverse beneath the first line. Although I couldn't read the writing, I saw that it was completely unbroken: one thing. When I put out my hand to receive the cheque, the woman refused, saying I'd get it later when I'd done what she'd requested.

For an hour I stood next to Maria Campbell as we both fished where the Rapid River flows dramatically into a lake called Nistowiak, the Cree word for "converging waters." I went over to the rocks by the bottom of the rapids to cast. Maria was standing on a smooth rock and casting haphazardly. I introduced myself and we talked; we discussed language, dreams, and art. She told me that this ground constituted what she called "a power place." There were many spirits here, where water vapour filled the air ceaselessly as the river coursed over a steep fall nearby and emptied into another lake. She said there were many islands in this region and the spirits of First Nations people still lived on those islands. If you pitched your tent on one of them, they might knock it down. She said she came here, to this same fishing camp that my family often visited, to work on a Cree dictionary with her friend and colleague, Anne Acco. They were trying to write down all the words of that language, to preserve it and other Indigenous languages before they perished. They were worried. The Cree language was connected to the earth while English was a language of the oppressor and was long ago disconnected from the earth.

When I told Maria about my dream, she knew what I was saying. I had never talked to anyone about these dreams, let alone someone I had never met before, yet I felt safe with Maria, connected. She knew the identity of the old woman with the whiskers. She said I had met the Mother. "Your people are afraid of her but we are not.

We know her quite well. She is the one at the bottom, the one some of you call Hecate. She meets us at birth and at death, ushers us into and out of life. She is gentle, yet terrifying to some. You may come across her as a bird or some other form." Maria observed the balance of the returning line on my cheque.

Everything comes back again, nothing is broken.

The sun was setting, pelicans had landed on a small island nearby, and all the while the rapids continued on their ancient way filling the air around us with sound and mist. The spirit world seemed here like a momentous reality. Nothing was merely what it appeared to be.

87 Digger was finally beaten badly in Calgary. He was found by his father, Arnold, after a vicious assault by several men in a barn at the racetrack. By that time—he was now nineteen—Digger was drinking heavily, and in the aftermath of the beating needed a quick drink to prevent withdrawal from setting in. He acquired a case of beer and drank it slowly using a straw since he could hardly open his mouth, nursing himself over two or three days. He knew from his father what this could look like if left unattended.

Arnold by that time had found counselling and sobriety. More, he discovered Elders who helped him to understand the world through new eyes and to accept himself with all his known flaws. The Elders taught him about the four directions, the four sacred plants—sage, tobacco, sweetgrass, and cedar—and released him from the tyranny of John's God. He'd found real and lasting peace through these Elders. He would be their hungry student always after that.

Once we visited Margaret's grave together. He stood there and shook his head like he still couldn't believe it. He'd been through so much by now. His career as a competitive driver of the harness horse had come to a sudden, catastrophic end one night in Edmonton, when during a race the horse in front of his collapsed. In the moment that followed Arnold was flung forward, breaking many bones and almost dying in the hospital. By this time, he was already a recovering alcoholic.

I wasn't totally afraid of Arnold anymore.

Later, on one of many return visits to pay my respect and love to my grandmother Margaret and her unborn son, I spotted a snakeskin lying in a coil near the headstone. Gabe saw the skin too. We decided to leave it there.

I was considering many things in that moment.

Like how just down the road a lone Peters man lived in the ramshackle farmyard overgrown with weeds and grasses. Also overrun with ticks. You couldn't really walk there anymore during tick season, and in any case the distant cousin didn't welcome visitors. He often sat out on the driveway, where he built a fire and drank beer and threw the cans out onto the road.

Like how John took a photo of Margaret wrapped in a shawl covering her head, standing alone on the prairie expanse.

Like how an archaic trouble lies upon the land, brought from the Old World. Still it travels up and down. Still it runs along the descending lines of settler men who need release from their guilt and God.

That work must never end.

88 When I return to Saskatoon in late June to see my parents, my father and I go to the Tim Hortons coffee shop on the Louis Riel Trail. This particular Tim Hortons stands where the Heide bungalow stood on June 29, 1940. Crossing the widened boulevard, the two of us are now in the place where Margaret was that day. It's about 6:30 p.m. for us, as it was for her. We stand with her. We look north as we know she did. Traffic from the south whizzing past. I wonder how many times I have driven by this place where Harry D. Reid hit her. Great fires are burning in the north and a pall of smoke hangs in the air. Willard my father, at my behest, returns to the Tim Hortons parking lot ahead of me. I want to take a picture of him, now in his ninth decade, cradling his coffee in the drifting smoke while looking back at me.

Driving back to his condo, we talk about Tim Horton, a popular NHL player who died in an alcohol-fuelled car accident in 1974, two years past the peak of vehicular deaths in the twentieth century. We also discuss the news of the day—this concerning the farm at Langham that John purchased as a retirement project, where he planted windbreaks that continue to stand. Where this story begins for me: my initial awareness, Digger and his scarred throat, John and his bees and a hand held out to me with raw honey and wax. Apparently, a smelting company wanted to buy up all that land. Dig a giant hole in which to bury a giant box to contain their toxic heavy metals. All the residue from all the smelting this company would ever produce into the future would, they promised, reside safely here, forever sealed in the same earth John had tilled.

They promised it will never leak.

But it will leak. And the communities in the area gather together to consider this fact carefully; and with one voice they say no to this. And so it isn't done, after all—no buried box on John's dream farm, no more toxic leaks here.

In this same summer, an oil pipeline breaks open beneath the North Saskatchewan River, spilling more than two hundred thousand litres of heavy oil into the water flowing east. The pipeline belongs to Husky Energy. The rupture has taken place in Alberta, upstream from Prince Albert, and the city's engineers move swiftly to shut down the water intake before the oil can contaminate their water treatment facility and infrastructure. All of PA is forced to go without running water from the river for two months; in the meantime, city engineers rapidly build out a water pipeline to a temporary source miles away. Hardest hit are the First Nations communities located along the river, especially the James Smith Reserve. They have no alternative. They watch the oily waters flow past to meet the South Saskatchewan at the Forks.

Husky Energy brings in a scientist to speak to the media. The scientist, who worked on the Exxon Valdez spill, is quoted in all the papers. "Oil basically breaks down naturally," he says. "It's just the question of what is an acceptable timeframe."

Numerous charges are laid against Husky Energy, which also faces lawsuits filed by the City of Prince Albert as well as by local First Nations communities like James Smith. But ninety-three of the company's documents related to the spill are sealed when a judge rules on behalf of Husky because of "litigation privilege." The documents account for Husky's own investigation of the pipeline rupture; they cannot be seen by the people of Saskatchewan. A pipeline might leak, but the files that tell its story are sealed.

89 Edith's sons, James and Randy, cut up the strap later, after the family had finally left Neuhoffnung and moved to Langham, when John began to build his retirement home, the long bungalow with the blue garage door across the back alley from Zoar Mennonite Church, the Singing Church. They found the Black Doctor in its usual place, hanging from a nail on the wall where all could see it, and they seized it. Cut it into fragments using tinsnips. Took the pieces and parcelled them out one at a time in neighbours' garbage cans up and down the town's back alleys.

In that new house John fashioned his own den, a study lined with his books and University of Saskatchewan graduation portrait. But he never really used this space because he died, saying those words that still ring and echo: "That's enough."

Whenever we gathered at Edith's in the years after his death, I'd go to his den and sit at his desk, looking at his books, almost his student. There was *Alice Through the Looking Glass* alongside Frank Epp's *Mennonites in Canada: A History of a Separate People* in two volumes. Possibly I decided while in that room I'd study literature and philosophy. I read "The Hollow Men" there. Edith must have noticed because years onward, when she decided to leave that house, she gave me John's hard copy edition of Eliot's *Collected Poems: 1908–1935*. What was always of great interest to me were the marginalia, the familiar blue ink and hand of my grandfather, fragments of his readings. The residue of his encounter with another complicated sufferer and the high modernist anguish. When I open the book now, I see him taking it all in in a poem like "Ash Wednesday," its year of publication, 1930, conspicuous beneath the title, and beside that John's note: "Most beautiful—difficult" and "First Christian poem." A young teen seated in his den, I absorbed the opening lines of "Ash Wednesday" through his eyes.

Uncle Bill, on the other hand, while he knew his Eliot, rejected outright the politics and faith attached to that poet. He had no time for Eliot's kind of longing for the past, with its regret, bitterness, and nostalgia over failed Western institutions, though he repeatedly told me that he didn't envy my life going forward. The future was filled with environmental injuries and insults that, Bill thought, would grow to monstrous proportions and eventually swallow everything. If John shared his brother's politics, he held to the Mennonite faith that had brought the Boschmans to North America in the first place. If Bill knew his history better even than his older brother and friend, he saw it as a prelude to the future. One in which the only genuine long-term hope lay with Indigenous Peoples, their traditions and aspirations.

On one of their many wilderness walks together just before Bill joined the Canadian Army (a revolutionary act for a young Mennonite and one that earned him scorn and criticism), the brothers discussed the politics of the Left. They'd both been called communists. Bill was a disillusioned Liberal; John was an impoverished teacher. The party of Woodrow Lloyd and Tommy Douglas had won them over. The brothers declared, "If they're communists, then we are too."

After Bill returned from the war, John informed him that he'd been offered a position by the Government of

Saskatchewan to be its provincial apiarist. He wanted the job badly, although it meant moving to Fort Qu'Appelle, far to the south. Bill was excited for his brother. But when John discovered there was no Mennonite church in Fort Qu'Appelle, he turned the offer down. He could never leave the church.

No one save Margaret and Edith knew John better than Bill. The terrible temper, worst of the ten Boschman brothers. "He was like my mother," Bill would say. "She reached for the strap if there was any fighting. Any fighting, she'd do it. One little woman amongst a bunch of boys, the damage was spread out. But with a man, a man who had little boys, well one trigger and he hauled off like that and it wasn't good. John wasn't big but he was still a man and a strong one too."

"How do you think the death of Margaret played into that whole scenario, his temper already being what it was?"

I had asked him this question in one form or another many times.

"Well, I think it made it much worse. . . . He was a very much changed man. Margaret. Margaret and he were just a real love. When that happened, his world was destroyed."

In 1995 I walked on a beach on the South China Sea with Bill. He was almost eighty then. We had journeyed there together to see his only child, a grown son who'd married a woman from the Philippines and had three young children. Bill said he wanted to see his grandchildren with his own eyes and asked me to come along as his travel partner. We talked about Margaret and John one afternoon out on the ash-strewn strand where countless charcoal barbeques burned and smoked, and Bill said he thought the second marriage was one of convenience. And I said if it was then it was the most convenient marriage of convenience in the history of such relationships. Because John *loved* Edith. Uncle Bill and I stood together beneath a banyan tree to have our picture taken, and he agreed.

Before we left, he invited his grandchildren to photocopy their hands with his—like leaves young and old, they grace the page together.

90 Just before Grandma Funk's death, I bring Gabriel to visit her. They sit side by side on her bed in the nursing home. Gabe holds a lollipop so big it matches his round face; I am annoyed that he has it at all—given to him on the way in by an elderly man trolling the hallways—but at least now I can say no to the equally large chocolate bar that his great-grandmother produces with a flourish and a grin.

Gabe's face turns florid as he attacks the lollipop and my grandmother and I speak of the past. She misses Jake and Kerby. She misses men in general. When she greets me, she manages to stand and give me a hug. "It's so good to hold a man in my arms," she says, long past any concerns about what is appropriate to say to a grandson. She giggles. Other family members have warned me that she might reminisce about her sex life with Jake. After all, they were together for over six decades. But she doesn't.

Instead, she says, "I want to go find Jake. I need to know what he's doing."

Months later, she makes good on her word. Lying in her grand casket, she wears a dress of royal blue and holds a knitting needle in the hand with the amputated finger. Next to the needle is a deluxe chocolate bar.

91 In the thirty years since Crystal reunited with her biological family, she has seen them regularly. She drives north often, taking her daughter Bella to visit with family and go fishing and hunting. Both have their status cards as members of their band under the terms of Treaty 10, which covers almost all of northern Saskatchewan.

In the summer of 2016, Crystal invites everyone—both her families and all her friends—to her wedding in the Parkland Hotel in Saskatoon. Along the South Saskatchewan River, blocks away from the Bessborough Hotel. The streets and riverside are brimming with people, walking, jogging, riding bicycles.

Crystal has been studying at the University of Saskatchewan for years and is a teacher in Saskatoon's Catholic school system.

She's finally met someone she considers marriage material, she says. And with that, asks me to make the toast to the bride. I am nervous about this but also honoured and humbled.

Her kinship network fills the room in the basement of the hotel, as I, her white settler brother, try my best to make my words matter. I decide to say what I know. I tell them about my first encounter with her when she was five months old and I was ten, and how much I loved her from the first instant. I tell a bit of my story, what happened, what I witnessed. How we drove through the heat in our 1966 Chev Bel Air, how she lay between my parents on the red bench seat in the front and cried because unbeknownst to us a pin was stuck in her side. How we passed Duck Lake, where I knew that Gabriel Dumont had once lived. How our parents said she would give more to us than we to her, and how they were right.

From the back of the hall, Crystal's biological mother started walking with her daughter. The two walked together arm in arm. Her mother wore a green sweater, blue pants, and beaded leather slippers trimmed in fur. She walked slowly with grace and the dignity of the moment. Halfway down the aisle she met up with my parents, who tearfully joined the procession.

At the reception that followed, the three parents sat together at a table Crystal reserved for them. The table was the closest one to her.

92 Sometimes the wind blows hard from the east. A nor'easter blows across the land. This place called Saskatchewan. Across the running waters large and small it blows and blows. The snow comes in heavy and lies in drifts, sharp and wave-like. They won't accept your weight if you try to walk over them. They'll let you down and rub you raw. Then the snow melts and the wind drops and just when you think it's all settled, back it comes with triple force. Gale force. Blinding. Animals and humans hunkering down. Some dying out there in the freeze.

At night I hear that wind from my warm bed and I think of my grandparents' remains lying in the packed, tight ground in their places at Aberdeen and Langham, towns whose names come from another continent, with their histories and projections, transplanted here by folks I may not have cared for much had I known them.

I think of my sister Crystal's people. I think of them living their lives upon the earth amid snow and runoffs, season in and season out, repeated endlessly. Every year, they hunt moose and sometimes I get a roast with bits of hide and hair clinging to the flesh.

There is no development here; I dislike that word. Nothing like progress or a denouement—instead a circle that turns among other circles. Surely this is what Indigenous Peoples have said all along, that this thing called "progress" is a bad idea. Letting it go would be progress. Saying "No more" to hate and violence and "Yes" to the findings of the Truth and Reconciliation Commission would be progress: "Reconciliation must become a way of life." We are all treaty people, every one of us.

I teach my son Gabriel this. He also learns it from Crystal, his aunt (who loves him as her own), and from Bella, his cousin, and from his sisters, mother, and four grandparents. Together we tell him the truth as we know it. We are proud of him when he acknowledges the land every morning at school.

I cast my imagination over the landscape between the two rivers with their settler towns and their histories. Their assumptions about land and ownership and a linear, forward-marching history. About the human beings who were already here and had been for millennia. That there was some place every person could go and start again at no one else's expense. The ice surfaces and hockey sticks and steeples and songs and violence and attempts to forget or dismiss in a century we call the twentieth.

In my imagination I stand for a while in each place next to the hard settler stones. I think of Edith and John and Margaret. I think of the unborn uncle. Amphibious creatures emerge and burrow and then emerge again. Spores wait. Earthworms wait. Erosions and rivulets and eddies of grit.

Sometimes I'm afraid in those places. But that's only because of my ingrained settler ways. All these markers, spots on the land, will fall back into nature.

Perhaps I still fear what others are being born into.

All I can do is to say what I know and put my hand on Gabriel's shoulder.

One day the two of us will go to the place where Uncle Bill's ashes were left in a big rock in the far north, unmarked, not laid to rest or buried in any cemetery. Pay our respects and give acknowledgement, recall good decisions for future reference, and learn from mistakes. I'll hold my son's hand and tell him the things I know and watch him put his nose to the wind. I'll tell him that a Prince Albert is a piercing. That his Great-Great-Uncle Bill once wrote a letter to the PA *Herald* arguing that Prince Albert should change its name and that the local First Nations and Métis Peoples would know what to call it instead.

ACKNOWLEDGEMENTS
AND NOTES

I grew up on Treaty 6 (1876) territory, a traditional meeting ground, gathering place, and travelling route for the Cree, Saulteaux, Blackfoot, Dene, and Nakota Sioux; it is also home to many Métis.

I acknowledge the Treaty 7 (1877) lands where my family and I lived while I wrote this book: the ancestral and traditional territory of the Kainai, Piikani, and Siksika as well as the Tsuu T'ina, İyârhe Nakoda, and the Métis.

Many readers, including friends, colleagues, and family members, have helped me throughout this project. An early draft of the opening pages appeared in *FreeFall* xxv, number 1 (Winter 2015), and was enthusiastically supported by publisher/poet Micheline Maylor and editor Ryan Stromquist. Jeffery Donaldson, at McMaster University, read encouragingly during this period.

Although I began writing *White Coal City* in the summer of 2009, I'd spent the previous decade and a half investigating the facts of Margaret Peters's life and death. Susan Gingell and Don Kerr were early readers and supporters of this story. The latter's history of Saskatoon, co-authored with Stan Hanson, was instrumental. In 1998, I recorded an interview with my Uncle Bill on video tape (unpublished) with help from filmmaker Laurence Green. Saskatchewan filmmaker Donna Caruso directed a one-hour documentary called *The Honey Children* (1999) based on my research and script. My poem "Dear Johnny Boy," published in *ARIEL: A Review of International English Literature* (vol. 30, no. 1, January 1999), constituted an early draft for some of the scenes described in the first and third parts of this book. During this period, archivists at the provincial courthouse in Saskatoon responded quickly to my requests for extant documentation. Finding and speaking with Elsie Heide so many years after the accident was a watershed moment, and I appreciate her generosity in taking my cold call. Catherine Hainstock and Geoffrey Cochrane have given time and crucial suggestions, especially regarding the city where we met as kids. The religious scholar Lisa Sideris, at the University of Indiana, has been a source of wisdom and good advice. Sam McKegney has been a detailed reader out of his expertise in Indigenous histories in Canada as well as toxic masculinities and hockey. At the eleventh hour, Tracey Harding in the UK appeared almost as a miracle to translate over sixty pages of shorthand from an inquest held in 1940.

My colleagues at Mount Royal University have been very supportive of this project. Several have read with care, pushing me to make it better. For this, I appreciate Kit Dobson, Richard Harrison, and Natalie Meisner.

For their friendship and support, I owe thanks to Mario Trono, Randy Schroeder, Cliff Werier, and Bill Bunn. For her legal insight concerning laws governing alcohol intoxication in Canada over the course of the last century, I am grateful to my colleague Dunia Scharie Tavcer. To philosopher Ada Jaarsma I owe special gratitude for sharing her expertise in epigenetic theory and for championing this work. Likewise, I thank historian Liam Haggarty for advising me concerning the Métis in Saskatchewan.

The Peters children provided rich details about their older sister. In speaking to Bill, Dan, Pete, Helen, Mary, Abe, Betty, and Jim, I witnessed their century-spanning love for Margaret and was proud to know them as my kin. My friendship with their (and Margaret's) mother, Helena, was an important part of my early adulthood, and I cherish our many conversations.

Before their passing, Grandma Edith and Uncle Bill Boschman, two people who knew John Boschman well, gave of their time, wisdom, writings, and photographs, and are of course integral actors in this story. Like them, Arnold Boschman, James Boschman, Marvin Boschman, Randy Boschman, Lola Antefaev, and my parents Willard and Elaine, provided interview material and correspondence. My cousins, Dean (Digger) and Stuart, have acted as touchstones and readers, as have Joni Funk, Sheila Funk, and my brother Ben. Any mistakes are my own.

Some of the names appearing in this memoir have been changed or withheld. There are no composite characters.

To my old friend, Barry Henry, thank you for reading and commenting.

To my sister, Crystal, *megwich*: you have given the most, my friend. Thank you for your honesty, wisdom, and integrity in all things.

My partner and love, Sari MacPherson, a terrific reader, has stood by me through the years of my work on this story.

The great poet Louise B. Halfe read the manuscript with an eye for, among other things, the history of the traditional lands covered by Treaty 6.

Finally, this book could not exist without the steady guiding hand of Karen Clark, acquisitions editor at the University of Regina Press. To all the folks at URP, thank you. I owe a special debt of gratitude and appreciation to copy editor Ryan Perks and proofreader Rachel Taylor.

ABOUT THE AUTHOR

ROBERT BOSCHMAN is a professor of American Literature and the Environmental Humanities at Mount Royal University in Calgary, Alberta. He is the author of *In the Way of Nature: Ecology and Westward Movement in the Poetry of Anne Bradstreet, Elizabeth Bishop and Amy Clampitt* (2009) and has co-edited and contributed to *Found in Alberta: Environmental Themes for the Anthropocene* (2014) and *On Active Grounds: Agency and Time in the Environmental Humanities* (2019). He co-founded the award-winning Under Western Skies biennial conference series on the environment held at Mount Royal from 2010 to 2016, and contributed to *Critical Zones: The Science and Politics of Landing on Earth* (2020) edited by Bruno Latour and Peter Weibel.

PHOTO CREDIT: ROBERT BOSCHMAN PHOTOGRAPHY.
PAINTING: "STORMKING" (2014) BY WALT PASCOE.

A NOTE ABOUT THE TYPE

The body of this book is set in WARNOCK PRO. This Adobe originals type font began as a private font requested by Chris Warnock for co-founder of Adobe, and his father, John Warnock's personal use. It was designed by award-winning long time Adobe staff designer Robert Slimbach, who began work on the font design in the year 1987. Slimbach wanted to design a font that mirrored the visionary spirit that Warnock embodied for Adobe, and found it in this classic and yet still contemporary family of fonts.

The Warnock Pro font was among the winners of the 2001 Type Directors Club Type Design Competition. In December of 2010, Warnock Pro was released as a webfont. In August of 2007, *Smashing Magazine* named Warnock Pro as one of the "80 Beautiful Typefaces for Professional Design."

The accents are set in AACHEN, a heavy-stroked slab serif font designed by Alan Meeks under the supervision of Colin Brignall and released by Letraset in 1969. Aachen is a bold typeface with heavy strokes and stubby serifs, which make it very readable. The heavy strokes and sharp outlines make Aachen usable for posters and anywhere bold headlines are needed. Aachen is also suitable for strong-looking book titles.